Turbocharge Your GMAT: Sentence Correction Guide

part of the 6th Edition Series

April 20th, 2016

☐ *Detailed Grammar Review*
  · *Nouns & Pronouns*
  · *Adjectives & Adverbs*
  · *Preposition Types & Errors*
  · *Idioms*
  · *Verb Voices & Tenses*
  · *Participles & Gerunds*
  · *Mood, Punctuation & Clauses*

☐ *Grammatical Errors to Avoid*

☐ *Tested Topics in Detail*

☐ *Tips & Strategies*

☐ *300 Realistic Practice Questions*
  · *Detailed explanations*
  · *Concept-wise discussion of errors*
  · *Concept-wise categorization*

www.manhattanreview.com

©1999-2016 Manhattan Review. All Rights Reserved.

Copyright and Terms of Use

Copyright and Trademark

All materials herein (including names, terms, trademarks, designs, images, and graphics) are the property of Manhattan Review, except where otherwise noted. Except as permitted herein, no such material may be copied, reproduced, displayed or transmitted or otherwise used without the prior written permission of Manhattan Review. You are permitted to use material herein for your personal, noncommercial use, provided that you do not combine such material into a combination, collection, or compilation of material. If you have any questions regarding the use of the material, please contact Manhattan Review at info@manhattanreview.com.

This material may make reference to countries and persons. The use of such references is for hypothetical and demonstrative purposes only.

Terms of Use

By using this material, you acknowledge and agree to the terms of use contained herein.

No Warranties

This material is provided without warranty, either express or implied, including the implied warranties of merchantability, of fitness for a particular purpose and noninfringement. Manhattan Review does not warrant or make any representations regarding the use, accuracy or results of the use of this material. This material may make reference to other source materials. Manhattan Review is not responsible in any respect for the content of such other source materials, and disclaims all warranties and liabilities with respect to the other source materials.

Limitation on Liability

Manhattan Review shall not be responsible under any circumstances for any direct, indirect, special, punitive, or consequential damages ("Damages") that may arise from the use of this material. In addition, Manhattan Review does not guarantee the accuracy or completeness of its course materials, which are provided "as is" with no warranty, express or implied. Manhattan Review assumes no liability for any Damages from errors or omissions in the material, whether arising in contract, tort or otherwise.

GMAT is a registered trademark of the Graduate Management Admission Council.
GMAC does not endorse, nor is it affiliated in any way with, the owner of this product or any content herein.

10-Digit International Standard Book Number: (ISBN: 1-62926-067-3)
13-Digit International Standard Book Number: (ISBN: 978-1-62926-067-9)

Last updated on April 20th, 2016.

Manhattan Review, 275 Madison Avenue, Suite 1429, New York, NY 10016.
Phone: +1 (212) 316-2000. E-Mail: info@manhattanreview.com. Web: www.manhattanreview.com

About the Turbocharge your GMAT Series

The Turbocharge Your GMAT Series is carefully designed to be clear, comprehensive, and content-driven. Long regarded as the gold standard in GMAT prep worldwide, Manhattan Review's GMAT prep books offer professional GMAT instruction for dramatic score improvement. Now in its updated 6th edition, the full series is designed to provide GMAT test-takers with complete guidance for highly successful outcomes. As many students have discovered, Manhattan Review's GMAT books break down the different test sections in a coherent, concise, and accessible manner. We delve deeply into the content of every single testing area and zero in on exactly what you need to know to raise your score. The full series is comprised of 16 guides that cover concepts in mathematics and grammar from the most basic through the most advanced levels, making them a great study resource for all stages of GMAT preparation. Students who work through all of our books benefit from a substantial boost to their GMAT knowledge and develop a thorough and strategic approach to taking the GMAT.

- ☐ GMAT Math Essentials (ISBN: 978-1-62926-057-0)
- ☐ GMAT Number Properties Guide (ISBN: 978-1-62926-058-7)
- ☐ GMAT Arithmetics Guide (ISBN: 978-1-62926-059-4)
- ☐ GMAT Algebra Guide (ISBN: 978-1-62926-060-0)
- ☐ GMAT Geometry Guide (ISBN: 978-1-62926-061-7)
- ☐ GMAT Word Problems Guide (ISBN: 978-1-62926-062-4)
- ☐ GMAT Sets & Statistics Guide (ISBN: 978-1-62926-063-1)
- ☐ GMAT Combinatorics & Probability Guide (ISBN: 978-1-62926-064-8)
- ☐ GMAT Data Sufficiency Guide (ISBN: 978-1-62926-065-5)
- ☐ GMAT Quantitative Question Bank (ISBN: 978-1-62926-066-2)
- ■ GMAT Sentence Correction Guide (ISBN: 978-1-62926-067-9)
- ☐ GMAT Critical Reasoning Guide (ISBN: 978-1-62926-068-6)
- ☐ GMAT Reading Comprehension Guide (ISBN: 978-1-62926-069-3)
- ☐ GMAT Integrated Reasoning Guide (ISBN: 978-1-62926-070-9)
- ☐ GMAT Analytical Writing Guide (ISBN: 978-1-62926-071-6)
- ☐ GMAT Vocabulary Builder (ISBN: 978-1-62926-072-3)

About the Company

Manhattan Review's origin can be traced directly back to an Ivy League MBA classroom in 1999. While teaching advanced quantitative subjects to MBAs at Columbia Business School in New York City, Professor Dr. Joern Meissner developed a reputation for explaining complicated concepts in an understandable way. Remembering their own less-than-optimal experiences preparing for the GMAT, Prof. Meissner's students challenged him to assist their friends, who were frustrated with conventional GMAT preparation options. In response, Prof. Meissner created original lectures that focused on presenting GMAT content in a simplified and intelligible manner, a method vastly different from the voluminous memorization and so-called tricks commonly offered by others. The new approach immediately proved highly popular with GMAT students, inspiring the birth of Manhattan Review.

Since its founding, Manhattan Review has grown into a multi-national educational services firm, focusing on GMAT preparation, MBA admissions consulting, and application advisory services, with thousands of highly satisfied students all over the world. The original lectures have been continuously expanded and updated by the Manhattan Review team, an enthusiastic group of master GMAT professionals and senior academics. Our team ensures that Manhattan Review offers the most time-efficient and cost-effective preparation available for the GMAT. Please visit www.ManhattanReview.com for further details.

About the Founder

Professor Dr. Joern Meissner has more than 25 years of teaching experience at the graduate and undergraduate levels. He is the founder of Manhattan Review, a worldwide leader in test prep services, and he created the original lectures for its first GMAT preparation class. Prof. Meissner is a graduate of Columbia Business School in New York City, where he received a PhD in Management Science. He has since served on the faculties of prestigious business schools in the United Kingdom and Germany. He is a recognized authority in the areas of supply chain management, logistics, and pricing strategy. Prof. Meissner thoroughly enjoys his research, but he believes that grasping an idea is only half of the fun. Conveying knowledge to others is even more fulfilling. This philosophy was crucial to the establishment of Manhattan Review, and remains its most cherished principle.

The Advantages of Using Manhattan Review

▶ **Time efficiency and cost effectiveness.**

- For most people, the most limiting factor of test preparation is time.
- It takes significantly more teaching experience to prepare a student in less time.
- Our test preparation approach is tailored for busy professionals. We will teach you what you need to know in the least amount of time.

▶ **Our high-quality and dedicated instructors are committed to helping every student reach her/his goals.**

International Phone Numbers and Official Manhattan Review Websites

Manhattan Headquarters	+1-212-316-2000	www.manhattanreview.com
USA & Canada	+1-800-246-4600	www.manhattanreview.com
Argentina	+1-212-316-2000	www.review.com.ar
Australia	+61-3-9001-6618	www.manhattanreview.com
Austria	+43-720-115-549	www.review.at
Belgium	+32-2-808-5163	www.manhattanreview.be
Brazil	+1-212-316-2000	www.manhattanreview.com.br
Chile	+1-212-316-2000	www.manhattanreview.cl
China	+86-20-2910-1913	www.manhattanreview.cn
Czech Republic	+1-212-316-2000	www.review.cz
France	+33-1-8488-4204	www.review.fr
Germany	+49-89-3803-8856	www.review.de
Greece	+1-212-316-2000	www.review.com.gr
Hong Kong	+852-5808-2704	www.review.hk
Hungary	+1-212-316-2000	www.review.co.hu
India	+1-212-316-2000	www.review.in
Indonesia	+1-212-316-2000	www.manhattanreview.id
Ireland	+1-212-316-2000	www.gmat.ie
Italy	+39-06-9338-7617	www.manhattanreview.it
Japan	+81-3-4589-5125	www.manhattanreview.jp
Malaysia	+1-212-316-2000	www.review.my
Mexico	+1-212-316-2000	www.manhattanreview.mx
Netherlands	+31-20-808-4399	www.manhattanreview.nl
New Zealand	+1-212-316-2000	www.review.co.nz
Philippines	+1-212-316-2000	www.review.ph
Poland	+1-212-316-2000	www.review.pl
Portugal	+1-212-316-2000	www.review.pt
Qatar	+1-212-316-2000	www.review.qa
Russia	+1-212-316-2000	www.manhattanreview.ru
Singapore	+65-3158-2571	www.gmat.sg
South Africa	+1-212-316-2000	www.manhattanreview.co.za
South Korea	+1-212-316-2000	www.manhattanreview.kr
Sweden	+1-212-316-2000	www.gmat.se
Spain	+34-911-876-504	www.review.es
Switzerland	+41-435-080-991	www.review.ch
Taiwan	+1-212-316-2000	www.gmat.tw
Thailand	+66-6-0003-5529	www.manhattanreview.com
Turkey	+1-212-316-2000	www.review.com.tr
United Arab Emirates	+1-212-316-2000	www.manhattanreview.ae
United Kingdom	+44-20-7060-9800	www.manhattanreview.co.uk
Rest of World	+1-212-316-2000	www.manhattanreview.com

Contents

1 Welcome	**1**
2 Grammar Review	**3**
2.1 Nouns	3
2.1.1 Common and Proper Nouns	3
2.1.2 Singular and Plural Nouns	3
2.1.3 Countable and Uncountable Nouns	4
2.1.4 Collective Nouns	5
2.2 Pronouns	6
2.2.1 Pronoun Types	6
2.2.2 Nominative and Objective Cases	6
2.2.3 Possessive Forms	7
2.2.4 Agreement & Reference	7
2.3 Adjectives	8
2.4 Adverbs	10
2.4.1 Adverbial Forms	10
2.4.2 Adverbial Positions	10
2.5 Adverbs vs. Adjectives	12
2.5.1 Position and Meaning	12
2.5.2 Adverbs and Adjectives	12
2.5.3 Adjectives Only	14
2.6 Prepositions	16
2.6.1 Preposition Types	16
2.6.2 Prepositions Frequently Misused	16
2.6.3 Idioms with Prepositions	18
2.7 Verbs	23
2.7.1 Transitive and Intransitive Verbs	23
2.7.2 Active and Passive Voices	23
2.7.3 Major Tenses	23
2.7.4 Moods: Indicative, Imperative and Subjunctive moods	26
2.7.5 Participle	28
2.7.5.1 Present Participle	29
2.7.5.2 Past Participle	29
2.7.5.3 Special Situations	30
2.7.6 Gerunds & Infinitives	30
2.8 Conjunctions	33
2.9 Helpful Topics	33

	2.9.1 Punctuation	33
	2.9.2 List of Irregular Verbs	35
	2.9.3 Words Frequently Confused	37
	2.9.4 American vs. British Usage	40
	2.9.5 Standard vs. Non-standard Usage	42

3 Sentence Correction Strategy 45
3.1 How to Tackle 46
3.2 Special Advice 47
3.3 Common Errors and Tested Topics 49
    3.3.1 Misplaced Modifiers (and Dangling Participles) 49
    3.3.2 Agreement (Concord) 50
    3.3.3 Tense 51
    3.3.4 Parallelism 53
    3.3.5 Comparisons 54
    3.3.6 Pronoun Agreement & Reference 56
    3.3.7 Idioms, Usage, and Style 57
        3.3.7.1 GMAT Idiom List 59
        3.3.7.2 Words Frequently Misused 60
3.4 What to Do If You Are Completely Stumped 62
3.5 Detailed List of Typical Errors 63
    3.5.1 Modifiers 63
    3.5.2 Agreement 65
    3.5.3 Verb Tense, Voice & Mood 67
    3.5.4 Parallelism 68
    3.5.5 Comparisons 68
    3.5.6 Pronoun Agreement & Reference 68
    3.5.7 Idioms, Usage and Style 69
3.6 Useful Examples 72

4 Practice Questions 75
4.1 Subject-Verb agreement (SVA) 76
4.2 Parallelism 81
4.3 Comparison 88
4.4 Modifiers 94
4.5 Pronouns 101
4.6 Meaning 105
4.7 Rhetorical construction 110
4.8 Redundancy 112
4.9 Grammatical construction 113
4.10 Concision 117
4.11 Idioms 119
4.12 Diction 124
4.13 Tenses 128
4.14 Conjunctions & Mood 131
4.15 Assorted questions 133

5 Answer key 163

Sentence Correction Guide

6 Solutions — 169
- 6.1 Subject-Verb agreement (SVA) — 170
- 6.2 Parallelism — 178
- 6.3 Comparison — 192
- 6.4 Modifiers — 205
- 6.5 Pronouns — 217
- 6.6 Meaning — 223
- 6.7 Rhetorical construction — 232
- 6.8 Redundancy — 236
- 6.9 Grammatical construction — 237
- 6.10 Concision — 247
- 6.11 Idioms — 250
- 6.12 Diction — 259
- 6.13 Tenses — 267
- 6.14 Conjunctions & Mood — 272
- 6.15 Assorted questions — 276

7 Talk to Us — 305

Chapter 1

Welcome

Dear students,

At Manhattan Review, we constantly strive to provide the best educational content for preparation of standardized tests, putting arduous effort into improvement. This continuous evolution is very important for an examination like the GMAT, which also evolves constantly. Sadly, a GMAT aspirant is confused with too many options in the market. The challenge is how to choose a book or a tutor that prepares you to reach your goal. Without saying that we are the best, we leave it for you to judge.

This book differs in many aspects from standard books available on the market. Unlike any book from other prep companies, this book discusses GMAT sentence correction grammar, strategies, errors and questions in equal measures. This comes directly as a result of students' feedback after finding that there is a scarcity of enough material; while the book encompasses over 100 pages solely on grammar, tips and strategies, it provides you 300 GMAT-like questions with detailed explanations. The questions are categorized as per the concepts tested in questions with an emphasis on why the correct option is right and the incorrect options are wrong.

In a nutshell, Manhattan Review's GMAT-SC book is holistic and comprehensive in all respects; it has been created this way because we listen to what students need. Should you have any queries, please feel free to write to us at *info@manhattanreview.com*.

Happy Learning!

Professor Dr. Joern Meissner
& The Manhattan Review Team

Chapter 2

Grammar Review

2.1 Nouns

Nouns are used as subjects of sentences and as the objects of verbs and prepositions.

2.1.1 Common and Proper Nouns

Generally there are two types of nouns - common nouns and proper nouns.

- Common nouns refer to any place, person or thing, for example: girl, apartment, city.
- Proper nouns refer to particular places, persons and things, for example: Mark, New York, the White House.

2.1.2 Singular and Plural Nouns

Nouns can also be categorized as singular nouns and plural nouns. Sometimes certain nouns are used exclusively as either singular or plural nouns. That means they do not have a corresponding word in the other form.

- Singular nouns are used for a single occurrence, single person, single item, etc.
- Plural nouns are used for more than one occurrence, person, item, etc.

A quick comparison table of some tricky nouns in their singular and plural forms:

Singular form	Plural form
Alumnus	Alumni
Bacterium	Bacteria
Criterion	Criteria
Formula	Formulae
Medium	Media
Phenomenon	Phenomena

There are some singular nouns often mistaken as plural nouns because they end with "s."

Citrus

Economics

Glasses

Means

Measles

News

Physics

Scissors

Series

Species

Statistics

2.1.3 Countable and Uncountable Nouns

Another way to group nouns is by separating them into countable nouns and non-countable nouns. Countable nouns usually have both singular and plural forms. Uncountable nouns are used just as singular.

- Countable nouns can be counted by the numbers 1, 2, 3... Examples: desk, pen, person.

- Uncountable nouns cannot be counted in numbers. Rather, they are considered an entire item. Some commonly used uncountable nouns are: water, health, and money.

Other examples of uncountable nouns include:

Advice

Anger

Baggage

Beauty

Gasoline

Information

Luggage

Smog

Wheat

Sometimes a noun is used as an uncountable noun when it refers to the entire idea or substance, but it can be used as a countable noun when used in a context involving:

$\implies$ Countable pieces or containers for things.

Uncountable: I prefer tea to coke.
Countable: Two teas (two cups of tea) for us, please.

$\implies$ Different brands, makes, or types.

Uncountable: I love cheese.
Countable: There are so many cheeses from which to choose.

⇒   A specific example.

Uncountable: She has shiny hair.
Countable: I found a hair today in my sandwich. How disgusting!

Uncountable: He is great at sports.
Countable: Skiing is a popular sport in Austria.

2.1.4 Collective Nouns

Certain nouns are used to describe a collection of people, items, or events in their entirety. Even though they are referring to more than one thing in the collection, they are singular. However, when they are used to represent a number of collections, then they are plural.

Examples include:

Audience

Business

Choir

Committee

Company

Crowd

Family

Flock

Government

Group

Majority

Nation

Pack

Team

The Public

Unit

2.2 Pronouns

2.2.1 Pronoun Types

A pronoun is a part of speech that is typically used as a substitute for a noun or noun phrase. There are **eight subclasses** of pronouns, although some forms belong to more than one group:

(1) **personal pronouns** (I, you, he/she/it, we, you, they)

  - Make sure sentences use them consistently.

(2) **possessive pronouns** (my/mine, his/her/its/hers, their/theirs, our/ours, etc.)

  - Do not change the gender of a noun (as some languages, such as French, do).

(3) **reflexive pronouns** (myself, yourself, him/herself, ourselves, themselves, etc.)

  - There are no reflexive verbs in English, as some languages have.

(4) **demonstrative pronouns** (this/these, that/those)

  - These show nearness in location.
  - Beware of the different between: that (pronoun) vs. that (conjunction)

(5) **reciprocal pronouns** (each other, one another)

(6) **interrogative pronouns** (who, what, when, where, why, etc.)

(7) **relative pronouns** (who, that, what, which, etc.)

  - These relate different clauses in a sentence to each other.
  - That vs. Which: restrictive vs. non-restrictive clauses
  - Who vs. Whom: take subject vs. take object (Please see explanation later.)

(8) **indefinite pronouns** (any, none, somebody, nobody, anyone, etc.)

  - none = singular (when it means "not one"); all = plural (if countable)
  - much = can't be counted (use with uncountable nouns); many = can be counted (use with countable nouns)
  - less = can't be counted (uncountable nouns); fewer = can be counted (countable nouns)

2.2.2 Nominative and Objective Cases

There are two pronominal cases: nominative (subject) and objective (object).

Subject: I, you, he/she/it, we, you, and they

Object: me, you, him/her/it, us, you, and them

Notice that the second person (both singular and plural) has only one form, *you*. The object case is used after verbs and prepositions:

We met *her* in a bookstore. She went to school with *us*.

Be careful of objects that consist of a proper noun (name) + a pronoun:

The puppy looked across the table at *Sarah* and *me*.

These situations can seem confusing, but there is an easy method to tell which pronoun (nominative or objective) is required. Just remove the other noun from the sentence to see if it still makes sense. If it does (as in "The puppy looked across the table at me"), then you have selected the correct pronoun; if it does not (as in "The puppy looked across the table at I"), then you should go back and check whether you selected the correct case for the pronoun (in this case it is the object of a preposition, *at*, so it should be in the objective case).

The relative pronoun *who* also has an objective case form, *whom*:

I kicked the girl *who* tried to steal my coat.

(I kicked the girl. *She* tried to steal my coat.)

I smiled at the girl *whom* I had kicked.

(I smiled at the girl. I had kicked *her*.)

2.2.3 Possessive Forms

All these pronouns have possessive forms that **do not** have apostrophes:

my, your, his/her/its, our, your, their

These act as adjectives, and are followed by nouns. If there is no noun and the possessive form is used by itself, this form is said to be disjunctive:

mine, yours, his/hers/its, ours, yours, theirs.

Again, there is no apostrophe. The relative pronoun *who* has the possessive form *whose*:

I comforted the dog *whose* tail had been stepped on.

One is used as a supplementary pronoun; it **does** have an apostrophe in the possessive:

One can only do *one's* best.

Note that *one's* is used only if the subject *one* is present; following with *his* would not be acceptable.

2.2.4 Agreement & Reference

There are several pronominal forms which seem to be plural but act as singular, taking singular verbs and singular pronouns, if they act as antecedents. The most common of these words are *another, any, anybody, anything, each, either, every, everybody, neither, no one, nobody, none (not one)*, etc.; they must be followed by a singular verb, whatever the meaning might indicate:

Not one of the bananas *was* ripe.

Everybody wanted *his or her* own way.

Always look back to see what the pronoun refers to; where there is a generalization, it is sometimes tempting to treat a singular as a plural:

Man, in all *his* glory, has ascended to the top of the food chain.

2.3 Adjectives

An adjective is a descriptive word which describes a noun, making it more specific:

The *red* car

The *old red* car

The *large old red* car

The two *young* professors lived in Greenwich Village.

A *bright* light flashed through the window of the house.

Adjectives are usually arranged in order of specificity. Words normally used to perform other grammatical functions may be used as adjectives. These can be recognized by their position before the noun to which they apply:

remote-control car

war effort

Christmas cookies

spring carnival

Adjectives can also be used to form a **predicate** with the verb to *be*:

Chocolate *is yummy*.

Normally, only "true" adjectives can be used to form this kind of predicate. It is not possible to say:

Wrong: The cookies were *Christmas*.
Wrong: The carnival was *spring*.

In such cases, it is necessary to use the prop-word, *one*:

The cookies were *Christmas ones*.

There are three forms of a "true" adjective.

Normal:	big	beautiful
Comparative:	bigger	more beautiful
Superlative:	biggest	most beautiful

No agreement to a noun is necessary for an adjective.

Student Notes:

2.4 Adverbs

An adverb is a part of speech used mainly to modify verbs, but also adjectives and other adverbs. Adverbs describe how, where or when.

2.4.1 Adverbial Forms

Adverbs are formed in a few different ways.

Most adverbs are formed from adjectives by the addition of the ending *"-ly"* (as in suddenly, playfully, interestingly) or *"-ally"* after words in *-ic* (as in, automatically). Some adverbs are formed from nouns in combination with other suffixes: *-wise* (as in, clockwise, lengthwise) and *-ward(s)* (as in, northward, westward, skyward).

Some common adverbs have **no** suffixes, as in: *here/there, now, well, just.*

Some adverbs can describe other adverbs (the most common are intensifiers, such as "very", as in "very quick").

Some adverbs have the **same** form as their adjective counterparts, e.g., *fast, long, first.*

Not all words ending in -ly are adverbs: *lovely, ungainly,* and *likely* are adjectives. The word *only* and *early* may be either.

2.4.2 Adverbial Positions

Adverbs modify verbs in the same way adjectives qualify nouns.
The adverb **often follows the verb** it modifies:

> I shouted *loudly* to my friends across the theater.

Sometimes it precedes the verb:

> I *really* wanted to talk to her.

Sometimes position determines meaning:

> I think *clearly*. (My thinking is clear.)
> I *clearly* think. (It is clear that I think.)

Where emphasis is needed, the adverb may be put first, and the verb and subject inverted:

> *Never* have I seen such an ugly dog.

Student Notes:

2.5 Adverbs vs. Adjectives

2.5.1 Position and Meaning

When adverbs are used to modify adjectives, it is important to work out the relationships between them:

> She heard an *odd*, chilling sound.
>
> She heard an *oddly* chilling sound.

If one is not careful, it is easy to confuse whether a word is an adverb or an adjective, and, in either case, which other word it is modifying in the sentence.

The change from adjective to adverb can change the meaning drastically:

> The centaur appeared *quick*.
>
> The centaur appeared *quickly*.

In this example when the adjective is used, it appears that the centaur is quick; whereas, when the adverb is used, it is the centaur's appearance which occurred quickly.

Good vs. well: Both *good* and *well* can be used as adjectives. When used as an adjective, *good* refers to morality or quality, and *well* refers to health. However, only *well* can be used as adverb and *good* is always an adjective.

Correct:

> I feel *good* about my work.
>
> I feel *well*.
>
> I am *well*.
>
> I'm doing *well*.

Wrong: I am doing *good*.

Note: This may feel like a correct sentence, as it is often used in colloquial English to express "how" are person is, but it is not grammatical in this instance.

Note also: "Good" can be a *noun* that refers to "good acts"

> I spend one day a month doing *good* for people in need.

2.5.2 Adverbs and Adjectives

Great care must be taken to align only with the word it actually modifies, because its positioning can affect the meaning of the sentence:

I ate some peas *only* yesterday - I don't need to eat any today.

I *only* ate some peas yesterday - I didn't do anything else.

I ate *only* some peas yesterday - I didn't eat anything else.

Only I ate some peas yesterday - nobody else had any.

Early may be both adjective and adverb:

I take the *early* train.

I get up *early* to take the train.

2.5.3 Adjectives Only

Notice that some verbs may take adjectives to complete the meaning required (complementary adjectives). These verbs cannot form a complete thought without the required adjectives:

He looks *confused* today.

The music seemed *loud*.

Likely

Special care must be taken with the adjective **likely**. It is often mistaken for an adverb because of its form, but this is not an acceptable usage, for example:

Correct: The Republic is *likely* to fall.

Wrong: The Republic will likely fall.

Like (used as an adjective or preposition)

Like, with its opposite *unlike*, should be treated as an adjective or a preposition; that is, it must always have a noun to relate to. A predicate is formed with the verb *to be*:

Life is *like* a box of chocolates. (Life resembles a box of chocolates.)

Used in the form of a phrase, *like* will link two nouns (or noun phrases) of the same kind. In this case, *like* functions as a preposition, a phrase-maker, and it is categorized so in some grammar books.

Like any politician, he often told half-truths.

Like vs. Such As

In the above example, *like* is used to introduce similarity between two items or persons. This is an accepted usage in Sentence Correction on the GMAT. In other words, *like* cannot be used to introduce examples or a subset of a category, which should used *such as*.

Correct: I enjoy playing musical instruments *such as* the piano and violin.

Wrong: I enjoy playing musical instruments *like* the piano and violin.

In sum, on the GMAT, use **like** before a noun or pronoun when emphasizing similar characteristics between two persons, groups or things. Use **such as** before a noun or phrase when introducing examples.

Like vs. As/As if/As though

Use *like* before a noun or pronoun.
Use *as* before a clause, adverb or prepositional phrase.
Use *as if* and *as though* before a clause.

Like is generally used as a preposition in such a context. *As* is generally used as an adverb while sometimes serving as a preposition with the meaning of "in the capacity of." As you can tell, the focus of the comparison shifts from the noun when used with *like* to the verb when used with *as, as if,* or *as though*.

> My mother's cheesecake tastes **like** glue.
>
> I love frozen pizza because there is no other snack **like** it.
>
> My mother's cheesecake tastes great, **as** a mother's cheesecake should.
>
> There are times, **as** now, that learning grammar becomes important.
>
> He golfed well again, **as** in the tournament last year.
>
> He served **as** captain in the navy.
>
> He often told half-truths, **as** any politician would.
>
> He acts **as if** he knows me.
>
> It looked **as if** a storm were on the way.
>
> He yelled at me **as though** it were my fault.

The same rule applies when you use the expressions *seem like* and *look like*.

> **Correct:**
> He *seemed like* a nice guy at first.
> That *looks like* a very tasty cake.
>
> **Wrong**: It *seemed like* he liked me.
> **Correct**: It *seemed as if* he liked me.

Here the comparison is with a clause, not a noun.

Due to

Due to is also used adjectivally, and must have a noun to attach itself to:

> My failure, *due to* a long-term illness during the semester, was disappointing.
>
> (That is, the failure was attributable to the long-term illness, not the disappointment, which would have had other causes, such as the failure.)

Owing to

If an adverbial link is needed, the expression *owing to* has lost its exclusively adjectival quality:

> My failure was disappointing *owing to* a long-term illness during the semester.
>
> (In this case, the disappointment at the failure was caused by the long-term illness during the semester.)

2.6 Prepositions

A preposition is a word that is placed before a noun making a particular relationship between it and the word to which it is attached.

2.6.1 Preposition Types

There are a few types of prepositions:

1) **Simple prepositions**: these are the most common prepositions, such as: *in, on, of, at, from, among, between, over, with, through, without*.

2) **Compound prepositions**: two prepositions used together as one, such as: *into, onto/on to (on to is British English, onto is American English), out of*.

3) **Complex prepositions**: a two- or three-word phrase that functions in the same way as a simple preposition, as in: *according to, as well as, except for, in favor of*.

Preposition, i.e. pre position – prepositions always occur before the thing they refer to.

In: I was born *in* that house. (Here that house is the object of the preposition *in*.)

Prepositional phrases may be adjectival or adverbial, according to what they modify:

>   The girl *in my science class* kissed me.

Here, *in my science class* qualifies *girl*, and it is adjectival, but in:

>   The girl kissed me *in my science class*.

in my science class modifies *kissed*, indicating where the kiss took place, and it is therefore adverbial.

Between refers to two things only; for more than two, use *among*.

>   I sat *between* two very large people.
>   We split the loot *among* the four of us.

2.6.2 Prepositions Frequently Misused

You should use prepositions carefully. Some prepositions are used interchangeably and carelessly.

For example:

beside vs. *besides*

>   *beside* - at the side of someone or something

Frank stood *beside* Henry.

besides - in addition to

Besides his Swiss bank account, he has many others in Austria.

Exception: some idioms do not refer directly to either direct meaning.

She was beside herself with emotion.

The use of 'of' phrases such as: *could of, must of* are **incorrect** forms for *could have, must have*, etc.

between vs. *among*

Use the preposition *among* in situations involving more than two persons or things and use *between* in situations involving only two persons or things.

The money was divided *among* the workers.
The money was divided *between* the two boxers.

at vs. *with*:

Usually *at* for a thing but *with* for a person. Exceptions include: throw something *at* somebody *with* something, be angry *at* someone, be pleased *with* something, and others.

For example,

I went at Roger *with* a bat.

What's wrong with this sentence? Nothing actually, as it is grammatically correct. It is simply an odd usage of the prepositions.

Be careful to use the right preposition for the meaning you want; *agree with* differs in meaning from *agree to, compare with* is distinct from *compare to*, and so on.

The expressions *superior to, preferable to* and *different from* are the only standard forms.

Student Notes:

2.6.3 Idioms with Prepositions

A

*a sequence **of***
*in accordance **with***
*be accused **of***
*acquiesce **in***
*access **to***
*adhere **to**, be an adherent **of** (follower)*
*affinity **with***
*be afraid **of***
*agree **with** (a person/idea)*
*agree **to** (a proposal or action)*
*aim **at***
*allow **for***
*an instance **of***
*analogy **with**, analogous **to***
*be attended **by** (not with)*
*attend **to***
*appeal **to** (a person)*
*approval **of***
*as a result **of***
*associate **with***
*attribute A **to** B (B is attributed to A)*
*authority **on***

B

*be based **on***
*have belief **in***
*be capable **of***
*be careful **of***

C

*care **about** – be considerate of; to think about*
*care **for** - like*

center **on**, center **upon** (not round)

collide **with** (not against)

comment **on**

compare **with**, in comparison **with** (used when emphasizing differences)

compare **to** (used when emphasizing similarities)

comply **with**

be composed **by** – be created by

be composed **of** – to be made up of

comprise **of**

be concerned **with**

concur **in** (an opinion)

concur **with** (a person)

conducive **to**

conform **to**

in conformity **with**

consist **of**

in contrast **to**

contrast A **with** B

credit **with** (not to)

give someone credit **for** (something or doing something)

D

in danger **of**

debate **on**, debate **over**

decide **on**

depend **on** (whether..., not if...), be dependent **on**, be independent **from**

determine **by**

differ **from** - to be unlike something; to be different from

differ **with** - to disagree with someone

discourage **from**

feel disgusted **with** (not at)

at one's disposal

distinguish **from**

be drawn **to**

E

be embarrassed **by** (not at)
end **with**, end **in** (not by)
be envious **of**, jealous **of**
be equal **to** (not as)
be essential **to**
except **for**, except that...

F

be familiar **with**
be fascinated **by**

H

be hindered **by**

I

be identical **with**, be identical **to**
be independent **from**
be indifferent **towards**
inherit **from**
instill something **in** someone (not instill someone with)
invest **in**
involve **in** (not by)
insist **on**, insist that someone do something
be isolated **from**

J

judge **by** (not on)

M

mistake **for**

N

native *to*
a native *of*
necessity *of*, necessity *for*
a need *for*

O

be oblivious *of*, oblivious *to*

P

participate *in*
preferable *to*
prevent someone *from* doing something
profit *by* (not from)
prohibit someone *from* doing something
protest *against* (not at)

R

receptive *of*, receptive *to*
be related *to*
relations *with* (not towards)
repent *of*
in response *to*
result *from*
result *in*

S

be in search *of* (not for)
be sensible *of*
be sensitive *to*
separate *from* (not away from or out)
similar *to*
be sparing *of* (not with)

*be solicitous **of** (not to)*
*suffer **from** (not with)*
*be superior **to***
*subscribe **to***
*sacrifice **for***

T

*tendency **to** (not for)*
*tinker **with** (not at, although this is British English usage)*
*be tolerant **of** (not to)*

W

*wait **for** - to spend time in waiting for someone or something*
*wait **on** – to serve someone, typically used in a restaurant setting*

Sentence Correction Guide - Grammar Review

2.7 Verbs

Verbs are a class of words that serve to indicate the occurrence or performance of an action, or the existence of a state or condition. English verbs, when discussed in grammar terms, are normally expressed in the infinitive form, together with "to." For example: to run, to walk, to work, etc.

2.7.1 Transitive and Intransitive Verbs

A verb is said to be **transitive** if it needs an object to complete the meaning:

Joern *kicked his brother.*

Whereas a verb is said to be **intransitive** if the meaning is complete in itself:

I *smiled.*

Leaves *fall.*

Some verbs may be either transitive or intransitive (meaning that they do not require an object to be complete, but they can take one to add detail):

I *ate.*

I *ate pudding.*

2.7.2 Active and Passive Voices

Transitive verbs may appear in **active** or **passive** constructions. In active verb constructions, the subject is directly concerned with the verbal process; it is the agent:

The hitman *killed* my boyfriend.

When an active construction is made passive, the object becomes the subject, and the relationship is reversed, so that the subject is now acted upon, and is thus 'passive':

My boyfriend *was killed* by the hitman.

2.7.3 Major Tenses

You will not have to memorize all of the commonly used tenses for the GMAT, but a quick review of the tenses and their respective meanings will help you make sense of what can be a confusing topic.

Tense	Example
Simple Present (action frequently happening in the present)	He laughs. They laugh.
Perfect Progressive (action ongoing at this moment)	He is laughing. They are laughing.
Present Perfect (action started previously and completed thus far)	He has laughed. They have laughed.
Simple Past (completed action)	He laughed. They laughed.
Present Perfect Progressive (action started previously and ongoing at this moment)	He has been laughing. They have been laughing.
Past Perfect (action completed before another past time)	He had laughed. They had laughed.
Future (action to occur later)	He will laugh. They will laugh.
Future Progressive (action ongoing at a later time)	He will be laughing. They will be laughing.
Future Perfect (action regarded as completed at a later time)	He will have laughed. They will have laughed.
Future Perfect Progressive (action started at a later time and ongoing)	He will have been laughing. They will have been laughing.

Sentence Correction Guide – Grammar Review

A few Tense Examples

Present	Past	Past Participle
ring	rang	rung
walk	walked	walked

More examples

Present	Past	Future	Present Perfect	Past perfect	Future perfect	Present progressive	Conditional
dance	danced	will dance	has danced	had danced	will have danced	am dancing	would dance

Common Irregular Verbs

Infinitive Participle	Past Participle	Future Participle
do	did	done
go	went	gone
take	took	taken
rise	rose	risen
begin	began	begun
swim	swam	swum
throw	threw	thrown
break	broke	broken
burst	burst	burst
bring	brought	brought
lie	lay	lain
lay	laid	laid
get	got	got or gotten

An extensive list of irregular verbs can be found in Helpful Topics.

2.7.4 Moods: Indicative, Imperative and Subjunctive moods

Mood is a set of verb forms expressing a particular attitude. There are three main types of mood in English:

⇒ **Indicative**　　　⇒ **Imperative**　　　⇒ **Subjunctive**

The indicative mood is the most common one and it is used to express factual statements.

> I love playing the piano.

The imperative mood is used to express commands.

> Please close the window immediately!

The subjunctive mood expresses possibilities and wishes.

> If I were you, I would tell him my feelings.

The subjunctive is rarely used, but it is more often found in formal American usage than in British. The present subjunctive is very rare, having been overtaken by the present indicative, which it resembles in all parts except the third person singular: the subjunctive has no *-s* ending. The verb *to be*, however, has the form *be* for every person.

> I'll call you if need *be*.

The past subjunctive is identical with the ordinary past tense, but again, the verb *to be* is different, having the form *were* for all persons.

> If I *were* you, I would not do that.

Since the subjunctive expresses possibility, not fact, it is therefore found in:

(1) Clauses beginning with *if, as if, though, as though*, and

(2) After verbs expressing some kind of wish, recommendation, proposal, desire, regret, doubt, or demand.

The *if* (in subjunctive mood), *as if, though, as though* clauses express a condition that is NOT true.

Dependent Clause	,	Main Clause	Example
Present (True Condition)	,	Will/Can + Verb (base form)	**If you put your heart into it, you will be the winner.**
Past (Untrue Condition)	,	Would/Could + Verb (base form)	**If you put your heart into it, you could be the winner.**
Past Perfect (Untrue Condition)	,	Would have/Could have + Verb (past participle)	**If you had put your heart into it, you could have been the winner.**

When the subjective is used after verbs expressing some kind of wish, recommendation, proposal, desire, regret, doubt, or demand, there is a degree of uncertainty related to the final outcome.

Wrong

> She recommended that John *should* take the ferry.
>
> She recommended that John *takes* the ferry.
>
> She recommended that John *had taken* the ferry.

Correct

> She recommended that John *take* the ferry.

Note that you should ALWAYS just use the base form of the verb in such a subjunctive construction involving the *that* clause.

Regarding a list of words that are associated with the subjunctive mood, unfortunately, there's no hard and fast principle for it. This is what the linguists would call a lexical issue; the particular word and its meaning determine whether or not it can take an infinitive complement.

The following verbs can be used with a subjunctive that-clause:

> advise
>
> advocate
>
> ask
>
> beg
>
> decide
>
> decree
>
> demand

desire

dictate

insist

intend

mandate

move (in the parliamentary sense)

order

petition

propose

recommend

request

require

resolve

suggest

urge

vote

Of these, the following can ALSO take an infinitive, X to Y construction:

advise

ask

beg

order

petition

request

require

urge

The infinitive group is to some degree distinguished by their being directed at a person, rather than at a state of affairs.

2.7.5 Participle

There are several parts of the verb system which function as if they were different parts of speech (in the case of a participle, an adjective). In grammar, the PARTICIPLE is the term for two verb forms, the PRESENT PARTICIPLE (the "-ing" participle) and the PAST PARTICIPLE (the "-ed" participle, also ending in "-d' and "-t"). Both participles may be used like adjectives, but only if the participle indicates some sort of permanent characteristic: "running water," "the missing link," "lost property."

The PRESENT PARTICIPLE ends in "-ing" and is used in combination with the auxiliary "be" for the progressive continuous, as in: "am driving," "has been talking," etc.

The PAST PARTICIPLE ends in "-ed," "-d" or "-t" for all regular verbs and many irregular verbs, but many irregular verbs end in "-en" and "-n" (as in, "stolen" and "known") or with a change in the middle vowel (as in, "sung").

2.7.5.1 Present Participle

The present participle ends in *-ing*. Like an adjective, it may be used to form a predicate with the verb *to be*:

> Her feelings for Bob *were burgeoning* quickly.
>
> She *is stunning* in that dress.

Used as an adjective, it holds the normal adjectival position:

> Her *burgeoning* feelings for Bob surprised her.
>
> The *stunning* woman looked straight at me.

Participles are commonly found in phrases alongside the main part of the sentence:

> *Burgeoning* rapidly, *her feelings* for Bob rose to an untenable level.

If there is no appropriate noun, the sentence becomes nonsensical. The falsely assigned participle is known as 'dangling' or 'misrelated':

> **Wrong:** *Burgeoning* rapidly, *she* was soon unable to control her feelings for Bob.

As we will discuss in the Sentence Correction section, this is one of the most common errors on the GMAT, so learn to recognize a misplaced modifier (dangling participle), and you will have great success with these questions.

2.7.5.2 Past Participle

The past participle ends in *-(e)d* or *-t* in most verbs. A few archaic forms remain; these are verbs which make the past tense by changing the internal vowel, e.g., *write, wrote; see, saw*. These have participles that end in *-(e)n*, e.g. *written, seen*. The past participle forms a compound tense (perfect) with the addition of the verb *to have*. This denotes the perfected or completed action:

> I have *decided* to leave you.

It is useful to be able to recognize tenses in the Sentence Correction section because another of the most common errors on the GMAT is changing tenses needlessly in the middle of a sentence. Make sure that the answer you select does not have a change of tense which is not justified by the meaning of the sentence.

Used adjectivally, however, the past participle may also form a predicate with the verb *to be*.

I *have slain* you.
You *are slain*.

As with the present participle, the past participle must be related to its proper noun when forming a modifying phrase:

Embarrassed by her faux pas, *Ellen* left the room.

If the participle is misrelated (misplaced), comic results will occur:

Wrong: *Covered* with aluminum foil, I popped the lasagna into the oven.
(Here it is me, and not the lasagna, that is covered with aluminum foil!)

2.7.5.3 Special Situations

Absolute participle constructions are rare, and normally consist of a noun and participle - the noun to which the participle refers is actually present, although it does not have a function in the rest of the sentence:

The game being over, the players all went home.
Weather permitting, the wedding will be held outdoors.

A similar construction has the preposition *with*:

I returned to school *with my essay revised*.

A few participles have virtually become prepositions in their own right. These are:

barring, considering, excepting, including, owing (to), regarding, respecting, seeing, touching;

and the past forms,

excepted, provided, given.

Student Notes:

2.7.6 Gerunds & Infinitives

The GERUND is a verbal noun, ending in "-ing." Many grammarians of English use the term PARTICIPLE to include the gerund. Take the word "visiting" in the sentence: "They appreciate my visiting their parents regularly."

Like participles, gerunds are verbal elements which take on the role of another part of speech (in this case, that of a noun).

More common is the form ending in *-ing*, and this is identical with the form of the present participle. The two are distinguished only by function:

>Taking this route was a mistake. (subject, *taking*)
>
>Why are we going this way? (participle, *going*)

There is no preferred version, but it is important to maintain parallelism in your constructions.

If an ordinary noun can be substituted for the *-ing* form, then it is a gerund, e.g.,

>*Taking it* was the fun part.
>
>*Its capture* was the fun part.

The gerund retains its verbal function by taking an object:

>*Owning a monkey* is very unconventional.

Less commonly, the noun function dictates the form:

>*The wearing of pink* by red-headed people is a major fashion crime. (Wearing pink ...)

Where a noun or pronoun is used with a gerund, it should be in the possessive case:

>*My admonishing him* will not change his mind.
>
>It was *his winning* that bothered me, not *my losing*.
>
>I can't stand *my mother's telling* my friends embarrassing stories about me.

Any word may be used as an attributive (adjective) if placed before a noun. A gerund may be used this way (called a *gerundive*); its form is identical with the present participle, but the meaning will be different:

>A *building* reputation - participle (a reputation that is building)
>
>Some *building* blocks - gerund (blocks for building with)
>
>A *working* appliance - participle (an appliance that works)
>
>*working* papers - gerund (papers which allow you to work)

The infinitive form of a verb has the word "to" proceeding it:

>to + verb

The infinitive form may be used in this function:

>To err is human, to forgive, divine.
>
>(= Error is human; forgiveness is divine.)

Care must be taken not to use a mixture of the two forms:

> Talking to him was one thing, but kissing him was entirely another!
>
> To talk to him was one thing, but to kiss him was entirely another!
>
> **Not:** Talking to him was one thing, but to kiss him was entirely another!

Do avoid inserting a word or a phrase between the "to" and the "verb" in the infinitive form. This error is known as a *split infinitive*.

Wrong

> I asked him to quickly clean the table.

Correct

> I asked him to clean the table quickly.

Student Notes:

2.8 Conjunctions

Conjunctions are used to connect words or constructions. You should simply keep in mind that the most common conjunctions are AND, BUT, OR, which are used to connect units (nouns, phrases, gerunds, and clauses) of equal status and function. The other conjunctions, BECAUSE, IF, ALTHOUGH, AS, connect a subordinate clause to its superordinate clause, as in "We did it BECAUSE he told us to."

In general, don't begin sentences with conjunctions - *however* is better than *but* for this, but *however* goes best after semicolons, or use the adverb *instead*.

Correlative expressions such as *either/or, neither/nor, both/and, not only/but also* and *not/but* should all correlate ideas expressed with the same grammatical construction.

Special care has to be taken with clauses: only clauses of the same kind can be joined with a conjunction. Similarly, a phrase cannot be joined to a clause.

American usage is extremely fastidious in making constructions parallel, and this is another one of the common tricks in the Sentence Correction questions. Keep a lookout for conjunctions and lists, and you will be able to catch these errors.

2.9 Helpful Topics

2.9.1 Punctuation

Punctuation is the practice in writing of using a set of marks to regulate text and clarify its meaning, mainly by separating or linking words, phrases, and clauses. Currently, punctuation is not used as heavily as in the past. Punctuation styles vary from individual, newspaper to newspaper, and press to press in terms of what they consider necessary.

Improper punctuation can create ambiguities or misunderstandings in writing, especially when the *comma* is misused. For example, consider the following examples:

"They did not go, because they were lazy."

In this case, the people in question did not go for one reason: "because they were lazy."

But consider the sentence again:

"They did not go because they were lazy."

In this case, without the comma, the people probably DID go, but not because they were lazy, and instead for some other reason (they did not go because they were lazy, they went because they were tired).

Periods and Commas

(1) **Periods and Commas**: These are the most common form of punctuation. The period ends a sentence, whereas the comma marks out associated words within sentences. Commas are used for pauses, prepositional phrases, and appositive clauses offset from the rest of the sentence to rename a proper noun (Thomas, a baker,). They are the rest stop in the English language.

(2) **Colons, Semicolons, and Dashes (or Hypens)**: Many people avoid the use of the colon and semicolon because of uncertainty as to their precise uses. In less formal writing, the dash is often used to take the place of both the colon and the semi-colon. The rule is that both colons and semicolons must follow a complete independent clause. A semicolon must be followed by another complete clause, either dependent or independent. A colon may be followed by a list or phrase, or by a complete clause.

- The APOSTROPHE (') is used to show possession: Those books are Thomas's books.
- The COLON (:) is normally used in a sentence to lead from one idea to its consequences or logical continuation. The colon is used to lead from one thought to another.
- The SEMICOLON (;) is normally used to link two parallel statements.
- Consider the following examples:
  - COLON: "There was no truth in the accusation: they rejected it utterly."
    * Points to a cause/effect relationship, as a result of...
  - SEMICOLON: "There was no truth in the accusation; it was totally false." (Here two parallel statements are linked - "no truth" and "totally false." In the COLON example, the consequence is stated after the insertion of the colon).
    * Re-states initial premise, creates relation between disparate parts
    * Technically these sentences could be broken down into two separate sentences and they would remain grammatically sound. Two sentences, however, would suggest separateness (which in speech the voice would convey with a longer pause) that might not always be appropriate.
- HYPHENS or DASHES: The hyphen, or dash, is perhaps most important in order to avoid ambiguity, and is used to link words. Consider the following example:
  - "Fifty-odd people" and "Fifty odd people." When the hyphen is used, the passage means "approximately fifty people," while the second passage means "fifty strange(odd) people."

Otherwise, the use of the hyphen is declining. It was formerly used to separate vowels (co-ordinate, make-up), but this practice is disappearing.

For example: House plant → house-plant → houseplant

Sentence Correction Guide - Grammar Review

2.9.2 List of Irregular Verbs

To correctly use the verbs in different tense forms, please study the list carefully.

Base Form	Past Tense	Past Participle
Awake	Awaked; awoke	Awaked; awoken
Be	Was/Were	Been
Beat	Beat	Beat; beaten
Become	Became	Become
Begin	Began	Begun
Bend	Bent	Bent
Bite	Bit	Bitten
Bleed	Bled	Bled
Blow	Blew	Blown
Break	Broke	Broken
Bring	Brought	Brought
Build	Built	Built
Burst	Burst	Burst
Buy	Bought	Bought
Catch	Caught	Caught
Choose	Chose	Chosen
Come	Came	Come
Cost	Cost	Cost
Cut	Cut	Cut
Deal	Dealt	Dealt
Dig	Dug	Dug
Dive	Dived; dove	Dived
Do	Did	Done
Draw	Drew	Drawn
Dream	Dreamed; dreamt	Dreamed; dreamt
Drink	Drank	Drunk
Drive	Drove	Driven
Eat	Ate	Eaten
Fall	Fell	Fallen
Feed	Fed	Fed
Feel	Felt	Felt
Fight	Fought	Fought
Find	Found	Found
Fit	Fitted; fit	Fitted; fit
Fly	Flew	Flown
Forget	Forgot	Forgotten
Freeze	Froze	Frozen
Get	Got	Gotten; got
Give	Gave	Given
Go	Went	Gone
Grow	Grew	Grown

Base Form	Past Tense	Past Participle
Hang (an object)	Hung	Hung
Hang (a person)	Hanged	Hanged
Hear	Heard	Heard
Hide	Hid	Hidden; hid
Hit	Hit	Hit
Hold	Held	Held
Hurt	Hurt	Hurt
Keep	Kept	Kept
Kneel	Knelt; kneeled	Knelt; kneeled
Knit	Knit; knitted	Knit; knitted
Know	Knew	Known
Lay (put down)	Laid	Laid
Lead	Led	Led
Lean	Leaned	Leaned
Leave	Left	Left
Lend	Lent	Lent
Let	Let	Let
Lie (recline)	Lay	Lain
Light	Lighted; lit	Lighted; lit
Lose	Lost	Lost
Make	Made	Made
Mean	Meant	Meant
Meet	Met	Met
Pay	Paid	Paid
Prove	Proved	Proved; proven
Put	Put	Put
Quit (leave a place uncommon in American English)	Quit; quitted	Quit; quitted
Quit (end a job)	Quit	Quit
Read	Read	Read
Rid	Rid	Rid; ridden
Ride	Rode	Ridden
Ring	Rang	Rung
Run	Ran	Run
Say	Said	Said
See	Saw	Seen
Sell	Sold	Sold
Send	Sent	Sent
Set	Set	Set
Shake	Shook	Shaken
Shine	Shone; shined (polish)	Shone; shined (polish)

Base Form	Past Tense	Past Participle
Shoot	Shot	Shot
Show	Showed	Showed; shown
Shrink	Shrank	Shrunk
Shut	Shut	Shut
Sit	Sat	Sat
Sleep	Slept	Slept
Slide	Slid	Slid
Speak	Spoke	Spoken
Speed	Sped; speeded	Sped; speeded
Spend	Spent	Spent
Spin	Spun	Spun
Spring	Sprang	Sprung
Stand	Stood	Stood
Steal	Stole	Stolen
Stick	Stuck	Stuck
Sting	Stung	Stung
Strike	Struck	Struck; strucken
Swear	Swore	Sworn
Swim	Swam	Swum
Swing	Swung	Swung
Take	Took	Taken
Teach	Taught	Taught
Tear	Tore	Torn
Tell	Told	Told
Think	Thought	Thought
Throw	Threw	Thrown
Wake	Waked; woke	Waked; woken
Wear	Wore	Worn
Win	Won	Won
Wring	Wrung	Wrung
Write	Wrote	Written

2.9.3 Words Frequently Confused

The following words are often misused, even by experienced writers:

accumulative, cumulative

adverse, averse

affect, effect

affluent, effluent

allusion, illusion, delusion
alternate, alternative

amiable, amicable, amenable

anomaly, analogy

apposite, opposite

appraise, apprise
ascent, assent, accent

belated, elated

beneficent, benevolent

biannual, biennial

censer, censor, censure

colloquy, obloquy

complement, compliment

contemptuous, contemptible

continual, continuous, contiguous

credible, credulous

decry, descry

deduce, deduct

deficient, defective

denote, connote

deprecate, depreciate

dependent, dependant

derisive, derisory

devolve, evolve
digress, regress

disburse, disperse

discrete, discreet

disquisition, inquisition

economic, economical

edible, eatable

efficient, effectual, effective

eject, inject

elusive, illusive

erotic, exotic

erupt, disrupt

euphony, cacophony

Sentence Correction Guide – Grammar Review

fallacious, fallible

fictitious, factitious

further, farther

grouchy, grungy

historic, historical

hoard, horde
homogenous, homogeneous

human, humane

hypercritical, hypocritical

inchoate, chaotic

induce, indict

ineligible, illegible

ingenious, ingenuous

insidious, invidious

intermediate, intermediary

introspection, retrospection

judicial, judicious

lie, lay

lightening, lightning

luxurious, luxuriant

monitory, monetary

negligible, negligent

notable, notorious

observance, observation
obtrude, intrude

ordinance, ordnance

oral, aural

overt, covert

peaceful, peaceable

perspective, perceptive

perspicacious, perspicuous

precipitate, precipitous

precede, proceed

preclude, prelude

prescribe, proscribe

principle, principal

prospective, prosperous

raise, rise

reputed, imputed

resource, recourse

salutary, salubrious

seasonal, seasonable

spasmodic, sporadic

tacit, taciturn

temperature, temperament

temporize, extemporize

tortuous, torturous

uninterested, disinterested

urban, urbane

veracious, voracious

vocation, avocation

If you think you may not know the difference between any of these pairs, or would like to brush up on the meanings of any of these words, please ask your instructor to clarify them, or look them up in a dictionary before your test date.

Student Notes:

2.9.4 American vs. British Usage

American spelling often differs from British usage, but this is **not** one of the factors tested in the GMAT examination. Examples include:

- The use of *-or* instead of British *-our*, e.g., *color, harbor, favor*, and the use of *-er* for *-re*, e.g., *center, fiber, theater*.

- The final or internal *e* is dropped in *ax, acknowledgment, judgment, jewelry*. Other modifications include: *plow, wagon, check* (cheque), *pajamas, gray, mold, program, draft, marvelous, traveler*.

- The double *-ll* is retained in *skillful, fulfill, install*; the endings *-ise, -isation*, are written, *-ize, -zation*.

If such American spelling forms appear in the sentences for correction, no alternatives will be given, so there is in fact no problem.

Some nouns have given rise to new usages, such as *service*, and this is acceptable in both American and British English. Others are not, e.g., *suspicion* for 'suspect.' Again, the presence of other forms in the choices given will indicate whether this usage is to be considered non-standard. The word *loan* is used only as a noun in British English, but is an acceptable verb form in American English.

Standard American words frequently differ from their British equivalents -

Frequently Used in America	**Frequently Used in Britain**
apartment	flat
boardwalk	promenade
bug	insect
drapes	curtains
elevator	lift
fall	autumn
fix a flat	change a tire
garbage can, trashcan	dustbin
gas	petrol
hardware store	ironmonger's
mad	angry
peek	peer, glimpse
pillow	cushion
pitcher	jug
round trip	return trip
salesgirl	shop assistant
sidewalk	pavement
sick	ill, diseased
smokestack	chimney

There are many more of these, but as these are not 'diction' errors, no alternative version will be given among the multiple choice answers in the Sentence Correction section.

Student Notes:

2.9.5 Standard vs. Non-standard Usage

There are many American expressions that do not meet standard requirements; most of these are easily recognized, but some may raise doubts. As a general rule, *kind of* and *sort of* are to be avoided altogether:

> I was *sort of* hurt by that.

If used adjectivally - and this would be possible - *kind of* does not have an article:

> I thought I saw you with some *kind of* food.

The expression *those (these) kind of things* is particularly offensive, since *kind* and *sort* are singular and would properly be preceded by *that* or *this*. Similarly, the ending *-s* should never be attached to compounds of *-where*, e.g., *somewhere*. The *-s* ending is, however, to be found in the compounds of *-ways*, e.g., *always, sideways, longways, lengthways*, but *anyways* and *ways* are nonstandard forms, as are *someway, noway* and *nohow*. Nonstandard also are the expressions *can't seem to*, for 'seem unable to' and *go to*, meaning 'intend.' *Any* should not be used adverbially:

> **Wrong:** I don't think I hurt him *any*.

The correct expression is *at all*. I don't think I hurt him *at all*.

Adjectives should not be used as adverbs:

> **Wrong:** We agreed on the specifics *some*; (use *some* for 'somewhat')
>
> **Wrong:** I thought my plan would *sure* succeed; (use *sure* for 'surely,' 'certainly.')
>
> **Wrong:** I noticed a guy who was *real* cute standing outside; (use *real* for 'really.')

Non-standard usages would include verbs used as nouns, as in *eats* or *invite* (invitation), prepositions used in conjunctions, or *on account of* for 'because':

> **Wrong:** I liked him *on account* he made me toys and things.

All should not be followed by *of* unless a pronoun follows:

> I hate *all those people*.
>
> I hate *all of you*!

Other nonstandard expressions include:

Nonstandard	Standard
be at	be
both alike	either 'both' or 'alike'
bring	take
equally near	equally
have a loan of	borrow
have got	have
human	human being
in back of	behind
inside of	within
lose out	lose
no account, no good	worthless
no place	nowhere
nowhere near	not nearly
off of	from or completely
out loud	aloud
outside of	outside or except
over with	over/ended
plenty, mighty	very

Student Notes:

Chapter 3

Sentence Correction Strategy

The Grammar Review in the previous section touches on nearly all of the flaws you are likely to encounter in Sentence Correction questions on the GMAT.

The Sentence Correction section tests your knowledge of written English grammar by asking you which of the five choices best expresses an idea or relationship. This section gives you a sentence that may or may not contain errors of grammar or usage. You must select either the answer that best corrects the sentence or the answer stating that the sentence is correct as is. The questions will require you to be familiar with the stylistic conventions and grammatical rules of standard written English and to demonstrate your ability to improve incorrect or ineffective expressions.

This section tests three broad aspects of language proficiency:

- Correct expression

- Effective expression

- Proper Diction

A correct sentence is grammatically correct and structurally sound. It conforms to all the rules of standard written English such as subject-verb agreement, verb tense consistency, modifier reference and position, idiomatic expressions and parallel construction.

In addition to being grammatically correct, a sentence needs to be effective. It should express an idea or relationship clearly and concisely, as well as grammatically. The best choice should have no superfluous words or unnecessarily complicated expressions. This does not mean that the shortest choice is always the best answer.

Proper diction is another important part of effectiveness. It refers to the standard dictionary meanings of words and the appropriateness of words in context. In evaluating the diction of a sentence, you must be able to recognize whether the words are well-selected, correctly presented, and suitable for the context.

3.1 How to Tackle

The following is a step-by step-process that you should follow to tackle Sentence Correction questions:

(1) **Read the whole sentence for structure and content.**

You have to understand the entire sentence to be able to pick the best choice later. You should read the sentence for meaning as well as structure. Two questions you should ask yourself are:

- What is the author trying to say?

    Some answers to GMAT questions are grammatically correct but change the meaning of the sentence. Such answers are wrong.

- What is the structure of the sentence?

    As you read the sentence, try to identify the subject, verb, prepositions, conjunctions, and participles. These parts of speech are associated with the common errors found in Sentence Correction questions. You won't have to identify the grammatical function of each word, phrase and clause in the sentence, but be familiar with common errors and watch for **signals** (which we will discuss later) that the question is testing a specific error.

(2) **Try to predict the correct answer.**

You may already have an idea of how to correct the sentence. Before you plunge into the answers for the question, try to predict what the correct answer is going to be.

For example, in the sentence "Shelly <u>have three items</u> in her pocket," the correct answer choice is likely to contain the verb "has."

While your ability to predict the correct answer will improve with practice, you will not be able to correctly predict the correct answer choice all the time.

(3) **Don't read the first answer choice.**

Reading the first answer choice is **always** a waste of your time. You have already read it in the original sentence! The first answer choice is **always** the same as the underlined portion of the original sentence.

Remember that only one out of five options in Sentence Correction questions contains no error. If you think that the original sentence is correct, then go ahead and scan through answers 2-5, but do not become flustered if none of the answers are correct. After all, **20% of the Sentence Correction problems need no correction**.

(4) **Scan through the answer choices.**

Each Sentence Correction problem in the GMAT is usually created with two or three different possible errors where you have to pay attention. The various combinations of these possible errors result in the options you are given.

If you have predicted the correct answer, you need only to identify the choice which matches your prediction. Sometimes you will find an exact match, but more often you will be able to narrow the answer choices to two or three.

If you were not able to predict the correct answer, look for evidence in the answer choices to determine what is being tested in the question in order to pick the best answer. For example, if more than one answer choice is similar except for a few words, your investigation should begin with the answers that are similar.

When you have found the parts of the sentence that vary, look for evidence in the remaining part of the sentence to determine which option to choose. Start with whatever is dictated by the unchanging part of the sentence. For example, if a verb is provided in singular and plural forms, find the subject of the sentence.

(5) **Eliminate wrong answers.**

By now, you should have an idea of what answers are grammatically or stylistically incorrect. Eliminate these answers and focus on the differences among the remaining choices.

(6) **Put your choice back into the sentence as you read once again.**

Remember that the GMAT test-writers will often create answer choices which are grammatically correct, but either change the meaning of the sentence or are not stylistically the best answer. Since the GMAT tests not only grammar, but also the efficiency and effectiveness of communication, you have to look for redundancy, ambiguity, and uncommon or confusing expressions.

Putting your choice back into the sentence will help you decide which answer communicates the meaning of the sentence most effectively and prevents you from making careless errors.

3.2 Special Advice

Sentence Correction accounts for 13-16 of the 41 questions in the verbal section of the GMAT. While you have an average of less than 2 minutes to answer each question on the verbal section, we recommend that you spend less time on each Sentence Correction question. **In fact, we recommend that you practice getting your speed down to one minute or less!**

Answering Sentence Correction questions rapidly will allow you to "bank" time in the verbal section that you can later use to concentrate on a difficult reading comprehension passage or to focus on a challenging critical reasoning question. Remember that the verbal section is the last section on the GMAT, and your endurance is likely to be fading at this point in the test. You may find that you need a few moments of the additional time you have saved to recover your energy to push through to the last question.

The Sentence Correction questions on the GMAT have several types of errors, most of which reoccur frequently throughout this section of the test. A close and thorough study of our grammar review segment will help you rapidly identify and correct these errors. We often recommend to students who are pressed for preparation time that they spend the lion's share of their study time on Sentence Correction. The time you spend concentrating on Sentence Correction and practicing spotting common errors quickly is among the most productive time you may spend studying for the GMAT.

While trying to answer each question correctly in such a short amount of time may seem daunting, practicing the steps outlined earlier will help you answer the questions efficiently, effectively, and most importantly, correctly.

Student Notes:

3.3 Common Errors and Tested Topics

3.3.1 Misplaced Modifiers (and Dangling Participles)

Modifiers are phrases that modify another part of the sentence. In order to be correct, the modifying phrase must be as close as possible to what it modifies. For example:

Disgusting and pus-filled, Enrico nursed his festering wound.

In this example, it sounds as if Enrico is disgusting and pus-filled, rather than his wound. As soon as you read this sentence, you should immediately realize that the correct answer choice will place *disgusting and pus-filled* as close as possible to *wound*. To wit:

Enrico nursed his *disgusting and pus-filled* festering wound.

Signals

- An introductory phrase is a common signal of a misplaced modifier.

- Any modifying phrase which is not close to what it modifies may also indicate this error.

Another example – Note: answers to examples appear at end of chapter.

Career switchers often schedule interviews with high-level managers, believing that the insight of professionals will help narrow down the many choices of careers available to graduating MBAs.

(A) Career switchers often schedule interviews with high-level managers, believing that the insight of professionals will help narrow down the many choices of careers available to graduating MBAs.

(B) Career switchers, believing that the insight of professionals will help narrow down the many choices of careers available to graduating MBAs, often schedule interviews with high-level managers.

(C) Career switchers believing that scheduling interviews with the insight of high-level professional managers will help narrow down the many choices of careers available to graduating MBAs.

(D) Career switchers, believing that interviews with high-level managers whose insight will help narrow down the many choices of careers available to graduating MBAs, often schedule them.

(E) Career switchers often schedule interviews to narrow down the many choices of careers available to graduating MBAs, believing that the insight of professionals with high-level managers will help them.

3.3.2 Agreement (Concord)

A very common Sentence Correction error centers on the agreement between the subject of a sentence and the verb. The subject and verb must agree in number; that is, a plural verb must have a plural subject and a singular verb must have a singular subject.

This is particularly important with *of* constructions:

A *flock* of birds, flying south for the winter, *was* above us.

Another example:

Wrong: My *group* of fourth graders *are* so well behaved.

The singular subject group demands a singular verb *is*.

Correct: My *group* of fourth graders *is* so well behaved.

If the verb is inverted, care must be taken to find the subject:

I journeyed to the graveyard *where once stood my father's tomb.*

Agreement is based on formal grammar, and plurals do not depend on meaning but on the grammatical relationships between words. Two single subjects joined by *and* take a plural verb, but an addition inside two commas using words such as *as well as*, or *not to mention*, takes a singular verb.

My mother, as well as my father, *is* from Venezuela.

Signals

- Collective nouns such as team, audience, staff, family, public or committee are singular.
- An intervening phrase which separates the noun from the verb is used to confuse the unwary test-taker.
- A sentence structure with the verb before the subject may indicate an agreement error.
- A conjunction such as *and*, *either/or*, and *neither/nor*, can be used as a trap.

3.3.3 Tense

Many GMAT questions center upon the relationships between tenses. While the tenses in a sentence do not have to be the same, they must relate to each other in a way that makes the sequence of actions clear to the reader. The term sequence of tenses refers to the rules which govern how we alter verb tenses to make clear that all events - past, present or future - are not simultaneous.

> As soon as I *hear* the dog bark, I *knew* you *were* at the door.

The above sentence sets forth a likely condition anticipated by the speaker. The use of the past tense is **incorrect**. The sentence may be corrected thus:

> As soon as I *hear* the dog bark, I *will* know you *are* at the door.

In the above example, the future tense makes clear that the dog's barking is anticipated by the speaker.

Errors in the sequence of tenses often occur with the perfect tenses, all of which are formed by inserting an auxiliary (or auxiliaries) before the past participle, the third principal form of a verb.

Some common auxiliaries are "had," "has," and "have." They are used with the past participle to form perfect tenses.

Unfortunately, the rules governing sequence of tenses are a bit of a jumble. Often you will have to rely on your ear and common sense to guide you with these questions. But below are some guidelines you can use in order to sort out what the correct sentence should look like.

- In complex sentences, the tense of the verb in the main clause governs the tenses of the verbs in subsequent or dependent clauses.

Tense in Main Clause	Purpose of Dependent Clause	Tense in Dependent Clause	Example
Simple Present	To show same-time action	Simple Present	**I am eager to go for a walk because I enjoy exercise.**
Simple Present	To show earlier action	Simple Past	**He feels that she made a mistake last year.**
Simple Present	To show a period of time extending from some point in the past to the present	Present Perfect	**The congregation believes that it has selected a suitable preacher.**

Simple Present	To show action to come	Future	My teacher says that he will grade the test next week.
Simple Past	To show another completed past action	Simple Past	She cooked the salmon because she knew it was fresh.
Simple Past	To show an earlier action	Past Perfect	He cooked the salmon well because he had attended culinary school.
Simple Past	To state a general truth	Simple Present	Copernicus believed that the universe is like a giant clock.
Present Perfect	To show an earlier action	Simple Past	The lawyer has handled many cases since he passed the bar.
Present Perfect	To show action happening at the same time	Present Perfect	She has grown a foot because she has taken steroids.
Past Perfect	To show the second of two actions in the past	Simple Past	The bird had flown for miles before it landed.
Future	To show action happening at the same time	Simple Present	I will be a senator if they vote for me.
Future	To show an earlier action	Simple Past	You will go to the concert if you waited in line beforehand to get the ticket.
Future	To show future action earlier than the action of the independent clause	Present Perfect	My grandmother will finish the puzzle soon if her dog has not eaten the pieces.

Future Perfect	For any purpose	Simple Present or	The factory will have produced many widgets long before it closes.
		Present Perfect	The factory will have produced many widgets long before it has closed.

Do not get confused between the present perfect ("has walked") and the past perfect ("had walked"). While both verbs convey past action, the present perfect verb actually represents present tense.

Signals

- Several actions occurring in different time frames.
- Multiple tenses.

Another example – answer at end of chapter

When he phones her, she tells him to stop calling, but he acted as if he had not understood her.

(A) she tells him to stop calling, but he acted as if he had not understood her.

(B) she told him to stop calling, but he acted as if he had not understood her.

(C) she tells him to stop calling, but he acts as if he did not understood her.

(D) she tells him to stop calling, but he acts as if he has not understood her.

(E) she tells him to stop calling, but he acted as if he does not understand her.

3.3.4 Parallelism

Parallelism is the most mathematical of the errors tested on the GMAT. Just as the expressions on each side of an algebraic equation must be equivalent, so too must the parts of speech on either side of a conjunction be the same. By thinking about a conjunction in a sentence as an equal sign, you can identify and correct this error. For example:

Which do you like best, *to swim, a drive, or jogging*?

Predicting the correct answer for these types of errors presents some difficulty, as often there is more than one way of restating the sentence correctly. For example, the previous sentence may be corrected in three different ways:

Which do you like best, *to swim, to drive, or to jog*?

Which do you like best, *a swim, a drive, or a jog*?

Which do you like best, *swimming, driving, or jogging*?

Any of the above is correct as long as the words or phrases connected by the conjunction *or* are the same part of speech.

Signals

- Items in a list

- Long phrases or clauses connected by a conjunction

Another example – answer at end of chapter

Our firm is best suited to undertake the project because we have the financial wherewithal, vast experience undertaking similar projects, and can use our large employee base - all of which is necessary to complete the work on-time and under-budget.

(A) the financial wherewithal, vast experience undertaking similar projects, and can use our large employee base - all of which is necessary

(B) the financial wherewithal, vast experience undertaking similar projects, and a large employee base - all necessary

(C) the financial wherewithal, vast experience undertaking similar projects, and a large employee base - all of whom are necessary

(D) the financial wherewithal, vast experience undertaking similar projects, and can use our large employee base necessary

(E) the financial wherewithal, vast experience undertaking similar projects, and can use our large employee base since they are necessary

3.3.5 Comparisons

Comparisons are a first cousin to parallelism. Frequently, a sentence with a comparison will appear at first glance to be correct, but will actually compare two or more elements which are not expressed in similar form. For example:

The judge of the baking contest liked *the pastry* Sally made better than *Bob*.

In this sentence, the judge is evaluating the comparative merits of Sally's pastry and Bob himself. Put it another way, he is comparing Sally's pastry to Bob, rather than comparing Sally's pastry to Bob's pastry. The correct way of expressing the idea is thus:

The judge of the baking contest liked *Sally's pastry* better than *Bob's*.

Signals

- Key words such as *than, like, unlike, as, compared to, more than,* and *less than* should alert you to check what is being compared in the sentence.

Sentence Correction Guide – Sentence Correction Strategy

Another example – answer at end of chapter

Unlike <u>its competitors, Globex and MondoCorp, the revenues of Galactic Enterprises increased by cornering the widget market in the fourth quarter, thus making</u> Galactic Enterprises the world's most profitable company and a darling of Wall Street.

- **(A)** its competitors, Globex and MondoCorp, the revenues of Galactic Enterprises increased by cornering the widget market in the fourth quarter, thus making

- **(B)** Globex and MondoCorp, its competitors, the revenues of Galactic Enterprises increased by cornering the widget market in the fourth quarter, thus making

- **(C)** its competitors, Globex and MondoCorp, Galactic Enterprises increased its revenues by cornering the widget market in the fourth quarter, by making

- **(D)** Globex and MondoCorp, its competitors, Galactic Enterprises increased its revenues by cornering the widget market in the fourth quarter, thus making

- **(E)** its competitors, Globex and MondoCorp, the revenues of Galactic Enterprises cornered the widget market in the fourth quarter, thus making

3.3.6 Pronoun Agreement & Reference

Errors regarding pronouns fall into two broad categories: agreement and reference.

Agreement

Pronouns must agree with their antecedents in person, number, and gender. If the antecedent is third person singular male, then the pronoun must be third person singular male, as well.

Wrong: In recent years, Fred has tried to lose *its* excess weight through numerous diets.

Correct: In recent years, Fred has tried to lose *his* excess weight through numerous diets.

Reference

Pronoun reference errors occur when ambiguity exists as to the antecedent of the pronoun. Additionally, the pronouns must clearly refer to only one antecedent. The sentence must leave no doubt in the reader's mind as to what the pronoun refers to. Sentences with multiple nouns are a classic signal of a pronoun reference error.

The attorney argued that students who were denied the use of school facilities for political activities had lost *their* right of free assembly.

In the above sentence, the writer does not make clear to what *their* refers. It could refer to students, facilities, or activities. The sentence must be constructed so that the reader has no doubt about the antecedent of the pronoun *their*:

The attorney argued that students lost their right of free assembly when they were denied the use of school facilities for political activities.

In the above sentence, it is clear that *their* and *they* refer to students.

Signals

- Several nouns preceding a pronoun.

Another example

The *Federalist Papers* is a compilation of articles written by Alexander Hamilton and James Madison, as well as a few by John Jay, <u>since each of them were</u> advocates of the Constitution.

(A) since each of them were

(B) since they were each

(C) since all of them were

(D) each of which was

(E) because all of the men were

3.3.7 Idioms, Usage, and Style

Sentence Correction questions that revolve around idioms, usage, and style generally test subtle errors in expression. Idiomatic expressions often have no basis in grammar, or even logic, but have been accepted into the language.

Especially for non-native speakers, some of the trickiest errors in this section are incorrect idioms. This includes using the wrong preposition with a verb, among many other things. Unfortunately, the only thing to do about this problem is practice, so do as many practice questions as possible and take note of any examples in which two different versions of an idiom are used. After you check your answers, make a list of the idioms you did not know and memorize them.

Native speakers often use idioms without thinking about the literal meaning of the words. For example:

> We finished the rest of the tasks *in one fell swoop*.

The expression in *one fell swoop* makes little sense literally, but English speakers recognize it as meaning *all at once*.

Some conventions of standard English may seem nit-picky, but you should familiarize yourself with some rules which are commonly tested. For example:

Wrong

> When *compared to* Greg's ability to carry a tune, Marsha's musical skill is unimpressive.

The correct expression in this case is *compared with* because the items being compared are dissimilar: the relative musical abilities of Greg and Marsha. The construction using *compared with* points out the differences.

Correct

> When *compared with* Greg's ability to carry a tune, Marsha's musical skill is unimpressive.

Use *compared to* when illustrating similarities. For example:

> He *compared* his teacher *to* Bruce Greenwald, the esteemed professor famous for his Value Investing lectures at Columbia Business School.

> May I *compare* thee *to* a summer's day? (Shakespeare, Sonnet 18)

In sum, *compare to* is used when things are being likened. *Compare with* is used when the comparison is more specific and implies differences.

Each other refers to **two** entities; where more than two are concerned, use *one another*.

> The two of them hated *each other* with a passion.

The four of us looked at *one another* and laughed.

Student Notes:

3.3.7.1 GMAT Idiom List

a lot – The proper form is two words, not *alot*.

agree on – must be followed by the *-ing* form of a verb.

an instance of – is different in meaning from *an example of*. An *example* is one of a number of things while an *instance* is an *example* which proves or illustrates. People may be *examples* but never *instances*.

as vs. than – The words are not interchangeable. Use *as* for comparisons of similarity or equality and *than* for comparisons of degree or difference. Always use *than* with the comparative (-er) form of an adjective.

as good as or better than – is a cliché and should be avoided. Do not telescope a comparison of similarity - *as* with a comparison of degree - *than*. A better construction is to break the juxtaposition up into separate thoughts.

as ... as – is a grammatical way of expressing similarity: he is *as* tall *as* his sister.

such ... as – is grammatical when both words are used as prepositions in a comparison: *such* men *as* he. Avoid *as such* when meaning *in principle*.

based on – The phrasal verb *based on* is grammatical and can be used either actively or passively.

> The style of her cooking is *based on* Southern cuisine.

> She *bases* her thinking *on* sound logic.

depends on whether – The construction is generally accepted and is certainly preferable to *depends on if*.

> His fate *depends on whether* the governor calls back in time.

different from vs. different than (differ from) – Although strict grammarians say that *from* is the correct word to follow *different*, many authorities believe that *than* may follow in order to avoid elaborate constructions. In contrast, the authorities agree that *from* is the correct word when used with *differ*.

> He is a *different* man *than* he was in 1985.

Compare to:

> He is a *different* man *from the man that* he was in 1985.

Identical with/to – *Identical* may be used with either preposition without changing the intended meaning.

no less a ... than - The expression is an accepted idiom meaning great or not less impressive.

not only/but also - *Not only* is **always** followed by *but also* in a sentence.

> The subways in summer are *not only* hot, *but also* humid.

regard as - The verb *regard* may be used with *as* and either an adjective or a noun.

> We *regard* George's ranting *as* silly. The tribe *regards* shaking hands *as* taboo.

Do not use regard with an infinitive or *being*:

> Wrong: He is regarded to be an expert. He is regarded as being an expert.

regardless - Usage of the word *regardless* is acceptable. *Irregardless* is non-standard usage.

So ... - Avoid the use of the appealing *so* as an intensifier. The weather is *so* delightful. Very would be a better choice. Similarly, when using *so* with a participle, consider using *well* to qualify.

> Mary is *so well* suited to be an attorney.

3.3.7.2 Words Frequently Misused

Aggravate/annoy - *To aggravate* is to make a situation worse. *To annoy* is to irritate. In formal English, people cannot be aggravated, only annoyed.

> When the Chairman of the Federal Reserve lowered interest rates, he *aggravated* the flailing economy and *annoyed* many Wall Street bankers.

Ago/since - *Ago* carries a thought from the present to the past. *Since* carries a thought from the past to the present.

> It was twenty years *ago* that I first heard that song.

> It has been twenty years *since* I first heard that song.

Among/between - Use *between* when comparing two items and *among* when comparing three or more.

> I was torn *between* studying finance and studying marketing.

> After I was accepted into all three MBA programs, I had to choose *among* Harvard, Wharton, and Columbia.

Amount/number - Use *amount* when referring to an uncountable noun and *number* when referring to a countable word.

There is a large *amount* of water in the ocean.

There is a large *number* of fish in the ocean.

Fewer/less – Use *fewer* when referring to a countable noun and *less* when referring to an uncountable noun. The usage of fewer/less is similar to amount/number.

The supermarket express lane is open to customers with ten items or *fewer*.

There is *less* rudeness at Dean and Deluca than at Fairway.

Good/well - When used as adjectives, *good* refers to morality or quality and *well* refers to health. However, only *well* can be used as adverb and *good* is always an adjective.

I feel *good* about my work.

I feel *well*.

I am *well*.

I'm doing *well*.

It is *good* to hear that you feel *well* today.

Imply/infer – *To imply* is to express a thought indirectly. *To infer* is to derive a conclusion indirectly.

While the politician never *implied* that he would raise taxes, the audience *inferred* that he would soon do so.

Like/as – Use *like* before a noun, or pronoun. Use *as* before a clause, adverb or prepositional phrase. *Like* is generally used as a preposition in such a context; *as* is generally used as an adverb while sometimes serving as a preposition with the meaning of "in the capacity of."

My mother's cheesecake tastes *like* glue.

I love frozen pizza because there is no other snack *like* it.

My mother's cheesecake tastes great, *as* a mother's cheesecake should.

There are times, *as* now, that learning grammar becomes important.

He golfed well again, *as* in the tournament last year.

He served *as* a captain in the navy.

Less than/under – *Less than* is the correct expression when making a comparison of number or amount. *Under* is limited to describing spatial relationships.

I will host the party if the guest list is *less than* fifty people.

More than/over – *More than* is the correct expression when making a comparison of number or amount. *Over* is limited to describing spatial relationships.

We processed *more than* 1,000 applications in one hour.

Why is there a fuss *over* the morality of citizens?

Student Notes:

3.4 What to Do If You Are Completely Stumped

Sometimes you may find yourself with one or more answer choices which seem to be correct. If you have followed Manhattan Review's six-step process for Sentence Correction and still find yourself lost, take a step back and think about the answer choices.

Put the answers back into the sentence, again.

> You should have already done this, but if you are still stumped, do it again. Remember that a correct answer retains the meaning of the original sentence. You may be analyzing an answer choice which changes the idea which the author wished to convey. Make sure that word order has not been switched in the answer to suggest a different meaning.

Shorter is better.

> Wordy or long-winded ways of expressing thoughts are often not the best means of expression. Sometimes the best answer is the one with the fewest words, though there may be exceptions. In fact, the GMAT test-maker may make a trap option which seemingly looks concise.

Eliminate answers with passive voice.

> You will seldom encounter a correct answer that employs the use of the passive voice. While use of the passive voice is not in and of itself grammatically incorrect, expressing an idea actively is preferable. Given the choice between *The ball was hit by me* and *I hit the ball*, the latter is the better choice.

Avoid redundancy.

> The best answer should be clear and concise. An answer which repeats elements of the sentence unnecessarily is incorrect.

Don't choose the answer with the word "being".

> Don't choose such an option unless you are positive that *being* is a necessary and useful part of the sentence. It is probably just confusing the issue and is better left out.

If you review the rules discussed in the Grammar Review section and follow the six-steps for Sentence Correction questions, you should have little trouble identifying the best answer among your choices.

Answers to prior Examples

4.3.1 Misplaced Modifier (B)   4.3.3 Tense (D)   4.3.4 Faulty Parallelism (B)
4.3.5 Comparison (D)   4.3.6 Pronoun Agreement & Reference (E)

3.5 Detailed List of Typical Errors

Based on our close examination of all the Sentence Correction problems in the Official Guides and released old exams, we have compiled the following list for your easy reference.

TIP: PLEASE FOCUS YOUR INITIAL ATTENTION ON BASIC GRAMMAR ELEMENTS ONLY - SUBJECT, VERB AND OBJECT. Then examine the sentence in detail; that way, you will not get bogged down by verbiage.

Goal I: Effectiveness of the Language

To achieve conciseness & clarity in a sentence, you should pick the choices that contain:

(1) No wordiness or fragments

(2) No redundancy

>   Example: The remarkable growth in increased revenue
>
>   Here, both *growth* and *increased* refer to increase.

(3) No ambiguous double negative meanings

(4) No possibility of multiple interpretations of the sentence

(5) No change in meaning or intent

(6) Also, be suspicious of any answer choice containing:

>   "being"
>
>   "thing"

Goal II: Correctness of the Language

3.5.1 Modifiers

Be aware:

> **A participle at the start of a sentence must modify the subject of the sentence. Otherwise, it is a dangling participle.**

Wrong

Having read the book, there is no question the book is better than the film.

Correct

Having read the book, I have no doubt that the book is better than the film.

Also please pay attention to:

(a) **Misplaced modifying clauses**

   Wrong

   Whether baked or mashed, Tom loves potatoes.

   Correct

   Tom loves potatoes, whether baked or mashed.

(b) **Ambiguous modifying clauses**

   Example

   People who jog frequently develop knee problems.

   To eliminate ambiguity, you can change it to:
   People develop knee problems if they jog frequently.

   -or-

   People frequently develop knee problems if they jog.

(c) **Proximity of the modifier and the modified object**

Limiting modifiers (*just, only, hardly, almost*) must be used immediately before what they modify:

Wrong

The priest only sees children on Tuesdays between 4pm and 6pm.

Correct depending on meaning

The priest sees only children on Tuesdays between 4pm and 6pm.
-or-
The priest sees children only on Tuesdays between 4pm and 6pm.
-or-
The priest sees children on Tuesdays only between 4pm and 6pm.

(1) **Correct use of *that* vs. *which* modifying clauses**

As relative pronouns, the two words "*that*" and "*which*" are often interchangeable:

The house *that/which* stands on the hill is up for sale.

The school *that/which* they go to is just around the corner.

(When *that* or *which* is the object of a following verb, it can be omitted altogether, as in "The school they go to is just around the corner.")

When the relative clause adds incidental (non-essential) information rather than identifying the noun it follows, *which* is used and is preceded by a comma:

The house, *which* stands on the hill, is up for sale.

It means:

The house is up for sale. It just happens to be on the hill.

When the relative clause identifies the noun it follows with essential information rather than adding incremental information, *that* is used without a comma:

The house *that* stands on the hill is up for sale.

It implies:

The house <u>on the hill</u> is up for sale. Not the house on the lake.

In other words, you can remove *which* from the sentence without affecting the meaning, while you have to keep *that* in the sentence to understand it fully.

(2) **Correct usage of modifiers such as "little" vs. "few"**

Little is used with uncountable nouns (ex. I have little money in my pocket.)
Few is used with countable nouns (ex. I have few dollars in my pocket.)

3.5.2 Agreement

In grammar, concord (also known as agreement) refers to the relationship between units in such matters as number, person, and gender. Consider the following examples:

- "THEY did the work THEMSELVES" (number and person concord between THEY and THEMSELVES).

- "HE did the work HIMSELF" (number, person and gender concord between HE and HIMSELF).

If there is no agreement, then grammatical errors occur. Consider the following example:
"The apples is on the table."

(Apples is plural; therefore, for concord to occur, the sentence should read: "The apples are on the table.")

A) **Number and Person Concord:** In standard English, number concord is most significant between a singular and plural subject and its verb in the third person of the simple present tense:

"That book seems interesting" (singular BOOK agreeing with SEEMS), and

"Those books seem interesting" (plural BOOKS agreeing with SEEM).

Number concord requires that two related units must always both be singular or both be plural.

Both number and person concord are involved in the use of pronouns and possessives, as in "I hurt MYself," and "MY friends said THEY WERE COMING in THEIR car."

B) **Gender Concord:** Gender concord is an important part of the grammar of languages like German and French. In English, gender concord does not exist apart from personal and possessive pronouns, such as "Elizabeth injured HERself badly in the accident," and "Thomas lost HIS glasses." These errors are generally couched in a longer sentence, so the test taker is distracted and misses the simple error.

C) **Subject-Verb Agreement:** The easiest kind of trick the GMAT will pull is to give you subjects and verbs that do not agree in time or in number.

TIP: One of the things you always have to look out for is that the GMAT will throw in lots of extra words to confuse you about what subject to which the verb is referring to.

Example

   Wrong:
   Although the *sting* of brown honey locusts *are* rarely fatal, they cause painful flesh wounds.

   Here, there is an error of subject-verb agreement. The subject *sting* and verb *are* are not in agreement. **Locusts** falsely gives an impression that the subject is plural, which is incorrect.

   Correct:
   Although the *sting* of brown honey locusts *is* rarely fatal, they cause painful flesh wounds.

Remember:

   a. **Certain words ending in "*s*" such as "*Diabetes*" and "*News*" are singular.**
   Other examples include:
   two hundred dollars
   five hundred miles
   United States

   b. **A compound subject is plural.** Exception: "Romeo and Juliet" is a singular noun when it is referred to as a play.

c. **"Each" and "Everyone" are singular.**

d. **Collective nouns are singular.** Common examples include *group, audience,* etc.

   Note that if the subject of a sentence is an entire phrase or clause, you should use a singular verb, regardless of the plural words inside this phrase or clause.

   Example

   Networking with professionals certainly *helps* a lot when you first start your career.

e. **Indefinite pronouns are singular.**

   Examples: *each, either, anything, everything, nothing, anyone, everyone, no one, neither, anybody, everybody, nobody*

f. **No verb should be missing in a sentence.**

g. **Subject and verb should ALWAYS be in agreement.**

Singular	Plural
The number of ___ together with ___ (as well as, combined with, etc)	A number of ___ and ___

___ or ___
___ nor ___
(verb agrees with nearer subject)

none, all, any, some
(depends on context; pay attention to the object after "of")

majority, minority
(depends on context)
(Singular when referring to the total group; plural when referred to many individual members of the group)

3.5.3 Verb Tense, Voice & Mood

Remember to avoid:

a. Inconsistent tense

b. Passive voice

c. Incorrect use of verbs in the subjunctive mood

3.5.4 Parallelism

Pay attention to the inconsistent use of:

   a. Clauses

   b. Phrases (verb phrases, noun phrases, prepositional phrases, adjective phrases, etc.)

   c. Gerunds

   d. Infinitives (If an infinitive is repeated once in a list, it must be repeated each time.)

Wrong

   I like to jog, swim and to run.

Correct

   I like to jog, to swim and to run.
   (Occasionally acceptable: I like to jog, swim and run.)

3.5.5 Comparisons

Pay attention to the use of:

   a. *Like* vs. *As* vs. *Such As*

   b. *As Old As* vs. *Older Than*

   c. Illogical Comparison

   d. Ambiguous Comparison

3.5.6 Pronoun Agreement & Reference

Remember:

   a. Antecedent and pronoun should be in agreement.

   b. No ambiguity with antecedent

   c. No missing antecedent

   d. Use of the relative pronoun should be correct

   · Which is for things only; Who/Whom for people only

   · Who vs Whom – nominative vs. objective case forms

   · They/them is not correct as a singular pronoun, nor is it correct as a pronoun with no antecedent.

3.5.7 Idioms, Usage and Style

Here are some selected examples of common words and phrases tested on the GMAT.

From _____ to _____

Between _____ and _____

The same to _____ as to _____

No less _____ than _____

The more _____ the greater _____

Better served by _____ than by _____

Not only _____ but also _____

Both _____ and _____

Different from _____ (not "than" or "to")

Either _____ or _____

Neither _____ nor _____

Whether to do something or not

They do not know x or y (NOT x nor y)

Doubt that

At the urging of somebody

Between (2) vs. among (> 2)

Affect (verb) vs. effect (noun)

Assure (give an assurance) vs. ensure (make sure something happens) vs. insure (financially guarantee)

Equivalent in number (vs "as many people")

A number of (not "numbers of")

Whether vs. if - *"I had to decide whether"*, not *"I had to decide if"*

> "Whether" is typically used to introduce doubt regarding two equal possibilities or two alternatives.

We should try to have dinner with them *whether* it's snowing or not.

He wonders *whether* it's worth a try.

She said she'd get here, *whether* by train *or* by plane.

It is preferable to use "whether" over "if" when the word "if" is not used to signal a condition and instead takes the meaning of "whether." This is particularly true with the GMAT. Using "whether" exclusively avoids possible confusion between different possible meanings of "if."

Wrong

I don't know *if* I am ready to take the test now and *if* I will ever be ready in the future.

Correct

I don't know *whether* I am ready to take the test now and *whether* I will ever be ready in the future.

"Despite" is not the same as "Although." "Despite" means 'with intention, in the face of an obstacle'.

Wrong

Despite having 5% of the world's population, the USA uses 30% of the world's energy.

Correct

Despite his poor education, he succeeded in becoming wealthy.

Idiomatic Prepositions:

based *on*

composed *by* (meaning "created by") vs. composed *of* (meaning "made up of")

credit *with* (not credit to)

depend *on*

differ *with* (meaning "disagree with") vs. differ *from* (meaning "be different from")

discourage someone *from* doing something/encourage someone *to* do something ("from" is a preposition here; "to" is the infinitive here)

prefer _____ *to* _____

prevent someone *from*

prohibit someone *from*

Idiomatic Phrases Involving or Omitting "As"

consider x y (not *to be* y)

defined *as*

depicted *as*

regard x *as* y

regarded *as*

think of x *as* y

view x *as* y

Idiomatic Phrases Involving or Omitting the Infinitive "to"

Help someone do something
Make someone do something

Enable someone to do something
Forbid x to do y

Words Associated with the subjunctive mood in "that" clauses

Demand *that*
Mandate *that*
Request *that*
Require *that* something be (not *are/is*)

Different Applications Involving "use"

Use (verb):	I use a pencil to write.
Used to (*to* is the infinitive):	I used to teach every night.
Be used to something/doing something (*to* is preposition):	I am used to challenges.
	I am used to being challenged.

It + adjective

After verbs such as *believe, consider, feel, find, think,* we can use *it + adjective* before a "that" clause or the infinitive.

> I find *it* impulsive to talk to the CEO directly in an elevator without being introduced.
>
> He felt *it* dreadful that his wife was diagnosed with cancer.

Avoid Run-On Sentences

A run-on sentence consists of two or more main clauses that are run together **without** proper punctuation. People often speak in run-on sentences, but they make pauses and change their tone so others can understand them. In writing, however, we must break our sentences into shorter units so that readers can understand us.

Wrong

It is nearly six o'clock we have not gone through all the practice problems yet.

There are several acceptable ways to correct this:

- Insert a semicolon between the clauses:

    It is nearly six o'clock; we have not gone through all the practice problems yet.

- Write the two clauses as two separate sentences:

    It is nearly six o'clock. We have not gone through all the practice problems yet.

- Insert a comma and a conjunction between the clauses:

    It is nearly six o'clock, and we have not gone through all the practice problems yet.

3.6 Useful Examples

Here are some examples of the types of questions you will be faced with in the Sentence Correction section.

Q1.
Unlike Lee Ang, whose films transcend ideology, Zhang Yi Mou is frequently dismissed <u>with being merely a photographer</u> of visually impressive productions with little meaning.

(A) with merely being a photographer

(B) as being a photographer merely

(C) for being merely a photographer

(D) as a mere photographer

(E) merely for being a photographer

The problem with the sentence as it stands: <u>dismissed with</u> is not idiomatic; it should be *dismissed as* or *dismissed for*. These two idioms mean different things - you can be dismissed from a job *for* something, but by critics, etc., one is dismissed AS something.

This leaves you with choices B and D. B includes the word <u>being</u>, which automatically makes it suspect. Also, it is the longer choice, which makes it less likely to be correct. The adverb <u>merely</u> is placed very far away from the verb, causing an awkward construction.

This makes D a better choice. D is correct.

Q2.

Once almost covered under centuries of debris, <u>skilled artisans have now restored some original famous paintings from the Italian Renaissance.</u>

- **(A)** skilled artisans have now restored some original famous paintings from the Italian Renaissance.

- **(B)** some original famous paintings from the Italian Renaissance now have been by skillful artisans restored.

- **(C)** the restoration of some original famous paintings from the Italian Renaissance has been done by skilled artisans.

- **(D)** skilled artisans from the Italian Renaissance have now restored some original famous paintings.

- **(E)** some original famous paintings from the Italian Renaissance have now been restored by skilled artisans.

What was covered? *Some original famous paintings.*

With modifying phrases at the beginning of the sentence, just determine what is being modified and select the answer which places that item directly after the phrase. Which have the correct opening? B & E

B needlessly separates the subject from the verb, creating a very awkward construction.

This makes E the better choice. E is correct.

Q3.

<u>With</u> centuries of seasonal roaming in search of pasture for their herds, or food and water, the Nomads still found the goal of a bawdy, prolonged adventure an elusive one.

- **(A)** With
- **(B)** Following
- **(C)** Despite
- **(D)** Having spent
- **(E)** As a result of

C is the best choice to indicate the emphasis of the Nomads' unchanging mentality after all the journeys.

Q4.

<u>The uniformized set of characters, which some historians date</u> in the late Qing dynasty, was the key to the sustainability and prosperity of Chinese culture over thousands of years.

- **(A)** The uniformized set of characters, which some historians date

- **(B)** The uniformized set of characters, which some historians have thought to occur

(C) Uniformizing the set of characters, dated by some historians at

(D) The uniformization of a set of characters, thought by some historians to have occurred

(E) The set of characters' uniformization, dated by some historians to have been

Before we look at the answers, let's answer the question: What is occurring? Historians are dating something. What are they dating? Not the uniformized set of characters itself, but the time when the characters became uniformized (the uniformization of the characters).

Therefore, the correct answer must be D.

Student Notes:

Chapter 4

Practice Questions

4.1 Subject-Verb agreement (SVA)

1. Whereas it had been possible to at least consider the draft proposal of the directors, <u>none of the two options of the final bargaining round were acceptable because of</u> the bulk of the finance stipulated in the fine print depended on output.

   (A) none of the two options of the final bargaining round were acceptable because of
   (B) none of the two options by the final bargained round were acceptable because
   (C) neither of the two options of the final bargaining round were acceptable because
   (D) none of the two options in the final bargaining round was acceptable because of
   (E) neither of the two options during the final bargaining round was acceptable because

2. To encourage foreign investment in the country, <u>the new government have introduced reforms in its first budget that permits foreign companies to operate tax-free</u> as long as they offer financial advice to would-be investors.

   (A) the new government have introduced reforms in its first budget that permits foreign companies to operate tax-free
   (B) the new government has introduced reforms in its first budget that permit foreign companies to operate tax-free
   (C) the new government have introduced reforms in their first budget that permit foreign companies to operate tax-free
   (D) the new government might have introduced reforms in their first budget that permit foreign companies operating tax free
   (E) the new government will introduce reforms in its first budget that permits foreign companies to operate tax- free

3. Parents' disagreements on how to discipline their children <u>has made problems for teachers as they are teaching such</u> spoiled students.

   (A) has made problems for teachers as they are teaching such
   (B) has made problems for teachers teaching such
   (C) has made problems for teachers as they are teaching
   (D) have made it problematic for teachers to teach such
   (E) have made it problematic for teachers as they are teaching such

4. After Georgio's Café got a favorable review in a travel guidebook, the number of tourists eating there <u>were in excess of the number of local customers</u> going regularly.

   (A) were in excess of the number of local customers
   (B) had an excess over the local customers who were
   (C) exceeded the local customers who were
   (D) numbered more than the local customers
   (E) exceeded the number of local customers

5. The experiences of the captives held for years in dark, cramped isolation cells beneath the Lon Da camp was so monotonous and uneventful many ex-prisoners are not able to imagine, even less to remember, what captivity was like.

   (A) was so monotonous and uneventful many ex-prisoners are not able to imagine, even less to remember,

   (B) were so monotonous and uneventful many ex-prisoners are unable to imagine, even less to remember,

   (C) were uneventful so many ex-prisoners are unable to imagine and even less be able to remember,

   (D) were so monotonous that many ex-prisoners cannot imagine, even less remember,

   (E) had been so uneventful that many ex-prisoners are unable to imagine, even less to remember

6. Germany received huge sums of money after the Second World War from the United States under the auspices of the Marshall Plan which was used to build a modern industrial system.

   (A) Germany received huge sums of money after the second World War from the United States under the auspices of the Marshall Plan which was used to build a modern industrial system.

   (B) After the Second World War Germany received huge sums of money from the United States by the auspices of the Marshall Plan, which was used to build a modern industrial system.

   (C) Germany received huge sums of money from the United States after the Second World War in the auspices of the Marshall Plan, which were used to build a modern industrial system.

   (D) After the Second World War, under the auspices of the Marshall Plan, Germany received huge sums of money from the United States and used them to build a modern industrial system.

   (E) Through the auspices of the Marshall Plan, after the Second World War, Germany received huge sums of money from the United States and used it to build a modern industrial system.

7. The most important decision for newly married couples who are residents of the eastern seaboard states concern the kind of mortgages they could require when buying their first home.

   (A) concern the kind of mortgages they could require when buying their

   (B) concerns the kind of mortgages they could require while buying their

   (C) concern the kind of mortgage they could require to buy their

   (D) concerns the kind of mortgage they could require when buying a

   (E) concerns the kind of mortgage they could require as they bought their

8. The ruling party, taking into account its recent showing in local elections and popularity polls, <u>are determined to hang onto power at all costs in the hope that inflation will drop dramatically in the near future, improving the chance of re-election.</u>

   (A) are determined to hang onto power at all costs in the hope that inflation will drop dramatically in the near future, improving the chance of re-election.

   (B) are determined to hang onto power at all cost, hoping that inflation will drop dramatically in the near future, improve the chance of re-election.

   (C) is determined to hang onto power at all costs in the hope that inflation will drop dramatically in the near future, improving the chances of re-election.

   (D) have been determined to hang onto power at all costs in the hope that inflation will drop dramatically in the near future, improving the chances of re-election.

   (E) is being determined to hang onto power at all costs in the hope that inflation will drop dramatically in the near future, improving the chances of re-election.

9. Two differently-abled children, one with crutches and <u>the other one with a wheelchair, joins</u> the class on Monday.

   (A) the other one with a wheelchair, joins
   (B) the other one a wheelchair, join
   (C) the other with a wheelchair, joins
   (D) the other with a wheelchair, join
   (E) one with a wheelchair, joins

10. <u>His love of basketball, long legs, and athletic talent makes</u> him well suited for a place on the high school basketball team.

    (A) His love of basketball, long legs, and athletic talent makes
    (B) Long legs, his love of basketball, and athletic talent makes
    (C) Athletic talent, long legs, and his love of basketball makes
    (D) Long legs, athletic talent, and his love of basketball make
    (E) His love of basketball, as well as long legs and athletic talent, make

11. Praise for Johnny Starstruck and his entourage <u>are common, although statistics show Americans still associate his name with</u> ritualistic murders.

    (A) are common, although statistics show Americans still associate his name with
    (B) are common, although statistics shows Americans still associate his name with
    (C) are common, although statistics shows Americans still associate his name to
    (D) is common, although statistics show Americans still associate his name with
    (E) is common, although statistics shows Americans still associate his name to

12. The Great Wall Space Agency's recent attempts to launch a man into space, a major goal of their space program for the past few years, has not substantially decreased the gaps existing between the technology-rich and technology-poor cities around the space center.

    (A) has not substantially decreased the gaps existing
    (B) has not been substantial in decreasing the gap that exists
    (C) has not made a substantial decrease in the gap that exists
    (D) have not substantially decreased the gap that exists
    (E) have not been substantial in a decrease of the gap that exists

13. Declining values for bonds, the financial vehicles against which investors hedge to get through the bear market, is going to force currency trading to increase.

    (A) the financial vehicles against which investors hedge to get through the bear market, is
    (B) which investors use as financial vehicles to hedge against to get through the bear market, is
    (C) the financial vehicle which is hedged against by investors to get through the bear market is
    (D) which investors use as financial vehicles to hedge against to get through the bear market, are
    (E) the financial vehicles against which investors hedge to get through the bear market, are

14. Although the sting of Egyptian Scorpions are rarely dangerous, they cause red welts to appear, posing minor health risks to infants, who are particularly vulnerable to its venom.

    (A) Egyptian Scorpions are rarely dangerous, they cause red welts to appear, posing minor health risks to infants, who are particularly vulnerable to its
    (B) Egyptian Scorpions are rarely dangerous, they cause red welts to appear and pose minor health risks to infants, who are particularly vulnerable to their
    (C) Egyptian Scorpions is rarely dangerous, it causes red welts to appear, posing minor health risks to infants, who are particularly vulnerable to their
    (D) Egyptian Scorpions is rarely dangerous, it causes red welts to appear and poses minor health risks to infants, who are particularly vulnerable to the
    (E) Egyptian Scorpions is rarely dangerous, they cause red welts to appear, posing the greatest danger to the infant, who are particularly vulnerable to its

15. A derivative of the North American Echinacea flower, which has been effective in preventing colds, is grown by many small farmers out west.

    (A) A derivative of the the North American Echinacea flower, which has been effective in preventing colds,
    (B) A derivative, which has been effective in preventing colds, of the North American Echinacea flower,

(C) A North American Echinacea flower derivative, which has been effective in preventing colds,

(D) The North American Echinacea flower has a derivative which has been effective in preventing colds, that

(E) The North American Echinacea flower, a derivative of which has been effective in preventing colds,

4.2 Parallelism

16. Many police officers arrest African-Americans <u>not from their significance as perpetrators of suburban crime</u> but because they are members of an ethnic minority.

    (A) not from their significance as perpetrators of suburban crime
    (B) although they are not a significant perpetrators of suburban crime
    (C) not in that they are significant as suburban perpetrators of crime
    (D) not because they are significant perpetrators of suburban crime
    (E) not because being significant perpetrators of crime in suburban areas

17. Now, a decade after the Chernobyl disaster, central European atomic physicists find themselves simultaneously fighting a wall of suspicion <u>concerning the effects of fallout, begging for fresh funds and, in the wake of the Dresden case, have to hire</u> lawyers to defend themselves in court.

    (A) concerning the effects of fallout, begging for fresh funds and, in the wake of the Dresden case, have to hire
    (B) of the affects of fallout, begging for fresh funds and, in the wake of the Dresden case, have to hire
    (C) over the affects of fallout begging for fresh funds and, in the wake of the Dresden case, hiring
    (D) because of the effects of fallout, begging for fresh funds and, in the wake of the Dresden case, having to hire
    (E) concerning the effects of fallout, begging for fresh funds and, in the wake of the Dresden case, having to hire

18. <u>In 1962 when the idea of a united Europe was proposed and a draft charter drawing up, a number of tentative steps to put the concept into practice were taken and</u> now on the eve of monetary union what once seemed like a farfetched dream has been almost realized.

    (A) In 1962 when the idea of a united Europe was first proposed and a draft charter drawing up, a number of tentative steps to put the concept into practice were taken and
    (B) Since 1962 when the idea of a united Europe was first proposed and a draft charter had been drawn up, a number of tentative steps putting the concept into practice have been taken but
    (C) Since 1962 when the idea of a united Europe was first proposed and a draft charter drawn up, a number of tentative steps to put the concept into practice have been taken and
    (D) Before 1962 when the idea of a united Europe was first a proposal and a draft charter drawn up, a number of tentative steps to put the concept into practice were taken although
    (E) During 1962 when the idea of a united Europe was first proposed and a draft charter drawn up, a number of tentative steps that put the concept into practice have been taken if

19. Nowhere in Finland is the influence of light engineering <u>more apparent than their</u> mobile phones.

   (A) more apparent than their
   (B) so apparent as their
   (C) so apparent than in its
   (D) as apparent as in its
   (E) more apparent than in their

20. <u>While the occupier of a Grove West apartment has free use of tennis courts and swimming pool, provided membership of the recreation club has been taken out,</u> occupiers of Albany Estate apartments have no such facilities yet pay higher rents.

   (A) While the occupier of a Grove West apartment has free use of tennis courts and swimming pool, provided membership of the recreation club has been taken out,
   (B) Although the occupier of a Grove West apartment has the free use of tennis courts and swimming pool, providing membership of the recreation club has been taken out,
   (C) Whereas occupiers of Grove West apartments have free use of tennis courts and swimming pool, provided membership of the recreation club has been taken out,
   (D) The occupier of a Grove West apartment has the free use of tennis courts and swimming pool, provided membership of the recreation club has been taken out,
   (E) Grove West apartment occupiers have the free use of tennis courts and swimming pool provided membership of the recreation club has been taken out,

21. The pharmaceutical company must report to the FDA the number of casualties <u>suffered by its test subjects and that the statistics be released</u> to the public.

   (A) suffered by its test subjects and that the statistics be released
   (B) that their test subjects suffered and that the statistics be released
   (C) that was suffered by their test subjects with the statistics being released
   (D) suffered by its test subjects and release the statistics
   (E) suffered by their test subjects and release the statistics

22. Language immersion experiences are valuable because they can quickly teach students <u>who may be unlikely to learn the language in other settings or months of regular teaching</u>.

   (A) who may be unlikely to learn the language in other settings or months of regular teaching
   (B) whose learning the language is unlikely in other settings or months of regular teaching
   (C) who might not learn the language in other settings or during months of regular teaching

(D) who may not learn the language under other settings or months of regular teaching

(E) unlikely not to learn the language during months of regular teaching or in other settings

23. Students of violin can distinguish a good tone quality from a bad one long before <u>the identification that</u> a given instrument is out of tune.

(A) the identification that

(B) they can identify that

(C) identify

(D) they could have the identification of

(E) having the identification of

24. Experts believe that senior citizens who have higher than average cholesterol <u>and their families develop a predisposition toward cardiovascular disease</u> are more likely to die at an age below that of their life expectancy.

(A) and their families develop a predisposition toward cardiovascular disease

(B) and whose families have a predisposition toward cardiovascular disease

(C) and a predisposition toward cardiovascular disease runs in the family

(D) whose families have a predisposition toward cardiovascular disease running in them

(E) with a predisposition toward cardiovascular disease running in their family

25. If seriously mentally ill people do not receive medication, they can grow unable to support themselves, become irrational, <u>and perhaps even threatening</u> the safety of themselves or others.

(A) and perhaps even threatening

(B) and perhaps even threaten

(C) and may even threaten

(D) as well as possibly threatening

(E) as well as a possible threat to

26. As the journalist left to interview the convicted murderer, she was advised <u>of the man's short temper, told she should not anger him, and was</u> given a tape recorder.

(A) of the man's short temper, told she should not anger him, and was

(B) of the man's short temper, told she should not anger him, and

(C) of the man's short temper and that she should not anger him and

(D) that the man had a short temper, should not anger him, and was

(E) that the man had a short temper, that she should not anger him, and was

27. The manager of the plastic fork factory tried to convince the unruly factory workers they should join forces to optimize production on the belt rather than attempting to be contrary.

   (A) they should join forces to optimize production on the belt rather than attempting to be contrary

   (B) that they should join forces to optimize production on the belt rather than attempt to be contrary

   (C) about joining forces to optimize production on the belt instead of attempting to be contrary

   (D) for the joining of forces to optimize production on the belt rather than attempt to be contrary

   (E) to join forces to optimize production on the belt rather than attempting to be contrary

28. Recently discovered gravitational lensing around certain proximate stars strongly suggests that the nine planets of our solar system are a common phenomenon in the universe rather than developing incidentally from a unique galactic phenomenon several billion years ago.

   (A) rather than developing incidentally from

   (B) rather than a type that developed incidentally from

   (C) rather than a type whose development was incidental of

   (D) instead of developing incidentally from

   (E) instead of a development that was incidental of

29. Acme, the family-oriented entertainment company, has moved away from traditional family programming and now draws on the production both of adult entertainers who work for magazines and of those in the movie industry.

   (A) now draws on the production both of adult entertainers who work for magazines and of those

   (B) now draws on the works of adult entertainers, both those who work for magazines and those who work

   (C) it draws on the works of adult entertainers now, both those working for magazines and who work

   (D) draws now on the works both of adult entertainers working for magazines and who are working

   (E) draws on the works now of both adult entertainers working for magazines and those

Sentence Correction Guide – Questions

30. The catastrophic San Francisco Earthquake at the turn of the century destroyed numerous buildings and <u>many were led to believe that the city had become</u> a permanent disaster zone.

- (A) many were led to believe that the city had become
- (B) many had been led to believing of the city as if it were
- (C) the belief this led to was that the city had become
- (D) led many to the belief of the city as if it were
- (E) led many to believe that the city had become

31. The possibility of an attack on Indian Point, a nuclear power plant, has led local governmental officials to <u>plan evacuation routes, build shelters, and offering citizens potassium pills so there will be</u> fewer casualties in case of a leak.

- (A) plan evacuation routes, build shelters, and offering citizens potassium pills so there will be
- (B) plan evacuation routes, build shelters, and offer citizens potassium pills in order to have
- (C) planning evacuation routes, building shelters, and the offer of potassium pills to citizens so there will be
- (D) evacuation route planning, building shelters, and offering citizens potassium pills in order to have
- (E) a planning of evacuation routes, shelter building, and offering potassium pills to citizens to have

32. Trying to mimic some of the pitch variations of a dolphin chattering is <u>the same as attempting to sing like a sick parakeet when one is intoxicated</u>; the complete lack of harmony and apparent randomness of the noise means the human vocal chords are completely incapable of reproducing these sounds.

- (A) the same as attempting to sing like a sick parakeet when one is intoxicated
- (B) similar to an intoxicated person singing like a sick parakeet
- (C) like singing like a sick parakeet as an intoxicated person
- (D) the same as an intoxicated person singing like a sick parakeet
- (E) like the intoxicated person is singing like a sick parakeet

33. Forced to cut back their stock, automobile dealers in the area have cut prices; their pickup trucks <u>have been priced to sell, and they are</u>.

- (A) have been priced to sell, and they are
- (B) are priced to sell, and they have
- (C) are priced to sell, and they do
- (D) are being priced to sell, and have
- (E) had been priced to sell, and they have

34. When he could no longer play the violin himself, Howard taught, imparted his knowledge to students to encourage them to be as successful as he once was.

    (A) imparted his knowledge to students to encourage
    (B) and he imparted his knowledge to students and encouraged
    (C) and imparting his knowledge to students encouraged
    (D) imparting his knowledge to students, and encouraged
    (E) imparting his knowledge to students and encouraging

35. There is a considerable body of evidence that NASA, under extreme political pressure, skillfully faked the first moon landing in 1968 by doctoring TV transmissions, transposing a film of astronauts taken during gravity free training flights against a moon backdrop.

    (A) faked the first moon landing in 1968 by doctoring TV transmissions, transposing
    (B) faked the first moon landing in 1968 by doctoring TV transmissions and transposed
    (C) in 1968 faked the first moon landing by doctoring TV transmissions, transposing
    (D) faked the first moon landing in 1968, doctoring TV transmissions when transposing.
    (E) faked the first moon landing in1968 by doctoring and transposing TV transmission.

36. The Federal Prosecutor, William Starr, went on record to say that he suspected White House aides of secretly taping a conversation he had with Lewinsky and then used it to build a defense to discredit the witness.

    (A) he suspected White House aides of secretly taping a conversation he had with Lewinsky and then used it to build a defense to discredit the witness.
    (B) he suspected White House aides of secretly taping a conversation he had had with Lewinsky and then they used it to build a defense to discredit the witness.
    (C) although he suspected White House aides of secretly taping a conversation he had with Lewinsky and then used it to build a defense to discredit the witness.
    (D) he suspected White House aides of secretly taping a conversation he had had with Lewinsky while using it to build a defense to discredit the witness.
    (E) he suspected White House aides of secretly taping a conversation he had with Lewinsky and using it to build a defense to discredit the witness.

37. During the summer of 72, Kenyon is thought to have traveled the length and breadth of the continent interviewing the natives and recording his thoughts, the formulation of the theories that were the basis of his final text.

    (A) interviewing the natives and recording his thoughts, the formulation of the theories that were the basis of his final text.
    (B) interviewed the natives and recorded his thoughts, to formulate the theories that were the basis of his final text.

(C) interviewing the natives, recording his thoughts and formulating the theories that would be the basis of his final text.

(D) interviewing the natives and recording his thoughts, that formulated the theories leading on the basis of his final text.

(E) interviewing the natives and recording his thoughts, which formulated the theories that were the basis of his final text.

38. The new Xerox machine does more than simply copying documents; it can resize, lighten, and collate.

(A) The new Xerox machine does more than simply copying
(B) The new Xerox machine's functions are more than a simple copying of
(C) The new Xerox machine has done more than a simple copying of
(D) The new Xerox machine's functions have done more than copy simply
(E) The new Xerox machine does more than simply copy

4.3 Comparison

39. Punk teenagers infuriate adults as much by wearing provocative clothing <u>than by their disregard for authority</u>.

    (A) than by their disregard for authority
    (B) rather than by their disregard for authority
    (C) than by disregarding authority
    (D) as by their disregard for authority
    (E) as by disregarding authority

40. <u>No less an expert than</u> John H. McWhorter has claimed that African-American children do poorly in schools because of implicit social pressure to fail academically.

    (A) No less an expert than
    (B) Not less an expert
    (C) Not less expert
    (D) Not less an expert than
    (E) An expert not less than

41. <u>Whosoever compared the estimates to those of the preceding years would have found that</u> an error had been made in the final calculations.

    (A) Whosoever compared the estimates to those of the preceding years would have found that
    (B) If someone had compared the estimates with those of the preceding years, they would have found that
    (C) Whosoever compared the estimates with those of preceding years would have found that
    (D) Who compared the estimates to those of the preceding years would have found
    (E) If a person should compare the estimates to the estimates of the preceding years he or she would have found

42. Harry's workload, which including the audit is <u>as great as, if not greater than, the workload of John, can be classified as either</u> question finding or question solving.

    (A) as great as, if not greater than, the workload of John, can be classified as either
    (B) as great as, if not greater than, that of John, can be classified either as
    (C) so great, if not greater, that John's can be classified either as
    (D) as great, if not greater, than John's can be classified as either
    (E) too great, if not greater, for John's can be classified as either

43. By the year 2010, it is expected that the average weekly food expenditure of a medium-income American family will be <u>at least eight times more than a Sudanese</u> of similar size.

    (A) at least eight times more than a Sudanese
    (B) at least eight times more than a Sudanese family
    (C) as much as eight times greater than a Sudanese family
    (D) up to eight times more than that of a Sudanese family's
    (E) at least eight times more than a Sudanese one's

44. Dalmatians with their black spots appeal particularly to children, but owners with limited finances say that <u>Dalmatians cost twice as much as keeping an Alsatian.</u>

    (A) Dalmatians cost twice as much as keeping an Alsatian.
    (B) Dalmatians cost twice as much to keep as Alsatians do.
    (C) keeping Dalmatians cost twice as much as keeping Alsatians.
    (D) keeping Dalmatians cost twice as much as it does for Alsatians.
    (E) Dalmatians cost twice as much to keep as Alsatians.

45. <u>Incomparable with the impact of the Dewey Industries sell-off last year, the sale of US Fox, compounded by the Carolina closures, will have consequences</u> too dire to consider.

    (A) Incomparable with the impact of the Dewey Industries sell-off last year, the sale of US Fox, compounded by the Carolina closures, will have consequences
    (B) Unlike the impact of the Dewey industries sell-off last year, selling off US Fox, compounded by the Carolina closures, will have consequences
    (C) Differing to the impact of the Dewey Industries sell-off last year, the sale of US Fox and compounded by the Carolina closures will have consequences
    (D) Unlike last year's Dewey Industry sell-off, the sale of US Fox, compounded by the Carolina closures, will have consequences
    (E) The sale of US Fox, compounded by the Carolina closures, unlike the impact of the Dewey Industries sell-off last year, will have consequences

46. The speeds of the new variations of the car <u>are well below the Toyota models, despite the diminishing differences in the engine sizes.</u>

    (A) are well below the Toyota models, despite the diminishing differences in the engine sizes.
    (B) is well below the Toyota models, despite the differences in the engine sizes diminishing.
    (C) are much below the speed of the Toyota models, despite the differences in the engine sizes diminishing.
    (D) are well below those of the Toyota models, despite the differences in the engine sizes diminishing.
    (E) are well below those of the Toyota models, despite the diminishing differences in engine size.

47. Unlike a normal first car insurance policy, which focuses upon length of driving experience, <u>the Apex insurance policy buyer is judged for his or her driving competency.</u>

   (A) the Apex insurance policy buyer is judged for his or her driving competency

   (B) with an Apex insurance policy, buyers are judged for his or her driving competency

   (C) an Apex insurance policy buyer is judged on his or her driving competency

   (D) an Apex insurance policy judges a buyer on his or her driving competency

   (E) Apex insurance policy buyers are judged on their driving competency

48. <u>Unlike that of the French, who linger when they eat</u> meals, Americans are so enamored of eating quickly that they have a type of meal called "fast food."

   (A) Unlike that of the French, who linger when they eat

   (B) Unlike the French, who linger when they eat

   (C) Unlike the French, lingering when eating

   (D) Dissimilar to the French, lingering during

   (E) Lacking similarity to the French, who linger during

49. Factories can mass-produce beautiful glass vessels <u>that are valued almost as much as that of the old-fashioned glass-blowers that remain.</u>

   (A) that are valued almost as much as that of the old-fashioned glass-blowers that remain

   (B) of a value that is almost as much as that of the old-fashioned glass-blowers that remain

   (C) almost as much in value as those of the remaining old-fashioned glass-blowers

   (D) almost as much in value as that of the remaining old-fashioned glass-blowers

   (E) valued almost as much as those of the remaining old-fashioned glass-blowers

50. The PTA decided that <u>just as alcohol is discussed in health class to protect those who might actually abuse it</u>, other drugs should also be covered to prevent students from falling prey to addiction.

   (A) just as alcohol is discussed in health class to protect those who might actually abuse it

   (B) like alcohol, which is discussed in health class to protect those who might abuse it

   (C) similar to alcohol, which is discussed in health class in order to protect those who might actually abuse it

   (D) while, to protect those who might actually abuse it, alcohol is discussed in health class

   (E) similar to the discussion of alcohol in health class in order to protect those who might actually abuse it

Sentence Correction Guide – Questions 91

51. <u>Like their sister schools in England, the American School of Ethical Culture has always</u> embraced the philosophy of nonviolence.

  (A) Like their sister schools in England, the American School of Ethical Culture has always

  (B) Like that of their sister schools in England, the American School of Ethical Culture has always

  (C) Like its sister schools in England, the American School of Ethical Culture always have

  (D) Like that of its sister schools in England, the American School of Ethical Culture always has

  (E) Like its sister schools in England, the American School of Ethical Culture has always

52. During gladiator matches, the unfair match-up between a prisoner with a short sword and ten soldiers with horses and whips can drive the prisoner to a state of manic frenzy, <u>like a rampaging bull whose rage increases when its hide is pierced with swords.</u>

  (A) like a rampaging bull whose rage increases when its hide is pierced with swords

  (B) like the increased rage of a rampaging bull when its hide is pierced with swords

  (C) like a rampaging bull that increases rage while rampaging with its hide pierced with swords

  (D) just as a rampaging bull that increases rage by piercing its hide with swords

  (E) just as a rampaging bull's rage increases when it is pierced with swords

53. When the chorus divides the women into sopranos and altos, it will be able to sing songs many times more complicated <u>compared to those that can be sung</u> now.

  (A) compared to those that can be sung

  (B) compared to those it can sing

  (C) than that can be sung

  (D) than those that can be sung

  (E) than those singing

54. <u>Unlike that of</u> the colonies of Portugal, France, and Germany, those of England are still affected by the former imperial power in modern days.

  (A) Unlike that of

  (B) Unlike those of

  (C) Unlike

  (D) In contrast to that of

  (E) Dissimilar to

© 1999–2016 Manhattan Review   www.manhattanreview.com

55. A survey showed that children are much more psychologically stable when raised in a family with two parents than in a family where one parent only cares for the child.

   (A) a family where one parent only
   (B) of a family where only one parent
   (C) that for families in which only one parent
   (D) a family in which only one parent
   (E) those of families in which one parent only

56. In the United States, a larger percentage of the defense budget is spent on development of an anti-missile shield than is spent on nuclear missile technology in the People's Democratic Republic of North Korea.

   (A) In the United States, a larger percentage of the defense budget is spent on development of an anti-missile shield than is spent on nuclear missile technology in the People's Democratic Republic of North Korea.
   (B) In the United States they spend a larger percentage of the defense budget on development of an anti-missile shield than the People's Democratic Republic of North Korea does on nuclear missile technology.
   (C) A larger percentage of the United States' defense budget is spent on development of an anti-missile shield than the People's Democratic Republic of North Korea spends on nuclear missile technology.
   (D) The United States spends a larger percentage of its defense budget developing its anti-missile shield than the People's Democratic Republic of North Korea spending on nuclear missile technology.
   (E) The United States spends a larger percentage of its defense budget on developing its anti-missile shield than the People's Democratic Republic of North Korea does on nuclear missile technology.

57. By the end of the nineteenth century, five Western European countries had developed a railroad system, but only one in the East.

   (A) only one in the East
   (B) only one eastern country
   (C) in the East there was only one country
   (D) in the East only one country did
   (E) only one in the East had

58. The Chinese army consists of several million young men, about equivalent to the enrollment of colleges in India.

   (A) equivalent to the enrollment of
   (B) the equivalent of those enrolled in
   (C) equal to those who are enrolled in
   (D) as many as the enrollment of
   (E) as many as are enrolled in

59. <u>Unlike in the other states in the tri-state area, there are no gasoline taxes set by state or local authorities</u> in New Jersey.

   (A) Unlike in the other states in the tri-state area, there are no gasoline taxes set by state or local authorities

   (B) Unlike the other states in the tri-state area that have gasoline taxes set by state or local authorities, there are none

   (C) Although state or local authorities usually set gasoline taxes in the tri-state area, no such one has been set

   (D) Although state or local authorities usually set gasoline taxes in the tri-state area, no such tax has been set

   (E) Although there are usually gasoline taxes set by state or local authorities in the tri-state area, no such taxes has been set

60. *Time* magazine is known to have <u>a higher number of women and African American employees in relation to total work force than any major magazine.</u>

   (A) a higher number of women and African American employees in relation to total work force than any major magazine.

   (B) a higher number of women and African American employees in relation to total work force than do major magazines.

   (C) a higher number of women and African American employees in relation to total work force more than does any other major magazine.

   (D) a higher number of women and African American employees in relation to total work force than does any other major magazine.

   (E) higher numbers of women and African American employees in relation to total work force than any other major magazine.

61. As the United States Census showed, <u>college graduates are five times more likely to own houses as</u> apartments.

   (A) college graduates are five times more likely to own houses as

   (B) college graduates are five times as likely to own houses as it is for them

   (C) college graduates are five times more likely to own houses than

   (D) it is five times more likely for college graduates to own houses than they are

   (E) it is five times as likely that college graduates will own houses as they are

4.4 Modifiers

62. <u>Wretched and increasing prevalent panhandlers are requesting money on the streets, money that seems</u> to be hard to come by in the deteriorating economy.

    (A) Wretched and increasing prevalent panhandlers are requesting money on the streets, money that seems

    (B) Wretched and increasing prevalent panhandlers request money on the streets, money seeming

    (C) On the streets, wretched and increasingly prevalent panhandlers are requesting money that seems

    (D) Wretchedly and increasingly prevalent panhandlers request money on the streets seeming

    (E) Wretchedly and increasingly prevalent panhandlers are requesting money on the streets that seems

63. Upset by the litter around her neighborhood, <u>the idea of after-school cleanups were substitutes for detention by Jane.</u>

    (A) the idea of after-school cleanups were substitutes for detention by Jane

    (B) after-school cleanups were ideas for substitution for detention suggested by Jane

    (C) Jane suggested the after-school cleanup as a substitute for detention

    (D) Jane suggested that detention be substituted as after-school cleanups

    (E) the after-school cleanup was suggested to be a substitute for detention by Jane

64. Annabelle's pack-a-day smoking habit <u>has done seriously and potentially fatal damage</u> to her lungs.

    (A) has done seriously and potentially fatal damage

    (B) did damage that is seriously and potentially fatal

    (C) damaged, serious and potentially fatally

    (D) has done serious and potentially fatal damage

    (E) did damage, serious and potentially fatal

65. Unchallenged as a result of having 16th-century European firearms, <u>early Native Americans viewed the white man with suspicion, for they</u> feared the thunder sticks of death that were pointed at them.

    (A) early Native Americans viewed the white man with suspicion, for they

    (B) early Native Americans were suspicious of the white man, and they

    (C) the white man was viewed with suspicion by early Native Americans, who

    (D) the white man was suspicious to early Native Americans, and it was

    (E) the white man was viewed with suspicion by early Native Americans, it being

Sentence Correction Guide – Questions

66. Certain painkilling drugs such as Oxycodone have recently been shown to be addictive to patients, <u>which may limit their potential to reduce</u> pain.

- (A) which may limit their potential to reduce
- (B) which may limit their potential for reducing
- (C) which may limit such drugs' potential to reduce
- (D) an effect that may limit their potential to reduce
- (E) an effect that may limit the potential of such drugs to reduce

67. Fencing is a tantalizing sport, unappreciated at best, <u>where two opponents fight a pitched and lightning-fast battle with</u> electrically connected swords and metal vests.

- (A) where two opponents fight a pitched and lightning-fast battle with
- (B) when two opponents fight a pitched and lightning-fast battle having
- (C) in which two opponents have pitched and in lightning-fast battle fighting with
- (D) having two opponents who fight a pitched and lightning-fast battle that has
- (E) in which two opponents fight a pitched and lightning-fast battle with

68. The festival lasted throughout the summer, attracting thousands of spectators, with a number of concerts being held midweek <u>but the majority taking place on the weekend in which people were free to forget their wretchedly poor lives by listening to music.</u>

- (A) but the majority taking place on the weekend in which people were free to forget their wretchedly poor lives by listening to music.
- (B) and the majority taking place on the weekend when people were free to forget their wretchedly poor lives to listen to music.
- (C) but the majority took place on the weekend when people were free to forget their wretchedly poor lives and listen to music.
- (D) although the majority took place on the weekend in which people were free to forget their wretchedly poor lives and listen to music.
- (E) even though the majority took place on the weekend that people were free to forget their wretchedly poor lives by listening to music.

69. At the age of twenty, soon after he returned from England, <u>his father, albeit to save taxes, gave him total control of two companies upon which he</u> founded a fortune.

- (A) his father, albeit to save taxes, gave him total control of two companies upon which he
- (B) albeit to save taxes, his father gave him total control of two companies from which he
- (C) albeit to save taxes, he was given total control of two companies by his father with which he
- (D) albeit to save taxes, total control of two companies were given to him by his father upon which he
- (E) he was given total control of two companies by his father with which, albeit to save taxes, he

70. <u>Employing the elimination technique, the correct answer can usually be found if all the correct procedures are followed.</u>

   (A) Employing the elimination technique, the correct answer can usually be found if all the correct procedures are followed.

   (B) The answer can usually be found if all the correct procedures are followed, by employing the elimination technique.

   (C) The correct answer to following all the correct procedures can usually be found by employing the elimination technique.

   (D) When the correct procedures are followed using the elimination technique, the answer can usually be found.

   (E) Employing the elimination technique and the answer can usually be found although all the correct procedures are followed.

71. As well as having more vitamins than other breakfast cereals have, <u>the vitamins in Cap'n Crunch is better quality than any other cereal on</u> the market.

   (A) the vitamins in Cap'n Crunch is better quality than any other cereal on

   (B) Cap'n Crunch contain vitamins better in quality than those of any other cereal on

   (C) Cap'n Crunch contain vitamins of better quality than those of any other cereal in

   (D) Cap'n Crunch contains better quality vitamins than those of any other cereal on

   (E) the vitamin in Cap'n Crunch is better quality than any other cereal vitamins in

72. Allegedly recruited by the KGB during the dying days of communist Russia, <u>a cloud still hangs over Pointdexter despite all his denials about very absurdity of his</u> accepting a mere $1000 as a bribe.

   (A) a cloud still hangs over Pointdexter despite all his denials about very absurdity of his

   (B) a cloud still hangs over Pointdexter despite all his denials about the very absurdity of him

   (C) Pointdexter remains under a cloud despite all his denials about very absurdity of him

   (D) Pointdexter remains under a cloud despite all his denials about the very absurdity of his

   (E) a cloud still hangs over Pointdexter despite all his denials about the very absurdity of his

73. Despite the prevalence of this kind of allergic reaction to the drug Diatoxin, <u>for lack of any alternative treatment, doctors are still prescribing it, albeit in limited dosages.</u>

   (A) for lack of any alternative treatment, doctors are still prescribing it, albeit in limited dosages.

   (B) lacking any alternative treatment, doctors are still proscribing it, albeit in limited dosages.

(C) because any alternative treatment is lacking, doctors are still proscribing it, albeit in limited dosages.

(D) requiring an alternative treatment, doctors are still prescribing it albeit in limited dosages.

(E) for the lack of any alternative treatment, in limiting doses doctors are still prescribing it.

74. Three recent independent studies would seem to suggest that a child born into a family whose members have criminal pasts, particularly for those offenses that involve violence, will probably end up committing a violent crime too.

   (A) whose members have criminal pasts, particularly for those offenses that involve violence, will probably end up committing a violent crime too.

   (B) where members have criminal pasts, particularly for offenses involving violence, will probably end up committing a violent crime too.

   (C) whose members have criminal pasts, particularly for those offenses that involve violence, might probably end up committing a violent crime too.

   (D) in which members have criminal pasts involving violence, might probably end up committing a violent crime too.

   (E) whose members have criminal pasts, particularly for offenses involving violence, will probably end up committing a violent crime too.

75. Known throughout the world as a pioneer in the commercial uses of the Internet, very few people are aware that Hendry also is an expert drummer and a member of a successful jazz band, The Whiplash.

   (A) very few people are aware that Hendry also is an expert drummer and a member of a successful jazz band,

   (B) very few people are aware that Hendry is also a member of a successful jazz band and an expert drummer,

   (C) Hendry is known to very few people also an expert drummer and a member of a successful jazz band,

   (D) very few people know that Hendry is also an expert drummer and a member of a successful jazz band,

   (E) Hendry is known to very few people as also a member of a successful jazz band and an expert drummer,

76. Content though she seems, the unhappiness of the housewife is evident to those who know her well.

   (A) Content though she seems, the unhappiness of the housewife

   (B) Even though she seems content, the unhappiness of the housewife

   (C) Though content, the housewife's unhappiness

   (D) Though the housewife seems content, her unhappiness

   (E) The unhappiness of the housewife who seems content

77. Using the methods employed by Country X's agents, a new form of torture has been developed by rogue generals to aid in extracting information from unwilling captives.

    (A) Using the methods employed by Country X's agents, a new form of torture has been developed by rogue generals to

    (B) Using the methods employed by Country X's agents, rogue generals will develop a new form of torture that will

    (C) Using the methods of Country X's agents, rogue generals have developed a new form of torture to

    (D) Employing the methods of Country X's agents, there has been a development by rogue generals of a new form of torture that will

    (E) Employing the methods of Country X's agents, a new form of torture that was developed by rogue generals will

78. A high school student fanatically devoted to modern art, Fanny has toured five museums, perhaps most remarkably the enormous Museum of Modern Art.

    (A) Fanny has toured five museums, perhaps most remarkably the enormous Museum of Modern Art

    (B) perhaps the most remarkable of the five museums toured by Fanny was the enormous Museum of Modern Art

    (C) of the five museums toured by Fanny, perhaps the most remarkable was the enormous Museum of Modern Art

    (D) five museums were toured by Fanny, of which the enormous Museum of Modern Art is perhaps the most remarkable

    (E) the enormous Museum of Modern Art is perhaps the most remarkable of the five museums toured by Fanny

79. Many are confused that the Atkins Diet, which permits such seeming less healthy foods as bacon, forbids bread.

    (A) which permits such seeming less healthy foods as

    (B) which permits such seemingly less healthy foods as

    (C) which is permitting such seeming less healthy foods like

    (D) permitting such foods that seem less healthy, for example

    (E) permitting such seeming less healthy foods like

80. Rallies organized in conjunction with the dissemination of democratic principles which was once prohibited by Communist leaders, are beginning to take shape at a grass roots level permitted by the new leadership.

    (A) Rallies organized in conjunction with the dissemination of democratic principles which was once prohibited by Communist leaders, are

    (B) Rallies organized in conjunction with the dissemination of democratic principles, a practice that Communist leaders once prohibited, is

(C) Organizing rallies in conjunction with the dissemination of democratic principles, as once prohibited by Communist leaders, is

(D) Communist leaders once prohibited organizing rallies in conjunction with the dissemination of democratic principles, but they are

(E) Communist leaders once prohibited organizing rallies in conjunction with the dissemination of democratic principles, but such principles are

81. Riddled with bullets, shattered by bombs, and hidden in alleys, <u>the historic buildings in Lodz, Poland, were long ignored by tourists, traveling</u> instead to more well-known memorial museums.

    (A) the historic buildings in Lodz, Poland, were long ignored by tourists, traveling

    (B) the historic buildings in Lodz, Poland, were long ignored by tourists, who traveled

    (C) tourists long ignored the historic buildings in Lodz, Poland, traveling

    (D) tourists long ignored the historic buildings in Lodz, Poland and traveled

    (E) tourists long ignored the historic buildings in Lodz, Poland; they traveled

82. Besides offering such physiological rewards as toned muscles, <u>the practice of Karate, if practiced regularly, can turn the body into a dangerous weapon</u> and produce numerous other benefits.

    (A) the practice of Karate, if practiced regularly, can turn the body into a dangerous weapon

    (B) one can turn the body into a dangerous weapon through Karate, if it is practiced regularly

    (C) the body can be turned into a dangerous weapon as a result of Karate if practiced regularly

    (D) when Karate is practiced regularly, the body can be turned into a dangerous weapon

    (E) when practiced regularly, the results of Karate can be to turn the body into a dangerous weapon

83. Surprisingly obedient, the <u>Smiths have a cat that follows</u> simple instructions like "come" or "sit," words to which usually only dogs respond.

    (A) Smiths have a cat that follows

    (B) Smiths of their cat follows

    (C) cat belonging to the Smiths follows

    (D) cat belonging to the Smiths has followed

    (E) cat belonging to the Smiths, following

84. Germany's most infamous leader, Hitler's policies were responsible for the slaughter of 6 million Jews.

   (A) Germany's most infamous leader, Hitler's policies were responsible for
   (B) Germany's most infamous leader, the policies of Hitler caused
   (C) More infamous than other leaders of Germany, the policies of Hitler were responsible for
   (D) Germany's most infamous leader, Hitler caused
   (E) Hitler, Germany's most infamous leader, pursued policies that caused

85. The miners were reluctant to embrace the company's new unionization policy because they thought it was merely meant to be a publicity stunt with no commitment to contract negotiation and eventually increases in salary.

   (A) stunt with no commitment to contract negotiation and eventually increases in salary
   (B) stunt, having no commitment to contract negotiation and eventually increases in salary
   (C) stunt and did not reflect a commitment to contract negotiation and eventual increases in salary
   (D) stunt, reflecting a commitment to contract negotiation and eventual increases in salary
   (E) stunt, not one that reflected that contract negotiation and eventual increases in salary was a commitment

4.5 Pronouns

86. <u>Although its income barely increased from the oil fields over the past two decades,</u> careful budgeting and rationing have ensured that the country's economy remains in good shape.

    (A) Although its income barely increased from the oil fields over the past two decades,
    (B) Even though income from the oil fields barely increased over the past two decades,
    (C) Although there is barely any increase in its oil field income over the past two decades,
    (D) Despite there being barely any increase of its income from the oil fields for the past two decades,
    (E) Despite income from its barely increasing oil fields for the past two decades,

87. Ms. Kardon spent three years studying the puffin, one of the smaller species of sea birds, in order to learn more about <u>their social organization, mating rituals, and foods that they prefer</u>.

    (A) their social organization, mating rituals, and foods that they prefer
    (B) their social organization, mating rituals, and their preferred foods
    (C) its social organization, mating rituals, and preferred foods
    (D) its social organization, mating rituals, and about preferred foods
    (E) social organization, mating rituals, and foods that are preferred

88. The <u>percentage of investment over the past six months have risen sharply, although it could well be just temporarily and may possibly decline</u> in the near future.

    (A) percentage of investment over the past six months have risen sharply, although it could well be just temporarily and may possibly decline
    (B) percent of investment has risen sharply over the past six months, although it could well be just temporarily and may possibly decline
    (C) percentage of investment has risen sharply over the past six months, although the rise could well be just temporary and the percentage may possibly decline
    (D) percentage of investment over the past six months has risen sharply, although this investment could well be just temporary and it may possibly decline
    (E) percentages of investment over the past six months have risen sharply, although they could well be just temporary and may possibly decline

89. Doctors are loath to prescribe powerful painkillers because <u>their abuse as addictive drugs is</u> a danger for many patients.

    (A) their abuse as addictive drugs is
    (B) as addictive drugs, their abuse is
    (C) the abuse of such addictive drugs is
    (D) the abuse of such addictive drugs are
    (E) the abuse of them as addictive drugs is

90. The electronics manufacturer announced that while earnings grew by 5% in the last quarter, revenue decreased whereas, <u>it might have been expected for it to rise</u>.

- **(A)** it might have been expected for it to rise
- **(B)** it might have been expected to rise
- **(C)** it might have been expected that it should rise
- **(D)** its rise might have been expected
- **(E)** there might have been an expectation it would rise

91. The new government requires <u>employers to inform an employee of their</u> legal right to holidays and overtime pay.

- **(A)** employers to inform an employee of their
- **(B)** employers to inform employees that he has a
- **(C)** every employer to inform employees of their
- **(D)** that employers inform an employee of their
- **(E)** that employers inform the employees that they have a

92. Research has found that <u>a child born into a family whose members have schizophrenia will most likely themselves develop schizophrenia</u> in their adolescence.

- **(A)** a child born into a family whose members have schizophrenia will most likely themselves develop schizophrenia
- **(B)** children born into families whose members have schizophrenia are most likely themselves to develop schizophrenia
- **(C)** a child born into a family the members of which have schizophrenia will most likely themselves develop schizophrenia
- **(D)** in those families where members have schizophrenia, children are most likely to develop schizophrenia themselves
- **(E)** children born into families where there is schizophrenia will themselves most likely develop schizophrenia

93. <u>While the union finally acquiesced, albeit reluctantly, to impose the surcharge on their</u> repayments to pay the outstanding amount, many members were so angered that they marched on its headquarters.

- **(A)** While the union finally acquiesced, albeit reluctantly, to impose the surcharge on their
- **(B)** Although the union finally acquiesced, albeit reluctantly, to impose the surcharge to
- **(C)** When the union finally acquiesced, albeit reluctantly, to impose a surcharge on the
- **(D)** If the union finally acquiesced, albeit reluctantly, to impose the surcharge on its
- **(E)** Despite the unions finally acquiescing, albeit reluctantly, to impose a surcharge in the

Sentence Correction Guide – Questions

103

94. Despite the board's decision to publish its report before the interim figures <u>were announced, because of the emerging crisis over debt control they have since reconsidered this decision and called for an emergency meeting next month.</u>

   (A) were announced, because of the emerging crisis over debt control they have since reconsidered this decision and called for an emergency meeting next month.

   (B) were announced, because of the emergency crisis over debt control they have since reconsidered this decision and called for an emergency meeting next month.

   (C) had been announced, because of the emerging crisis over debt control it has since then reconsidered this decision and called for an emergency meeting next month.

   (D) were announced, because of the emerging crisis over debt control it has since reconsidered and called for an emergency meeting next month.

   (E) were announced, it has since reconsidered calling for an emergency meeting next month because of the emerging crisis over debt control.

95. Found throughout southern Africa, <u>these relations of the common sparrow build perfectly rounded balls as nests from mud, flitting from tree to tree with its tiny turquoise wings flashing fast enough</u> that specialized film has to be used to snap them in motion.

   (A) these relations of the common sparrow build perfectly rounded balls as nests from mud, flitting from tree to tree with its tiny turquoise wings flashing fast enough

   (B) a perfectly rounded mud nest is home to a relation of the common sparrow which flits from tree to tree with its tiny turquoise wings flashing so fast

   (C) perfectly rounded mud nests are home to a relative of the common sparrow which flits from tree to tree with its tiny turquoise wings flashing sufficiently fast

   (D) these relations of the common sparrow build a perfectly rounded mud nest, flitting from tree to tree with their tiny turquoise wings flashing so fast

   (E) these relations of the common sparrow build a perfectly rounded ball as a nest from mud, flits from tree to tree upon tiny turquoise wings and it flies so fast

96. The beginning of the show always brought in lots of money, yet the average singer ended the show <u>with a decrease in what their tip may be.</u>

   (A) with a decrease in what their tip may be
   (B) with what was a decrease in what their tips were able to be
   (C) having decreased that which their tips might be
   (D) decreasing in their tips
   (E) with a decrease in tips

97. The exhibit, created by painstaking craftsmanship in the jungles of Burma, consisted of hundreds of paintings, <u>each painting a tiny etched landscape inside its</u> own ceramic work of pottery.

   (A) each painting a tiny etched landscape inside its
   (B) all the paintings a tiny etched landscape inside their

© 1999-2016 Manhattan Review

www.manhattanreview.com

(C) all the paintings a tiny etched landscape inside its

(D) every painting a tiny etched landscape inside their

(E) each painting a tiny etched landscape inside their

4.6 Meaning

98. Bush, who is by far the most popular of the Republican front runners and well funded thanks to the generosity of a band of Texan oil tycoons, should announce his candidacy now and this is certainly no coincidence.

   (A) Bush, who is by far the most popular of the Republican front runners and well funded thanks to the generosity of a band of Texan oil tycoons, should announce his candidacy now and this

   (B) That Bush, by far the most popular of the Republican front runners and well funded thanks to the generosity of a band of Texan oil tycoons, should announce his candidacy now

   (C) Although Bush is by far the most popular of the Republican front runners arid well funded thanks to the generosity of a band of Texan oil tycoons, he may announce his candidacy now and this

   (D) Why should Bush, who is by far the most popular of the Republican front runners and well funded thanks to the generosity of a band of Texan oil tycoons, announce his candidacy now when this

   (E) Bush, by far the most popular of the Republican front runners and well funded thanks to the generosity of a band of Texan oil tycoons, will announce his candidacy when it

99. According to the ancient Egyptians, the rising of the moon as it peeked over the topmost tip of the Gaza Pyramid signaled the moment for the first sacrifice but this ritual was changed over the years.

   (A) the rising of the moon as it peeked over the topmost tip of the Gaza Pyramid signaled the moment for the first sacrifice but this ritual was changed over

   (B) the rise of the moon as it peeked over the topmost tip of the Gaza Pyramid signaled the moment for the first sacrifice but this ritual was changed over

   (C) the rise of the moon as it peeked over the tip of the Gaza Pyramid signaled the moment for the first sacrifice but this ritual was changed over

   (D) the rising of the moon as it peeked over the tip of the Gaza Pyramid signaled the moment for the first sacrifice but this ritual was changed over

   (E) the rise of the moon as it peeked over the topmost tip of the Gaza Pyramid signaled the moment for the first sacrifice but this ritual was changed over

100. Some vehicles that were destroyed and damaged beyond repair in the hurricane that continues to ravage the region are stolen goods from the nearby army camp.

   (A) Some vehicles that were destroyed and damaged beyond repair in the hurricane that continues to ravage the region are stolen goods

   (B) Some vehicles that were destroyed or damaged beyond repair in the hurricane that continues to ravage the region had been stolen goods

   (C) Some vehicles that were destroyed or damaged beyond repair in the hurricane that continues to ravage the region were stolen goods

(D) Some of the vehicles that were destroyed or damaged beyond repair in the hurricane continue to ravage the region are stolen goods

(E) Some vehicles that were destroyed and damaged beyond repair in the hurricane that is continuing to ravage the region had been goods stolen

101. Unlike the physically-challenged or those suffering any affliction that might disadvantage them if they participated under normal conditions, all candidates must take an obligatory entry examination.

   (A) Unlike the physically-challenged or those suffering any affliction that might disadvantage them if they participated under normal conditions, all candidates must take an obligatory entry examination.

   (B) Other than the physically-challenged or those suffering an affliction that could disadvantage them should they participate under normal conditions, all candidates are required to sit for an entry examination.

   (C) Unlike the physically-challenged or those suffering any affliction that might put them at a disadvantage if they participated under normal conditions, all candidates must take an obligatory entry examination.

   (D) Aside from the physically-challenged and those suffering any affliction that might disadvantage them were they to participate under normal conditions, all candidates are required to sit an obligatory entry examination.

   (E) Unless the physically-challenged or those suffering any affliction that might disadvantage them feel they would be disadvantaged if they participated under normal conditions, all candidates are required to sit an entry examination.

102. In of one of the most shocking and violent episodes of the trek, the Indian Agency, whose role was to protect the natives, surrendered to the will of thousands of pioneers who demanded them to hang an Indian boy who stole a lump of bread.

   (A) who demanded them to
   (B) who demanded that it
   (C) demanding that it should
   (D) demanding them to
   (E) and their demanding to

103. When Robert Hunter of the Interstate Insurance Committee claimed there was a concrete correlation between high insurance premiums and poor credit ratings has been denied by the Federal Association of Insurers.

   (A) When Robert Hunter of the Interstate Insurance Committee claimed there was a concrete correlation between high insurance premiums and poor credit ratings has been denied by the Federal Association of Insurers.

   (B) The Federal Association of Insurers denied why Robert Hunter of the Interstate Insurance Committee claimed there was a concrete correlation between high insurance premiums and poor credit ratings.

(C) The Federal Association of Insurers denied the claim made by Robert Hunter of the Interstate Insurance Committee that there was a concrete correlation between high insurance premiums and poor credit ratings.

(D) When Robert Hunter of the Interstate Insurance Committee claimed there was a concrete correlation between high insurance premiums and poor credit ratings which has been denied by the Federal Association of Insurers.

(E) Although Robert Hunter of the Interstate Insurance Committee claimed there was a concrete correlation between high insurance premiums and poor credit ratings but this has been denied by the Federal Association of Insurers.

104. Contrary to popular opinion, it may be true <u>increasing fatal automobile accidents as a result of producing</u> faster cars would be beneficial to society at large.

(A) increasing fatal automobile accidents as a result of producing
(B) increased fatal automobile accidents resulting from the production of
(C) increasing fatal accidents in automobiles resulting from the production of
(D) fatal automobile accidents that had increased from producing
(E) fatal automobile accidents that increased from producing

105. Isabelle so loved her dead husband that when forced to sell his collection of Genghis Khan's diaries to raise money, <u>she first made copies of more than 50</u>.

(A) she first made copies of more than 50
(B) first she made more than 50 copies
(C) more than 50 copies first were made
(D) copies of more than 50 were made
(E) she copies more than 50 of them beforehand

106. Eye movement occurs <u>more rapidly during dreams than when waking</u>.

(A) more rapidly during dreams than when waking
(B) when dreaming more rapidly than waking hours
(C) more rapidly during dreaming than waking
(D) more rapidly during dreams than when a person is awake
(E) more rapidly when dreaming than when waking

107. Marian Corey has developed a chest cold <u>that, with persistent coughing, could gravely strain</u> the five-octave voice that earned her fame.

(A) that, with persistent coughing, could gravely strain
(B) that, because of persistent coughing, could be a grave strain for
(C) with persistent coughing, and it could gravely strain
(D) with persistent coughing and could be a grave strain for
(E) with persistent coughing and could gravely strain

108. Hospitals are increasing the hours of doctors, significantly affecting the frequency of surgical errors, which already are a cost to hospitals of millions of dollars in malpractice lawsuits.

   (A) significantly affecting the frequency of surgical errors, which already are a cost to hospitals of
   (B) significantly affecting the frequency of surgical errors, which already cost hospitals
   (C) significantly affecting the surgical errors frequency , already with hospital costs of
   (D) significant in affecting the frequency of surgical errors, and already costs hospitals
   (E) significant in affecting the surgical errors frequency and already costing hospitals

109. When Henry dreams about his late wife, he sees her as she was during her youth.

   (A) he sees her as she was in
   (B) he sees her as she had been in
   (C) he sees her as if during
   (D) she appears to him as she did during
   (E) she appears to him as though during

110. In one of the most surprising victories in World War I, the newly-formed Soviet communist state was routed by the Polish general, Jozef Pilsudski, demanding that it should push back its borders east of Vilnius.

   (A) demanding that it should
   (B) demanding it to
   (C) and their demand to
   (D) who demanded that it
   (E) who demanded them to

111. Except for internal networks involve identical operating systems, whose identification protocol is the same, all legacy multi-system networks need software emulators to communicate.

   (A) Except for internal networks involve identical operating systems, whose identification protocol is the same
   (B) As well as internal networks involving identical operating systems with the same identification protocol
   (C) Unless internal networks involve identical operating systems, which have the same identification protocol
   (D) In addition to an internal network between identical operating systems with the same identification protocol
   (E) Together with internal networks between identical operating systems, whose identification protocol is the same

112. Statisticians from the Department of Motor Vehicles have calculated that <u>one human being should be struck every three minutes by a vehicle</u>, while each minute two animals can be expected to die from such collisions.

   (A) one human being should be struck every three minutes by a vehicle
   (B) a human being should be struck by a vehicle once in every three minutes
   (C) a vehicle will strike one human being once in every three minutes
   (D) every three minutes a human being will be struck by a vehicle
   (E) every three minutes a human being should be struck by a vehicle

113. New high-combustion models of engines show the potential of being able to produce high horsepower and performance without the costly <u>requirements of maintenance and consuming of special racing fuel by earlier high horsepower models</u>.

   (A) requirements of maintenance and consuming of special racing fuel by earlier high horsepower models
   (B) requirements by earlier high horsepower models of consuming of special racing fuel and maintenance
   (C) requirements for consuming of special racing fuel and maintenance of earlier high horsepower models
   (D) consumption of special racing fuel and maintenance that was required by earlier high horsepower models
   (E) maintenance and consumption of special racing fuel that were required by earlier high horsepower models

4.7 Rhetorical construction

114. <u>Though without understanding a word of what is being said, savvy communicators</u> can follow a conversation in a foreign language by interpreting tone of voice and body language.

    (A) Though without understanding a word of what is being said, savvy communicators
    (B) Without understanding a word of what is being said, savvy communicators
    (C) Even though the person has not understood a word of what is being said, a savvy communicator
    (D) Even when the person has not understood a word that is being said, savvy communicators
    (E) In spite of not understanding a word of what is being said, a savvy communicator

115. <u>When deer damage plants, it</u> can be prevented if human hair is spread around the garden.

    (A) When deer damage plants, it
    (B) The damage to plants caused by deer
    (C) The fact that deer cause damage to plants
    (D) When deer cause plant damage, it
    (E) Deer damage plants, which

116. Books to be added to the high school curriculum should be educational <u>and should have no profanity in them or be lewd</u>.

    (A) and should have no profanity in them or be lewd
    (B) and should not have profanity in them or not be lewd
    (C) and contain no profanity or lewdness
    (D) without containing profanity nor be lewd
    (E) without having any profanity or no lewdness in them

117. Sometimes it seems like Mary does things only <u>to make it more inconvenient for her husband to have</u> a good time when he's out with his friends.

    (A) to make it more inconvenient for her husband to have
    (B) to make more inconvenient for her husband the having of
    (C) making it more inconvenient for her husband so he can have
    (D) that her husband more inconveniently can have
    (E) for her husband to more inconveniently

118. Seven out of ten households in the United States own two or more televisions.

    (A) Seven out of ten households in the United States own two or more televisions.
    (B) Out of every ten, seven households in the United States owns two or more televisions.
    (C) Two or more televisions are owned by seven out of every ten households in the United States.
    (D) In the United States, seven out of every ten households owns two or more televisions.
    (E) Out of every ten households in the United States, two or more televisions are owned by seven.

119. Actors on Broadway have the difficult task of being singers who must also perform as dancers.

    (A) of being singers who must also perform as dancers
    (B) of singers who must also perform like dancers
    (C) that they are singers who must perform like dancer
    (D) that, as a singer, they must also perform as a dancer
    (E) to be a singer that must also perform as a dancer

4.8 Redundancy

120. Even though the profits of the store barely rose over a fraction for twenty years, thanks to careful bookkeeping and wise purchases of nonperishable goods at knockdown prices, the store has remained in the possession of the family.

    (A) Even though the profits of the store barely rose over a fraction for
    (B) Whereas profits from the store had been raised barely a fraction in
    (C) In spite of the store's profits barely rising over
    (D) Despite there being barely a rise in profits of the store in
    (E) Although there was a fractional raise in profits during

121. At the conclusion of a long and protracted meeting to converse about the reissuing of a new stock offer, the spokesman expressed his misgivings and doubts that the necessary finance could be raised before the deadline imposed by the banks.

    (A) a long and protracted meeting to converse about the reissuing of a new stock offer, the spokesman expressed his misgivings and doubts that the necessary finance could be raised before the deadline.
    (B) the protracted meeting to converse over the reissuing of a new stock offer, the spokesman expressed his misgivings and doubts that the necessary finance could be raised before the deadline.
    (C) a drawn out meeting on the stock reissuing offer, the spokesman expressed his skepticism that the money would be found before the deadline.
    (D) a protracted meeting to discuss the reissuing of a new stock offer, the spokesman expressed his doubts that ample finance could be raised before the deadline.
    (E) a lengthy meeting to finalize the reissuing of a new stock offer, the spokesman expressed his misgivings and doubts that ample finance could be raised before the deadline.

Sentence Correction Guide – Questions

4.9 Grammatical construction

122. <u>Elvis Presley, known by most of the world as being the King of Rock and Roll,</u> millions of his fans mourned his death.

    (A) Elvis Presley, known by most of the world as being the King of Rock and Roll,
    (B) Elvis Presley was known by most of the world's population for becoming the King of Rock and Roll and
    (C) Elvis Presley was known by most of the world for being the King of Rock and Roll and
    (D) Elvis Presley had been known around the world as the King of Rock and Roll but
    (E) Elvis Presley was known by most of the world as being the King of Rock and Roll so

123. <u>With regard to the complexity of the device, while many users have complained that even though it comes complete with an operating manual that explains in English the instructions necessary for operation and has such obtuse wording as to be impossible</u> to understand.

    (A) With regard to the complexity of the device, while many users have complained that even though it comes complete with an operating manual that explains in English the instructions necessary for operation and has such obtuse wording as to be impossible
    (B) With regard to the complexity of the device, many users have complained that even though it comes complete with an operating manual that explains in English the instructions necessary for operation and has such obtuse wording as to be impossible.
    (C) Regarding the complexity of the device, while many users have complained that even though it comes complete with an operating manual that explains in English the instructions necessary for operation, others complain it has such obtuse wording as to be impossible
    (D) With regard to the complexity of the device, many users have complained that even though it comes complete with an operating manual that explains in English the instructions necessary for operation, the wording is too obtuse
    (E) With regard to the complexity of the device, while many users have complained that despite coming with an operating manual that explains in English the instructions necessary for operation and also has such obtuse wording as to be impossible

124. Because of the mounting number of petty crimes attributable to children skipping school, a law is to be introduced requiring <u>that parents of absconding children between the ages of 12 and 16 will be kept at home.</u>

    (A) that parents of absconding children between the ages of 12 and 16 will be kept at home.
    (B) parents of between the ages of 12 and 16 absconding children to be kept at home.
    (C) which parents of absconding children between the ages of 12 and 16 will be keeping them at home.

(D) parents of absconding children between the ages of 12 and 16 to keep them at home.

(E) that parents of those children between the ages of 12 and 16 who abscond will be kept at home.

125. The handbook makes clear <u>each recruit is responsible to select one course of action over another one,</u> and that he or she must rely on self-initiative as well as trained skills to survive the ordeal.

(A) each recruit is responsible to select one course of action over another one

(B) that each recruit is responsible for selecting one course of action over another

(C) each recruit is responsible by selecting one course of action over another

(D) that each recruit is responsible to select one course of action over the other

(E) each recruit is responsible for selecting one course of action over other ones

126. Rarely in the history of the US, even if one includes the 1926 stock crisis, <u>the market has fluctuated to so many degrees in the course of just</u> twenty-four hours.

(A) the market has fluctuated to so many degrees in the course of just

(B) the market fluctuated so many degrees during only

(C) has fluctuated the market so much in the course of merely

(D) has the market fluctuated to such degrees in the course of only

(E) has the market fluctuated to such a degree in the course of a mere

127. It's an undisputed fact that Socrates experimented with a number of mind-altering drugs <u>but in attributing the ideas as he expresses to drugs in effect</u> implies he was just a tool in their creation.

(A) but in attributing the ideas as he expresses to drugs in effect

(B) while attributing the ideas he expresses to drugs in affect

(C) but in attributing a drug as the source for the ideas he expresses in effect

(D) but, if drugs are attributed for the ideas he expresses, this in effect

(E) but to attribute the ideas he expresses to drugs in effect

128. All the housing cooperative committees are enforcing a new contract and <u>have began to prohibit tenants from accepting sub-tenants in the event of them</u> taking a holiday.

(A) have began to prohibit tenants from accepting sub-tenants in the event of them

(B) have begun the prohibition of tenants to accept sub-tenants in the event of them

(C) have begun prohibiting of tenants to accept sub-tenants in the event of their

(D) have began prohibiting tenants accepting sub-tenants in the event of their

(E) have begun to prohibit tenants from accepting sub-tenants in the event of their

129. The field of mathematics, which in recent years was neglected by elementary school teachers, who prefer topics that can be easily illustrated by hands-on activities.

    (A) mathematics, which in recent years was

    (B) mathematics that was to be

    (C) mathematics, one which has, in recent years, been

    (D) mathematics is one that in recent years has been

    (E) mathematics, in recent years, is one that was

130. Most people think that women have achieved equality with men, but sociologists know that statistics for both post-graduate education and median income indicate as drastic of a gap as there was 10 years ago.

    (A) that statistics for both post-graduate education and median income indicate as drastic of

    (B) that statistics for both post-graduate education and median income indicate as drastic

    (C) that both the post-graduate education and median income statistics indicate as drastic

    (D) of both post-graduate education and median income statistics that indicate as drastic

    (E) of statistics for both post-graduate education and median income indicating as drastic of

131. A survey of men from ages 18 to 30 revealed homosexual experiences in 30 percent of them and they ranged from an isolated incident to a permanent lifestyle.

    (A) homosexual experiences in 30 percent of them and they ranged

    (B) experiences in 30 percent were homosexual and ranging

    (C) the ranging of homosexual experiences in 30 percent of them to be

    (D) that 30 percent had had homosexual experiences ranging

    (E) that 30 percent of them had had experiences that were homosexual; the range was

132. America's nuclear arsenal has expanded, but India's and Pakistan's too.

    (A) but India's and Pakistan's too

    (B) and also India's and Pakistan's

    (C) but so have India's and Pakistan's

    (D) and so also India's and Pakistan's

    (E) but so did India's and Pakistan's

133. Because memory weakens with age, for the experiment to be valid, it is important that a group to be tested for drug-induced memory loss be compared with a control group.

   (A) to be tested for drug-induced memory loss be compared with
   (B) being tested for memory loss induced by drugs are compared with
   (C) being tested for drug-induced memory loss should be compared to
   (D) being tested for drug-induced memory loss are to be compared to
   (E) that is to be tested for drug-induced memory loss are to be comparable with

134. Most MBA programs now mandate that potential applicants be finished with an undergraduate degree before applying.

   (A) mandate that potential applicants be finished
   (B) mandate potential applicants to be finished
   (C) mandate that potential applicants will be finished
   (D) have a mandate for a potential applicant finishing
   (E) have a mandate to finish potential applicants

135. The CEO has proposed a new policy requiring that employees should retain all pensions indefinitely or be allowed to cash them in at retirement.

   (A) that employees should retain all pensions
   (B) that all pensions be retained by employees
   (C) the retaining by employees of all pensions
   (D) employee's retention of all pensions
   (E) employees to retain all pensions

136. After the attack on the World Trade Center, the President ordered intelligence agencies should prepare lists of who were America's most wanted terrorists.

   (A) should prepare lists of who were America's most wanted terrorists
   (B) would do the preparation of lists of America's most wanted terrorists
   (C) preparing lists of most wanted terrorists in America
   (D) the preparing of a list of the most wanted terrorists in America
   (E) to prepare lists of the most wanted terrorists in America

4.10 Concision

137. Although he had fought against abortion while being a teenager, Saul Ludiminsky later went on to head the Planned Parenthood Association.

    (A) while being a teenager
    (B) as a teenager
    (C) during the time he was a teenager
    (D) in the years that he was a teenager
    (E) at the time of his being a teenager

138. The UN arms inspectors are reviewing Iraq's arsenal of weapons for the determination of whether they are meeting the requirements set by the Security Council.

    (A) for the determination of whether they are meeting the requirements set by the Security Council
    (B) for the determining of whether or not it meets the requirements set by the Security Council
    (C) for the determining of whether the requirements set by the Security Council are being met or not
    (D) determining whether the requirements set by the Security Council are being met
    (E) to determine whether the requirements set by the Security Council are being met

139. Although the initial setup of generators and a power grid by Edison and JP Morgan was rather costly, the electrification of lighting in lower Manhattan doubled work efficiency when the energy costs were cut in half.

    (A) the electrification of lighting in lower Manhattan doubled work efficiency when the energy costs were cut in half
    (B) the electrification of lighting in lower Manhattan doubled work efficiency while cutting energy costs in half
    (C) the electrification of lighting in lower Manhattan doubled work efficiency while costs were cut to half
    (D) lighting electrification in lower Manhattan doubled work efficiency while energy costs were cut in half
    (E) lighting electrification in lower Manhattan doubled work efficiency while costs were cut to half

140. Historians and philosophers in the late nineteenth century argued that Plato's work was perhaps the ultimate work of political philosophy, that it was the one paradigm of political discourse that there was no possibility to supersede.

    (A) it was the one paradigm of political discourse that there was no possibility to supersede

(B) the one paradigm of political discourse that could not be superseded

(C) for it was the one paradigm of political discourse, and that it was impossible to supersede

(D) a paradigm of political discourse that there was no possibility to supersede

(E) as being the one paradigm that could not be superseded in political discourse

4.11 Idioms

141. No school policies forbid <u>a teacher from scolding a student or to call</u> the student's parents based only on another child's accusations.

    (A) a teacher from scolding a student or to call
    (B) a teacher to scold a student or call
    (C) that teachers scold a student or call
    (D) the scolding by a teacher of a student or calling of
    (E) scolding by teachers of a student or calling of

142. Because of persuasive arguments made by both lawyers, juries often have difficulty distinguishing <u>the innocent from</u> the guilty; DNA testing helps prevent innocent people from being convicted.

    (A) the innocent from
    (B) the innocent and
    (C) between the innocent and that of
    (D) for the innocent or
    (E) among the innocent or

143. The pieces performed in their latest concert show <u>the chamber musicians have combined styles of music from the Middle East to that</u> of Russia.

    (A) the chamber musicians have combined styles of music from the Middle East to that
    (B) that the chamber musicians have combined styles of music from the Middle East to that
    (C) the chamber musicians have combined styles of music from the Middle East with that
    (D) that the chamber musicians have combined styles of music from the Middle East with those
    (E) that chamber musicians have combined styles of music from Egypt and those

144. At first sight the two proposals look very similar, but in fine print, sandwiched <u>between corollaries, almost opposing concepts are propounded on</u> how production could be expanded.

    (A) between corollaries, almost opposing concepts are propounded on
    (B) among the corollaries, are propounded almost opposing concepts
    (C) between corollaries, are propounded almost opposing concepts of
    (D) in the corollaries, almost opposing concepts are propounded at
    (E) between corollaries, are propounded concepts which are almost opposing on

145. As much as those preliminary ideas were derived from accessing the work of colleagues in the field, the Senate still insisted on independent verification.

    (A) As much as those preliminary ideas were derived from accessing the

    (B) As many as those preliminary ideas were derived from accessing the

    (C) Even though much of those preliminary ideas were derived from accessing in the

    (D) Although many of those preliminary ideas were derived from access into the

    (E) Despite those preliminary ideas deriving from accessing to the

146. Under the committee's latest proposal, the budget for research on inheriting disease, abiding to the stipulations in the will, be increased to ward off any criticisms from the trustees of the fund.

    (A) on inheriting disease, abiding to the stipulations in the will, be increased to ward off

    (B) on inheriting disease, abiding with the stipulations in the will, should be increased more to ward through

    (C) into inherited disease, abiding to the stipulations in the will, may be increased to ward by

    (D) into inherited disease, abiding by the stipulations in the will, will be increased to ward off

    (E) on inheriting disease, abiding by the stipulations in the will, has increased to ward off

147. However common in Southeast Asia, in reality the buffalo squirrels, famed for having garishly red fur and their human-like cries, are really native to South Africa but were introduced to India by British colonialists as pets.

    (A) in Southeast Asia, in reality the buffalo squirrels, famed for having garishly red fur and their human-like cries, are really native to

    (B) to Southeast Asia, in reality the buffalo squirrels, famed for their garishly red fur and their human-like cries, are really native to

    (C) in Southeast Asia, in reality the buffalo squirrels, famous for having garishly red fur and human-like cries, are really natives of

    (D) to Southeast Asia, in reality the buffalo squirrels, famed for their garishly red fur and human-like cries, are really native to

    (E) in Southeast Asia, in reality the buffalo squirrels, famed for their garishly red fur and their human-like cries, are really native to

148. Chemists at the Carnegie Research Center claim to have found the ultimate super glue, one that they believe is a type never seen before.

    (A) one that they believe is

    (B) one they believe to be of

(C) one that they believe it to be of

(D) one that is believed is

(E) one they believe that is

149. Even though <u>books about the Canadian wilderness portray grizzly bears as savage animals, roaring ferociously from the peaks of snow covered mountains,</u> in reality they are playful and sociable and only attack if they or their cubs are threatened.

   (A) books about the Canadian wilderness portray the grizzly bears as savage animals, roaring ferociously from the peaks of snow covered mountains,

   (B) in books about the Canadian wilderness portray grizzly bears as savage animals, roaring ferociously from the peaks of snow covered mountains,

   (C) grizzly bears are portrayed in books about the Canadian wilderness as savage animals, roaring ferociously from the peaks of snow covered mountains,

   (D) books about the Canadian wilderness portray grizzly bears as if they were savage animals, roaring ferociously from the peak tops of snow covered mountains,

   (E) books about the Canadian wilderness portray grizzly bears to be savage animals, roaring ferociously from the peaks of snow covered mountains,

150. The announcement made today by NATO spokesman Jamie O'Shea stressed that the UN mandate distinguishes <u>Serb councils, which were democratically elected prior to their being disbanded, from Albanian exile councils returning from</u> Macedonia.

   (A) Serb councils, which were democratically elected prior to their being disbanded, from Albanian exile councils returning from

   (B) from Serb councils, which were democratically elected prior to their being disbanded, from Albanian exile councils returning to

   (C) between Serb councils, which have been democratically elected prior to disbandment, and Albanian exile councils returning from

   (D) between Serb councils, which had been democratically elected prior to their being disbanded, from Albanian exile councils returning from

   (E) from Serb councils which were democratically elected prior to disbandment, from Albanian exile councils returning from

151. In his speech last night, the mayor acknowledged Citizens for Communities, a grassroots organization that has <u>provided aid in drawing residents of impoverished neighborhoods together</u>.

   (A) provided aid in drawing residents of impoverished neighborhoods together

   (B) provided aid in the drawing together of residents of impoverished neighborhoods

   (C) provided aid to draw together residents of neighborhoods that are impoverished

   (D) provided aid to drawing together residents of impoverished neighborhoods

   (E) provided aid to draw together neighborhoods that are impoverished

152. The pharmaceutical company hired a consultant to supervise a division <u>studying lower salaries as to their effects on employees' morale</u>.

    (A) studying lower salaries as to their effects on employees' morale

    (B) studying the effects of lower salaries on employees' morale

    (C) for studying what are the effects in employees' morale that lower salaries would cause

    (D) studying the effects of employees' morale on lower salaries

    (E) studying what the effects lower salaries would have on employees' morale

153. The local orchestra, which used to perform everything from <u>Bach and Handel to Bartok, appears to have</u> reduced its repertoire to only baroque music.

    (A) Bach and Handel to Bartok, appears to have

    (B) Bach, Handel, and Bartok, appears having

    (C) Bach, Handel, and Bartok, appears that it has

    (D) Bach and Handel to Bartok, appears that it has

    (E) Bach and Handel as well as Bartok, appears to have

154. <u>The average American may not think of sexual harassment to be</u> a widespread issue, but 75 percent of all women report experiencing it in the workplace.

    (A) The average American may not think of sexual harassment to be

    (B) The average American may not think of sexual harassment being

    (C) An average American may not think of sexual harassment being

    (D) The average American may not think of sexual harassment as

    (E) Sexual harassment may not be thought of by the average American as

155. The recently discovered notes of the writer suddenly revealed <u>that this most timid and shy of women was an intellectual giant guided in both emotional and</u> spiritual activities by a sharp sense of moral courage.

    (A) that this most timid and shy of women was an intellectual giant guided in both emotional and

    (B) that this most timid and shy of women was an intellectual giant also guided both in emotional as well as

    (C) this most timid and shy of women was an intellectual giant and that she was guided in both emotional and

    (D) this most timid and shy of women was an intellectual giant and that she was guided in both emotional as well as

    (E) that this most timid and shy of women to have been an intellectual giant and that she guided herself in both emotional as in

Sentence Correction Guide – Questions

156. Although coffee is not usually considered a drug, <u>it is so addictive that it has become a critical</u> part of breakfast for many people.

    (A) it is so addictive that it has become a critical
    (B) it is of such addiction, it has become a critical
    (C) so addicting is it as to become a critical
    (D) such is its addiction, it becomes a critical
    (E) there is so much addiction that it has become a critical

157. In the most bizarre court case this month, the judge ruled <u>that two ping-pong ball manufacturers owed restitution to four national ping-pong teams for the illegal weighting of</u> the ping-pong balls in an effort to fix the tournament.

    (A) that two ping-pong ball manufacturers owed restitution to four national ping-pong teams for the illegal weighting of
    (B) that two ping-pong ball manufacturers owed restitution to four national ping-pong teams because of their illegal weighting of
    (C) that two ping-pong ball manufacturers owe restitution to four national ping-pong teams for their illegal weighting of
    (D) on two ping-pong ball manufacturers that owed restitution to four national ping-pong teams because they illegally weighted
    (E) on the restitution that two ping-pong ball manufacturers owed to four national ping-pong teams for the illegal weighting of

158. In an effort to shorten the time span and cut the costs needed to raise full-size beef stock, many ranchers substitute cornmeal and ground bones <u>for their cattle's regular diet, branded by them</u> to become generic-grade beef.

    (A) for their cattle's regular diet, branded by them
    (B) for the regular diet of their cattle that have been branded
    (C) for the regular diet of their cattle, having been branded
    (D) in place of their cattle's regular diet, for those of them branded
    (E) in place of the regular diet of their cattle to have been branded by them

159. Because the economic cycle in the United States changes little during its 20-year interval <u>between recessing</u>, it is fairly easy for analysts to predict analogous trends in the stock market.

    (A) between recessing
    (B) of recessing
    (C) between its recessions
    (D) of its recessions
    (E) as it recesses

4.12 Diction

160. If the draft is not re-instated, <u>less people will join the army in the coming 10 years than</u> did in any other 10-year period in our nation's history.

    (A) less people will join the army in the coming 10 years than
    (B) less people will be joining the army in the coming 10 years as
    (C) fewer people will join the army in the coming 10 years as
    (D) fewer people will be joining the army in the coming 10 years as
    (E) fewer people will join the army in the coming 10 years than

161. Many fear the epidemic of obesity in America; the amount of food consumed per person in America is <u>as much as thrice that consumed in Japan</u>.

    (A) as much as thrice that consumed in Japan
    (B) as much as thrice that of Japan's consumption
    (C) up to three times of Japan's consumption
    (D) up to three times what Japanese consumed
    (E) up to triple the amount the Japanese consumed

162. The president's ill-advised economic policies affected <u>the employed and the jobless alike; vast quantities of people were precariously balanced</u> on the edge of poverty.

    (A) the employed and the jobless alike; vast quantities of people were precariously balanced
    (B) both the employed and the jobless alike; large amounts of people precariously balanced themselves
    (C) the employed and the jobless alike; a great number of people were precariously balanced
    (D) both the employed and the jobless alike; vast numbers of people precariously balanced themselves
    (E) both the employed and the jobless; great quantities of people were precariously balanced

163. Although the prime interest rate has been fluctuating dramatically for almost a month and there has been a considerable flight <u>of capital, the economy in terms of production, currency level and exports have remained stationery.</u>

    (A) of capital, the economy in terms of production, currency level and exports have remained stationery.
    (B) by capital, the economy, as regards to production, currency level and exports remained stationary.
    (C) of capital, the economy with regard to production, currency level, and exports has remained stationary.

(D) from capital, the economy in terms of production, currency level and exports has remained stationery.

(E) from capital, the economy regarding production, currency level and exports remained stationary.

164. The Bhopal inquiry only reluctantly acknowledged that <u>no amount of money or staff members</u> could have prevented the emission of the poisonous gases as the plant itself was fundamentally flawed.

    (A) no amount of money or staff members
    (B) neither large amounts of money nor staff members
    (C) no matter how large the staff or how enormous the amount of money
    (D) neither an enormous amount of money nor a large staff
    (E) neither enormous amounts of money nor increasing staff members

165. The survey revealed that thanks to the efforts of the aid organizations, the refugees living in the camp considered themselves <u>no worse off than do people living</u> in the US.

    (A) no worse off than do people living
    (B) not any worse than do people living
    (C) not any worse off than do people who live
    (D) no worse off than are people who are living
    (E) not as worse off as are people who live

166. Despite the huge sums spent on the interception of drugs, <u>the amount of seizures in US cities increased by more than twice in the years between 1996 to 1998.</u>

    (A) the amount of seizures in the US cities increased by more than twice in the year between 1996 to 1998.
    (B) the size of seizures in US cities increased by more than two times between 1996 to 1998.
    (C) the number of seizures in some US cities increased twice more between 1996 and 1998.
    (D) the number of seizures in US cities more than doubled between 1996 and 1998.
    (E) the number of seizures in US cities more than doubled in the years between 1996 to 1998.

167. The three candidates all had similar qualifications and in every respect were <u>the ideal replacement for Jones so its no wonder that the committee had such difficulty choosing one between them.</u>

    (A) the ideal replacement for Jones so its no wonder that the committee had such difficulty choosing one between them.

(B) the ideal replacement to Jones so its no wonder how the committee had such difficulty choosing one among them.

(C) the ideal replacement for Jones so it's no wonder the committee found it difficult to choose one between them.

(D) the ideal replacement for Jones so it's no wonder that the committee had such difficulty choosing one among them.

(E) the ideal replacement for Jones so it was no wonder that the committee had so much difficulty choosing one between them.

168. The incidence of drug abuse in rural areas is <u>equally high or more so than in urban areas.</u>

(A) equally high or more so than in urban areas.

(B) equal to or higher than in urban areas.

(C) as high as in urban areas or more.

(D) equal to, if not more than, in urban areas.

(E) as high as, if not higher than, it is in urban areas.

169. <u>The shipping of raw materials being improved has become an economical</u> factor in the transformation of Japan into a world economic power.

(A) The shipping of raw materials being improved has become an economical

(B) The improved shipping of raw materials has become an economical

(C) That the shipping of raw materials is improved has become an economical

(D) The shipping of raw materials being improved has become an economic

(E) The improvement in the shipping of raw materials has become an economic

170. <u>During the late 1960's and the 1970's, funding for space missions fell by nearly 70 percent from its peak in 1968 down to its nadir in 1977.</u>

(A) During the late 1960's and the 1970's, funding for space missions fell by nearly 70 percent from its peak in 1968 down to its nadir in 1977

(B) During the late 1960's and the 1970's, funding for space missions fell by nearly 70 percent from its peak in 1968 to its nadir in 1977

(C) At the time of the late 1960's and the 1970's funding for space missions fell by almost 70 percent from its 1968 peak down to its 1977 nadir

(D) At the time of the late 1960's and the 1970's, funding for space missions fell from its peak in 1968, by nearly 70 percent, to its nadir in 1977

(E) During the late 1960's and the 1970's, funding for space missions fell from its peak in 1968 to its nadir in 1977 by nearly 70 percent

Sentence Correction Guide – Questions 127

171. The leader of the physics seminar was prepared to start discussions herself, <u>for not everyone in attendance was knowledgeable</u> that the material being discussed involved new theories of quantum mechanics unknown to many in the profession.

    (A) for not everyone in attendance was knowledgeable
    (B) for everyone in attendance did not know
    (C) with everyone in attendance not knowing
    (D) with everyone attending not knowledgeable
    (E) for not everyone attending knew

172. Despite her recent promise not to talk about her divorce with the media, she decided to <u>do so at the press conference because she thought that many women, likely most, would appreciate</u> her message of empowerment.

    (A) do so at the press conference because she thought that many women, likely most, would appreciate
    (B) talk at the press conference since she thought that many women, likely most, would have appreciated
    (C) so talk at the press conference due to her thinking that many women, even most, would likely appreciate
    (D) do so at the press conference because she thought that many women, if not most, would appreciate
    (E) do so at the press conference since she thought many women, and even most, would likely appreciate

173. At school, Miruko is antisocial and sullen, but <u>at home</u> she is a bubbly, even-tempered child.

    (A) at home
    (B) in her home, in which
    (C) it is in her home in which
    (D) at her home where
    (E) it is in her home and

174. More than one hundred years ago, students of ornithology reported that hummingbirds can hover <u>as insects, flitting gracefully from one flower to another</u>.

    (A) as insects, flitting gracefully from one flower to another
    (B) like insects, flitting gracefully from one flower to another
    (C) as insects do that flit gracefully from one flower to others
    (D) like insects do that flit gracefully from one flower to others
    (E) as do insects that flit gracefully from one flower to some other one

4.13 Tenses

175. Some civil libertarians insist that the best way to ensure freedom of religion for all citizens is to reduce the prominence of the Judeo-Christian god in politics.

   (A) insist that the best way to ensure freedom of religion for all citizens is to reduce
   (B) have insisted the best way freedom of religion can be ensure for all citizens is reducing
   (C) insist the best way to ensure freedom of religion for all citizens is the reduction of
   (D) are insistent that the best way freedom of religion can be ensured for all citizens is the reduction of
   (E) insist that the best way for the ensuring of freedom of religion for all citizens is to reduce

176. Scientists have determined that the inner ear assists in awareness of body orientation, since people with disorders of the inner ear were found to have increased difficulties in maintaining balance.

   (A) were found to have increased difficulties
   (B) have been found to have increased difficulty
   (C) were found to have increasing difficulty
   (D) had been found to have increased difficulties
   (E) have been found to have increasing difficulties

177. In a period of time when the differently-abled generally have had a limited range of opportunities, Campbell became a notable artist and poet as well as a leading spokesman for the rights of the mentally challenged.

   (A) In a period of time when the differently-abled generally have
   (B) Generally in a time when the differently-abled
   (C) At a time when the differently-abled generally
   (D) During a time in which the differently-abled generally have
   (E) Generally when the differently-abled have

178. Sociologists have discovered that caregivers subconsciously enjoy the chance to nurse someone; the workers are, in fact, disappointed when patients recover.

   (A) the workers are, in fact, disappointed when patients recover
   (B) and the workers are, in fact, disappointed when patients recovered
   (C) the workers are, in fact, disappointed when patients recovered
   (D) in fact, they are disappointed when patients recovered
   (E) the workers are disappointed at the recovery of patients, in fact

179. Al Gore was vice-president of the United States, <u>while earlier his father has been</u> a senator.

   (A) while earlier his father has been

   (B) where his father earlier had been

   (C) just as earlier his father had been

   (D) as his earlier father has been

   (E) his father earlier being

180. The Smiths lost all of their money gambling, and <u>they were forced to move to a suburb bordering the city from their apartment</u>.

   (A) they were forced to move to a suburb bordering the city from their apartment

   (B) they had been forced to move from their apartment to a suburb that bordered the city

   (C) they were forced to move from their apartment to a suburb bordering the city

   (D) they having been forced to, moved from their apartment to a suburb that bordered the city

   (E) they withdrew, because they were forced to, from their apartment to a suburb bordering the city

181. Stanford University gave the Musician of the Year Award to Joan White, <u>one of only eight musicians who had performed in the end-of-the-year concert</u>.

   (A) one of only eight musicians who had performed in the end-of-the-year concert

   (B) one of eight of the only musicians who have performed in the end-of-the-year concert

   (C) one of the only eight musicians who performs in the end-of-the-year concert

   (D) only one of eight musicians to perform in the end-of-the-year concert

   (E) only one of the eight end-of-the-year musicians who performs in the concert

182. George Brown <u>lost more than 180 pounds since having</u> an operation truncating his stomach three years ago.

   (A) lost more than 180 pounds since having

   (B) lost more than 180 pounds since having had

   (C) has lost more than 180 pounds since having

   (D) has lost more than 180 pounds after

   (E) has lost more than 180 pounds subsequently to

183. <u>Although he is as brilliant as, if not more brilliant than, many of his fellow students, he is very lazy and his thesis will be unfinished.</u>

   (A) Although he is as brilliant as, if not more brilliant than, many of his fellow students, he is very lazy and his thesis will be unfinished.

   (B) Although he is as brilliant as, if not more brilliant than, many of his fellow students, he is very lazy with his thesis remaining unfinished.

   (C) Although he is as brilliant as, if not more brilliant than, many of his fellow students, he is very lazy and will not finish his thesis.

   (D) Despite his being brilliant as, if not more brilliant than his fellow students, he is very lazy and will not finish his thesis.

   (E) Being as brilliant as, or more brilliant than, many of his fellow students, he is very lazy and his thesis will be unfinished.

184. The defending attorney weakened the prosecution's arguments so much that, at the end of the trial, the jury <u>doubted that the victim had even existed</u>.

   (A) doubted that the victim had even existed
   (B) doubts that the victim has even existed
   (C) was in doubt as to the existence of the victim
   (D) was doubtful concerning the victim's existence
   (E) had doubted about the victim's even existing

4.14 Conjunctions & Mood

185. The city of Montreal spends a large portion of its annual budget on the construction of tourist attractions such as amusement parks, <u>even if it is by no means certain that the construction of tourist attractions increases</u> revenue from tourism.

    (A) even if it is by no means certain that the construction of tourist attractions increases

    (B) even if the city is by no means certain that the construction of tourist attractions will increase

    (C) even if there is no certainty that the construction of tourist attractions increases

    (D) even though the city is by no means certain that the construction of tourist attractions increases

    (E) though there is no certainty as to the construction of tourist attractions increasing

186. During this phase, Picasso <u>would paint a bold stroke when inspiration struck</u>, after meditating for days, continue with lightening brushes before beginning to add color.

    (A) would paint a bold stroke when inspiration struck,

    (B) painting a bold stroke when inspiration struck,

    (C) but who would paint a bold stroke when inspiration struck,

    (D) would paint a bold stroke when inspiration struck and,

    (E) who, painting a bold stroke when inspiration struck,

187. The actors in *The Mystery of Edwin Drood* have become known as <u>a prime example of the interaction between performers with</u> the audience.

    (A) a prime example of the interaction between performers with

    (B) a prime example of the interaction of performers and

    (C) being prime examples of the interaction between performers with

    (D) prime examples of the interaction between performers with

    (E) prime examples of the interaction between performers and

188. At Pomona College, a rule has been passed that <u>permits students to cook and serve their food, as well as to buy it</u>.

    (A) permits students to cook and serve their food, as well as to buy it

    (B) permits students to cook, serve, and to buy their food

    (C) permits students to cook, to serve, and buy food

    (D) will permit the student to cook, serve, as well as to buy food

    (E) will permit food to be cooked, served, as well as bought by students

189. Regardless of the amount of dairy they consume in adulthood, people who consumed little dairy in childhood <u>seem to be prone to bone fractures</u>, a disadvantage that suggests a need for higher calcium consumption in childhood.

   (A) seem to be prone to bone fractures
   (B) seemingly are prone to bone fractures and have
   (C) seem to be prone to bone fractures and have
   (D) seemingly are prone to bone fractures, having
   (E) are, it seems, prone to bone fractures, and they have

190. Because both parents worked full-time, they had a nanny who not only watched the children <u>and also cleaned the house should it be</u> messy.

   (A) and also cleaned the house should it be
   (B) but also did the cleaning of the house if it were
   (C) and the house was cleaned if it were
   (D) but also cleaned the house when it was
   (E) and cleans the house if it were

4.15 Assorted questions

191. Many companies pay almost twice as much to men, if the effect of faster promotions, more bonuses, and better benefits <u>are regarded as salary, than</u> to women, who earn 77 cents for every dollar their male counterparts earn in base salary.

    (A) are regarded as salary, than
    (B) are regarded as salary, as
    (C) is regarded as salary, than it pays
    (D) is regarded as salary, as is paid
    (E) is regarded as salary, as they pay

192. The Planned Parenthood representative suggested that all sexually active teenagers <u>be protected from STDs as thoroughly as possible and also encouraged all parents who have post-pubescent children</u> to talk to their children about birth control.

    (A) be protected from STDs as thoroughly as possible and also encourages all parents who have post-pubescent children
    (B) should be protected from STDs as thoroughly as possible and also encourages all parents that have post-pubescent children
    (C) are protected from STDs as thoroughly as possible and also encourages those parents who are having post-pubescent children
    (D) be protected from STDs as thoroughly as possible and also encouraged all parents with post-pubescent children
    (E) should be protected from STDs as thoroughly as possible and also has encouraged all those parents with a post-pubescent child

193. SAS is a database-forming programming language, <u>a means to organize, in order to analyze, the huge amount</u> of seemingly unrelated facts on a topic.

    (A) a means to organize, in order to analyze, the huge amount
    (B) a means to organize, in order to analyze, the huge number
    (C) the means of organizing for analyzing the huge number
    (D) the means that organizes, in order to analyze, the huge amount
    (E) the means for organizing in order to analyze the huge amount

194. Unlike Christians, Jews only see Jesus as a prophet; they do not think of him as the Messiah, <u>nor do they view him</u> as the son of God.

    (A) nor do they view him
    (B) but they do not view him
    (C) neither do they view him
    (D) and they neither view him
    (E) while viewing him neither

195. Partial-birth abortion, a procedure <u>used in the third trimester of pregnancy involving the partial delivery and the euthanasia of a fetus, is now the subject of controversy because it involves</u> killing a fetus that could live outside the mother.

    (A) used in the third trimester of pregnancy involving the partial delivery and the euthanasia of a fetus, is now the subject of controversy because it involves

    (B) used in the third trimester of pregnancy involving the partial delivery and the euthanasia of a fetus, is now the subject of controversy because of involving

    (C) used in the third trimester of pregnancy, involves the partial delivery and the euthanasia of a fetus and is now the subject of controversy because it involves

    (D) in the third trimester of pregnancy that involves the partial delivery and the euthanasia of a fetus, is now the subject of controversy because it involves

    (E) in the third trimester of pregnancy involving the partial delivery and the euthanasia of a fetus, which is now the subject of controversy, involves

196. To end violent tendencies in young children, mothers want peaceful conflict resolution, readily available counseling, and <u>decreasing the prominence of television shows that contain abundant and often casual violence</u>.

    (A) decreasing the prominence of television shows that contain abundant and often casual violence

    (B) decreasing the prominence of television shows containing often casual but abundant violence

    (C) a decrease of the prominence of television shows, containing as they do often casual violence in abundance

    (D) a decreased prominence of the abundant and often casual violence contained in television shows

    (E) a decreased prominence of television shows that contain abundant but often casual violence

197. It may be many years before politicians <u>again attempt to revive the draft, a program known to be</u> unpopular with voters.

    (A) again attempt to revive the draft, a program known to be

    (B) attempt to revive the draft again, a program known for being

    (C) will attempt to revive the draft again, a program known as being

    (D) attempt to revive the draft again, a program that is known to be

    (E) will again attempt to revive the draft, a program known as being

198. Over the last 10 years, the population of deer in America <u>increased dramatically over the past decade, while the number of drivers who report car accidents with deer on highways is more than four times what it was</u>.

    (A) increased dramatically over the past decade, while the number of drivers who report car accidents with deer on highways is more than four times what it was

(B) increased dramatically, while the number of drivers reporting car accidents with deer on highways is more than quadruple what it was at that time

(C) has increased dramatically, while the number of drivers reporting car accidents with deer on highways has more than quadrupled

(D) has increased dramatically over the past decade, while the number of drivers reporting car accidents with deer on highways is more than four times what it was at that time

(E) has increased dramatically over the past decade, while the number of drivers who are reporting car accidents with deer on highways are more than quadruple what they once were

199. The organs of pigs genetically modified by human stem-cells are now viewed as forms of health insurance and as resources <u>a human is able to use to take care of one's</u> later illnesses.

(A) a human is able to use to take care of one's

(B) that a human is able to use to take care of oneself in

(C) a human is able to use to take care of oneself in

(D) humans are able to use to take care of them in

(E) humans are able to use to take care of themselves in

200. The mayor regretted that Hurricane Bradley affected the metropolitan area so much more dramatically than meteorologists <u>had expected may occur</u>.

(A) had expected may occur

(B) had expected

(C) expected the occurrence of

(D) expected may occur

(E) expected

201. The intense humidity emphasized the fact <u>that it was, which the records show</u>, the hottest day Ottawa had ever had.

(A) that it was, which the records show,

(B) it was, and it is the records that show it,

(C) of it being, as the records show,

(D) that the day was, as the records show,

(E) shown in the records, that it was

202. Animal Rescue is a non-profit organization that tries to find lost pets and that returns them to their owners.

    (A) to find lost pets and that returns them
    (B) to find lost pets and return them
    (C) to find lost pets for return
    (D) at finding lost pets so as to return them
    (E) finding lost pets and that returns them

203. Not since Communist crushed the democratic demonstrations has a country so brutally denied the right of its citizens that they could speak freely.

    (A) has a country so brutally denied the right of its citizens that they could speak freely
    (B) did a country so brutally deny the right of its citizens that they could speak freely
    (C) has a country so brutally denied the right of its citizens to speak freely
    (D) did a country so brutally deny the right of its citizens to speak freely
    (E) has a country so brutally denied whether its citizens had the right that they could be speaking freely

204. In recent years, despite the ethnocentrism of Western cultures, Eastern customs are understood in the international community.

    (A) are understood
    (B) are becoming better understood
    (C) which have gained understanding,
    (D) have become better understood
    (E) have since become understood

205. Lately, union leaders have been divided in arguments over if the union should fight for increased benefits or raised safety awareness.

    (A) over if the union should fight for increased benefits or raised safety awareness
    (B) over whether the union should fight for increased benefits or raised safety awareness
    (C) about the union fighting for increased benefits or raised safety awareness
    (D) about if increased benefits should come from the union or raised safety awareness
    (E) concerning the union and its fighting for increased benefits or raised safety awareness

206. Montreal, where the tourist industry is larger than any other Canadian city, has neighborhoods entirely composed of souvenir shops and cafes.

    (A) where the tourist industry is larger than any other Canadian city
    (B) which has a tourist industry larger than that of other Canadian cities
    (C) which had a tourist industry larger than any other Canadian city
    (D) whose tourist industry is larger than any other Canadian city
    (E) whose tourist industry is larger than that of any other Canadian city

207. With a salary of less than $15,000 dollars a year and fewer sources of alternate income than before, Mrs. Greenman is in financial difficulty.

    (A) of less than $15,000 dollars a year and fewer
    (B) lower than $15,000 dollars and less
    (C) lesser than $15,000 dollars and fewer
    (D) fewer than $15,000 dollars and less
    (E) of fewer than $15,000 dollars and of fewer

208. The Johnson family is to be pitied for, first of all, becoming ineligible for welfare, and secondarily, for their failure to find a well-priced apartment.

    (A) secondarily, for their failure to
    (B) secondly, for their failure to
    (C) secondly, that they failed and did not
    (D) second, that they failed to
    (E) second, failing to

209. Notice of the upcoming execution being given to convicted murderers two days before executing them is the standard practice in certain police states in Asia.

    (A) Notice of the upcoming execution being given to convicted murderers two days before executing
    (B) Giving notice of the upcoming execution to convicted murderers two days before executing
    (C) Notice of the upcoming execution to give to convicted murderers two days before executing
    (D) Giving notice of the upcoming execution two days before executing
    (E) To give notice of the upcoming execution two days before having to execute

210. Distressed by the nutritional content of the junk food sold in the school cafeteria, <u>the possibility of removing vending machines was discussed by the PTA at its monthly meeting</u>.

    (A) the possibility of removing vending machines was discussed by the PTA at its monthly meeting

    (B) the removal of vending machines was discussed as a possibility by the PTA at its monthly meeting

    (C) removed vending machines was discussed by the PTA at its monthly meeting as a possibility

    (D) the PTA discussed at its monthly meeting the possibility of vending machines being removed

    (E) the PTA, at its monthly meeting, discussed the possibility of removing vending machines

211. Robert Wood Johnson University requires <u>that a professor with classes of more than 60 students schedule smaller extra-help sessions for their students before or after the standard classes</u>.

    (A) that a professor with classes of more than 60 students schedule smaller extra-help sessions for their students before or after the standard classes

    (B) a professor with classes of more than 60 students schedule smaller extra-help sessions for their students before or after the standard classes

    (C) that professors with classes of more than 60 students schedule smaller extra-help sessions for their students before or after the standard classes

    (D) professors with classes of more than 60 students schedule smaller extra-help sessions for their students before the standard classes or after

    (E) that a professor with classes of more than 60 students to schedule smaller extra-help sessions for his students, before or after the standard classes

212. <u>Just as the Russian communists of the early 20th century believed that they were overcoming the tyranny of the czars, so too</u> did the Country X's communists believe they were avoiding the misrule of then government.

    (A) Just as the Russian communists of the early 20th century believed that they were overcoming the tyranny of the czars, so too

    (B) The Russian communists of the early 20th century believed that they were overcoming the tyranny of the czars, and in a similar way

    (C) Like the case of the Russian communists of the early 20th century who believed that they were overcoming the tyranny of the czars, so too

    (D) As in the belief that they were overcoming the tyranny of the czars held by the Russian communists of the early 20th century

    (E) Similar to the Russian communists which believed in the early 20th century that they were overcoming the tyranny of the czars

213. Jewish immigrants from Poland, Schwartz's Deli was opened by Eli and Rivka Schwartz in 1843 after unsuccessfully attempting to find office work.

    (A) Schwartz's Deli was opened by Eli and Rivka Schwartz in 1843 after unsuccessfully attempting to find office work

    (B) Eli and Rivka Schwartz opened Schwartz's Deli in 1843, after unsuccessfully attempting to find office work

    (C) after unsuccessfully attempting to find office work, Schwartz's Deli was opened by Eli and Rivka Schwartz in 1843

    (D) Schwartz's Deli was opened in 1843 by Eli and Rivka Schwartz after unsuccessfully attempting to find office work

    (E) Eli and Rivka Schwartz opened after unsuccessfully attempting to find office work Schwartz's Deli in 1843

214. After firing Danny, his boss discovered that not only had he skimmed money from the cash register, he in addition sexually harassed a female coworker.

    (A) he in addition sexually harassed a female coworker

    (B) he had sexually harassed a female coworker in addition

    (C) but he had also sexually harassed a female coworker

    (D) he had also sexually harassed a female coworker

    (E) but also his female coworker was sexually harassed as well

215. An attempt to elect a woman as president of the United States, begun 15 years ago, has had no success despite the willingness of the Democratic Party to back a female candidate.

    (A) to elect a woman as president of the United States, begun 15 years ago

    (B) begun 15 years ago, to elect a woman as president of the United States

    (C) begun for electing a woman as president of the United States 15 years ago

    (D) at electing a woman as president of the United States, begun 15 years ago

    (E) that has begun 15 years ago to elect a woman as president of the United States

216. After a murderer has been convicted, it is the judge who decides whether his crime calls for executing him or imprisoning him for life.

    (A) whether his crime calls for executing him or imprisoning him

    (B) if there is a crime that calls for an execution or an imprisonment of him

    (C) whether or not his crime calls for the execution or imprisonment of him

    (D) if there is a crime that calls for executing him or his imprisonment

    (E) if his crime would call for him being censured or that he be imprisoned

217. Because Albert is the most experienced <u>and he is therefore, the best ballet dancer in the company, he is being increasingly viewed</u> by the director as the best candidate for the role of the Nutcracker.

    (A) and he is therefore, the best ballet dancer in the company, he is being increasingly viewed

    (B) he is therefore, the best of ballet dancers, and it has increased the view

    (C) and therefore, the best ballet dancer, he is being increasingly viewed

    (D) and therefore, he is the best of ballet dancers, there is an increasing view

    (E) therefore, being the best of ballet dancers, it is increasingly viewed

218. The political and social forces that may facilitate a dictator's rise to power include sudden crashes in the economy, discrimination and other methods of finding scapegoats, <u>inciting the masses to rebellion, and their protesting that the current government may still be inadequate.</u>

    (A) inciting the masses to rebellion, and their protesting that the current government may still be inadequate

    (B) inciting the masses to rebellion, and a protest that the current government may still be inadequate.

    (C) an incitement of the masses to rebellion, and a protesting that the current government may still be inadequate.

    (D) an incitement of the masses to rebellion, and a protest of the still inadequate current government

    (E) an incitement of the masses to rebellion, and a protest that the current government may still be inadequate.

219. Like the play that came before it, <u>Shakespeare's Othello is the inspiration for the new play</u>.

    (A) Shakespeare's Othello is the inspiration for the new play

    (B) the inspiration for the new play is Shakespeare's Othello

    (C) Shakespeare's Othello is the new play's inspiration

    (D) the new play has been inspired by Shakespeare's Othello

    (E) the new play has an inspiration of Shakespeare's Othello

220. <u>To compare the thunderous brilliance of Beethoven with the bubble-gum pop tunes of Britney Spears is to compare the value of diamonds with that of plastic baubles.</u>

    (A) To compare the thunderous brilliance of Beethoven with the bubble-gum pop tunes of Britney Spears is to compare the value of diamonds with that of plastic baubles.

    (B) To compare the thunderous brilliance of Beethoven with the bubble-gum pop tunes of Britney Spears is comparing the value of diamonds with that of plastic baubles.

    (C) Comparing the thunderous brilliance of Beethoven with the bubble-gum pop tunes of Britney Spears is to compare the value of diamonds with plastic baubles.

Sentence Correction Guide – Questions

(D) Comparing the thunderous brilliance of Beethoven with the bubble-gum pop tunes of Britney Spears is like comparing the value of diamonds with plastic baubles.

(E) To compare the thunderous brilliance of Beethoven with the bubble-gum pop tunes of Britney Spears is to compare diamonds' value with plastic baubles' value.

221. When we visited the hospital, the doctors told us <u>that using a walker was much easier for Grandmother</u> than to try to walk on her own.

(A) that using a walker was much easier for Grandmother

(B) that for Grandmother, it was much easier to use a walker

(C) that for Grandmother, a walker was much easier to use

(D) for Grandmother, using a walker was much easier

(E) for Grandmother, a walker was much easier than

222. The steps of the ceramic process in which the students will be involved <u>is in the molding, smoothing of the shape, and in the decoration</u> of the finished item.

(A) is in the molding, smoothing of the shape, and in the decoration

(B) is the molding, smoothing of the shape, and also the decorating

(C) are the molding, smoothing of the shape, and in the decorating

(D) are the molding and smoothing of the shape, and the decorating

(E) is in the molding and smoothing of the shape, and the decorating

223. Since the President was caught having an affair, nearly 10,000 men have been sued for divorce, <u>which is more than had been sued</u> in the past five years combined.

(A) which is more than had been sued

(B) more than had been sued

(C) more than they had sued

(D) more than had experienced suits

(E) which is more than had experienced suits

224. Despite the doctor's urgings that she consider surgery, Marilyn decided not to go to the hospital because <u>she believed that herbal remedies would prove not only economical, but</u> ultimately effective in curing her malady.

(A) she believed that herbal remedies would prove not only economical, but

(B) herbal remedies will prove both economical and also

(C) she believed that herbal remedies would prove themselves to be both economical as well as

(D) she believed that herbal remedies would prove to be both economical and

(E) herbal remedies will prove to be both economical and

225. The pharmaceutical company should add many new strains of the disease to Prevnar, making the vaccine much more effective than 10 years ago.

(A) making the vaccine much more effective than 10 years ago

(B) and make the vaccine much more effective than 10 years ago

(C) making the vaccine much more effective than it was 10 years ago

(D) to make the vaccine much more effective than 10 years ago

(E) in making the vaccine much more effective than it was 10 years ago

226. The disciplinary decisions teachers make are less strict for girls than they are for boys because they usually cause less trouble and are more repentant.

(A) The disciplinary decisions teachers make are less strict for girls than they are for boys because they usually cause less trouble and are more repentant.

(B) Because they usually cause less trouble and are more repentant, the disciplinary decisions teachers make are less strict for girls than the disciplinary decisions are for boys.

(C) The disciplinary decisions teachers make are less strict for girls than boys because they usually cause less trouble and are more repentant.

(D) Because girls usually cause less trouble and are more repentant than boys, the disciplinary decisions that teachers make for girls are less strict than boys.

(E) The disciplinary decisions teachers make are less strict for girls than are for boys because girls are usually less troublesome and more repentant than boys.

227. In cities, teenagers get more independence than most suburbs.

(A) most suburbs

(B) most suburbs do

(C) most suburbs are

(D) they are in most suburbs

(E) they do in most suburbs

228. Once near-slums with cheap rent, neighborhoods in the South Bronx have been increasingly gentrified in recent decades as urban renewal drives away the poor.

(A) been increasingly gentrified

(B) been increasing gentrification

(C) been of increased gentrification

(D) gentrified, increasingly,

(E) increased gentrification

Sentence Correction Guide – Questions   143

229. Not until Hammurabi's code was enacted <u>had a government granted the right to its citizens that they could be aware</u> of their laws.

   (A) had a government granted the right to its citizens that they could be aware

   (B) did a government grant the right to its citizens that they could be aware

   (C) had the government granted the right to its citizens for the awareness

   (D) did a government grant the right to its citizens to be aware

   (E) had the government granted that its citizens had a right that they could be aware

230. Police are mystified by the serial murderer and have no explanation as to why he attacks some of the prostitutes with whom he has contact <u>when he spares</u> most others.

   (A) when he spares

   (B) while spares

   (C) where sparing

   (D) when sparing

   (E) while sparing

231. At the press conference, the President's spokesman <u>has announced that the government plans</u> to build up a reserve of the smallpox vaccine in case of a biological attack.

   (A) has announced that the government plans

   (B) announced that the government plans

   (C) has announced that the government will plan

   (D) announced that the government has a plan

   (E) has announced that the government planned

232. <u>Thought to emanate from a tiny gland on the underside of their bodies, ants leave behind pheromone trails that can be used</u> as signals or messages for other ants.

   (A) Thought to emanate from a tiny gland on the underside of their bodies, ants leave behind pheromone trails that can be used

   (B) Ants leave behind pheromone trails that are thought to emanate from a tiny gland on the underside of their bodies, and they can use this

   (C) Thought to emanate from a tiny gland on the underside of ants' bodies, pheromone trails left behind can be used

   (D) Emanating it is thought from a tiny gland on the underside of their bodies, ants leave behind pheromone trails they can use

   (E) Emanating, it is thought, from a tiny gland on the underside of their bodies, pheromone trails are left behind by ants that can be used

233. Although the public is accustomed to tax adjustments that benefit only the rich, economic experts were delighted to discover that both rich and the poor people would benefit from the President's tax plan.

   (A) rich and the poor people
   (B) rich people and the poor
   (C) the rich and the poor people
   (D) rich people and poor people
   (E) people who are rich and those who are poor

234. When buying electronics, one should request a guarantee for one's merchandise; the guarantee may be necessary if your new purchase breaks and you wish to have it replaced.

   (A) one should request a guarantee for one's merchandise
   (B) you should request a guarantee for your merchandise
   (C) a guarantee for your merchandise is what one should request
   (D) a guarantee for one's merchandise is what should be requested
   (E) a guarantee for your merchandise is what should be requested

235. At the suggestion of his guidance counselor, Brad applied to two Ivy League colleges and to the schools he knew would accept him.

   (A) At the suggestion of
   (B) When he was suggested by
   (C) A suggestion coming from
   (D) A suggestion that came from
   (E) After having a suggestion from

236. The 12-hour documentary on the Civil War revealed many interesting quirks that illustrates how complex and peculiar the war that pitched brother against brother really was.

   (A) that illustrates
   (B) which illustrates
   (C) that illustrate
   (D) and illustrate
   (E) who illustrate

237. He was an orphan, and Kyle founded the largest orphanage in China.

   (A) He was an orphan, and Kyle
   (B) An orphan, Kyle
   (C) Orphan that he was, Kyle
   (D) Kyle has been an orphan and he
   (E) Being an orphan, Kyle

238. Many historians regard the time of the Heian court as the greatest period in Japanese history.

    (A) regard the time of the Heian court as
    (B) regard the time of the Heian court to be
    (C) regard the time of the Heian court to have been
    (D) consider that the time of the Heian court is
    (E) consider the time of the Heian court as

239. As concerned citizens continue to investigate the activities of the CIA, their surprising similarity to Russia's infamous KGB has become impossible to ignore.

    (A) their surprising similarity to Russia's infamous KGB has become
    (B) the surprise of their similarity to Russia's infamous KGB has become
    (C) the surprising similarity between them and Russia's infamous KGB becomes
    (D) the surprising similarity between the CIA and Russia's infamous KGB becomes
    (E) the surprising similarity of the CIA with Russia's infamous KGB has become

240. Henry never showed effort, and his essays were always pedestrian; since his latest paper is nearly flawless, the obvious conclusion seems to be one of a more advanced student researching and writing at least part of Henry's impressive essay.

    (A) obvious conclusion seems to be one of a more advanced student researching and writing at least part of Henry's impressive essay
    (B) conclusion of a more advanced student researching and writing at least part of Henry's impressive essay seems obvious
    (C) conclusion seems obvious that at least part of Henry's impressive essay was researched and written by a more advanced student
    (D) conclusion of at least part of Henry's impressive essay having been researched and written by a more advanced student seems obvious
    (E) seemingly obvious conclusion is that a more advanced student would have researched and written at least part of Henry's impressive essay

241. To the distress of fans of musical theater, the producers are closing *Meet Pauline*, the first Broadway musical that had been written by a large group of composers and the inspiration for a plethora of similar works that crowded Broadway for years after.

    (A) that had been written by a large group of composers and
    (B) written by a large group of composers and which was
    (C) to be written by a large group of composers and which was
    (D) written by a large group of composers and
    (E) to have been written by a large group of composers and was

242. Based on the customs of countries such as Mexico and an analysis of ancient records, historians have inferred that the Aztecs fed prisoners sumptuous meals before using the prisoners as human sacrifices.

   (A) Based on the customs of countries such as
   (B) On the basis of the customs of countries such as
   (C) Based on the customs of countries like
   (D) On the basis of the customs of countries, like those of
   (E) Based on such customs as those of countries like

243. Golf games often turn out to be more tiring than they originally seemed.

   (A) they originally seemed
   (B) they originally seem to
   (C) they seemingly would tire originally
   (D) it would have seemed originally
   (E) it originally seemed they would

244. Unlike conservatives who wish to substitute abstinence training to full sex education, Mr. Jackson stresses how necessary it is to teach teenagers how to make adult decisions.

   (A) to full sex education, Mr. Jackson stresses how necessary it is to teach
   (B) for full sex education, Mr. Jackson stresses the necessity of teaching
   (C) to full sex education, Mr. Jackson stresses that it is necessary to teach
   (D) for full sex education, Mr. Jackson's stress is that it is necessary to teach
   (E) to full sex education, Mr. Jackson's stress is on the necessity of teaching

245. Those watching the libel suit might speculate if the company, swift to take offense, might have been as responsible for the perceived slander as the newspaper was.

   (A) speculate if the company, swift to take offense, might have been
   (B) speculate if the company, swift to take offense, had been
   (C) speculate if, in its swiftness to take offense, the company was
   (D) wonder as to whether, in its swiftness to take offense, the company was
   (E) wonder whether the company, swift to take offense, was

246. Added to the increase in monthly wages discussed last spring, the dining hall employees are currently seeking improved insurance coverage.

   (A) Added to the increase in monthly wages discussed last spring, the dining hall employees are currently seeking improved insurance coverage.
   (B) Added to the increase in monthly wages which had been discussed last spring, the employees of the dining hall are currently seeking an improved insurance coverage.

(C) The dining hall employees are currently seeking improved insurance coverage added to the increase in monthly wages that were discussed last spring.

(D) In addition to the increase in monthly wages that were discussed last spring, the dining hall employees are currently seeking improved insurance coverage.

(E) In addition to the increase in monthly wages discussed last spring, the employees of the dining hall are currently seeking improved insurance coverage.

247. Ripe peaches are marked not so much by their color <u>but instead</u> by their firmness and fullness of aroma.

   (A) but instead
   (B) rather than
   (C) than
   (D) as
   (E) so much as

248. <u>Ten percent of Clarkstown South High School students go on to Ivy League colleges, compared with from Clarkstown North High School it is five percent and Nyack High School, Pomona High School, and Ramapo High School, it is two percent.</u>

   (A) Ten percent of Clarkstown South High School students go on to Ivy League colleges, compared with from Clarkstown North High School it is five percent and Nyack High School, Pomona High School, and Ramapo High School, it is two percent.

   (B) Ten percent of Clarkstown South High School students go on to Ivy League colleges; from Clarkstown North High School it is five percent and from Nyack High School, Pomona High School, and Ramapo High School, it is two percent.

   (C) From Clarkstown South High School, ten percent of students go on to Ivy League colleges, compared with five percent from Clarkstown North High School and two percent from Nyack High School, Pomona High School, and Ramapo High School.

   (D) The percentage of students from Clarkstown South High School who go on to Ivy League colleges is ten, compared with Clarkstown North High School's ten, Nyack High School's two, Pomona High School's two, and Ramapo High School's two.

   (E) The percentage of Clarkstown South High School students going on to Ivy League colleges is ten, that from Clarkstown North High School is five, and that from Nyack High School, Pomona High School, and Ramapo High School is two.

249. The sharp contrast in sales of sports memorabilia <u>seen in sports in which most of the participants are male and such sales in sports in which most of the participants are female have</u> demonstrated that women's sports are still lacking dedicated fans.

   (A) seen in sports in which most of the participants are male and such sales in sports in which most of the participants are female have

   (B) seen in sports in which most of the participants are predominately male over those that are predominately female have

(C) that favors sports in which most of the participants are male over sports in which most of the participants are female have

(D) that favors sports in which most of the participants are male over sports in which most of the participants are female has

(E) seen is sports in which most of the participants are male and such sales in sports in which most of the participants are female has

250. The National Organization for Women has insisted that discrimination against women is still rampant in modern society and <u>that unanimous opposition to prejudice is necessary for improving any aspects of the situation.</u>

(A) that unanimous opposition to prejudice is necessary for improving any aspects of the situation

(B) unanimous opposition to prejudice is necessary if any aspects of the situation are to be improved

(C) that unanimous opposition to prejudice is necessary to improve any aspects of the situation

(D) unanimous opposition to prejudice is necessary in improving any aspects of the situation

(E) the prejudice needs to be unanimously opposed so that any aspects of the situation is improved

251. According to the editor of *Elle* magazine, <u>wearing the same clothes as are worn on undersized models will lead to a fashion failure for the plus-size woman, who</u> should shop at stores such as Lane Bryant that have clothing that will flatter her shape.

(A) wearing the same clothes as are worn on undersized models will lead to a fashion failure for the plus-size woman, who

(B) it will lead to a fashion failure for the plus-size woman to wear the same clothes as on the undersized models; they

(C) fashion failure will result from wearing the same clothes as undersized models to the plus-size woman, who

(D) fashion failure for the plus-size woman will result from wearing the same clothes as on the undersized models; they

(E) the plus-size woman wearing the same clothes as are worn on undersized models will lead to fashion failure; they

252. The nutritionist defined an obese individual <u>as one that is handicapped by an excess of weight with difficulty refraining from eating.</u>

(A) as one that is handicapped by an excess of weight with difficulty refraining from eating

(B) to be one that is handicapped by an excess of weight with difficulty refraining from eating

(C) as one who is handicapped by an excess of weight and who has difficulty refraining from eating

(D) to have difficulty refraining from eating and being handicapped by a severe excess of weight

(E) as having difficulty refraining from eating and handicapped by a severe excess of weight

253. The Constitution of the United States protects more rights <u>for its citizens than does the constitution of any other country</u>, but there are many areas in which it could provide more freedom.

   (A) for its citizens than does the constitution of any other country
   (B) to its citizens as the constitution of any other country
   (C) for its citizens as the constitution of any other country
   (D) to its citizens as the constitution of any other country
   (E) for its citizens than the constitution of any other country's

254. Answering machines and microwaves are to the modern age <u>just like a butler and cook were</u> to the Victorian era.

   (A) just like a butler and cook were
   (B) as have been a butler and cook
   (C) what butlers and cooks were
   (D) what butlers and cooks are
   (E) just the same as butlers and cooks had been

255. Teachers want students to be as well behaved as possible <u>for the reason that misbehavior on the part of students affect</u> the learning experience of the entire class.

   (A) for the reason that misbehavior on the part of students affect
   (B) for the reason because misbehavior on the part of students affects
   (C) in that misbehavior on the part of students affect
   (D) because misbehavior on the part of students affects
   (E) because misbehavior on the parts of students affects

256. After the Communist revolution in Country X, the Communist Party <u>embodied the dominant ideology of the citizens, replacing older ideologies</u> and political systems.

   (A) embodied the dominant ideology of the citizens, replacing older ideologies
   (B) embodied the dominant ideology of the citizens, replacing ideologies that were older
   (C) embodies the dominant ideology of the citizens and it replaced older ideologies
   (D) embodies the dominant ideology of the citizens and it replaced ideologies that were older
   (E) embodies the dominant ideology of the citizens, having replaced ideologies that were older

257. With a total population of <u>less than five thousand and fewer</u> well-trained soldiers than ever before, the army base is still unprepared for a real war.

   (A) less than five thousand and fewer
   (B) lower than five thousand and less
   (C) lesser than five thousand and fewer
   (D) less than five thousand and less
   (E) fewer than five thousand and of fewer

258. During the Stock Market crash in 1929, the run on the banks resulted in thousands of Americans losing hard earned savings <u>on which these depositors can</u> no longer rely.

   (A) on which these depositors can
   (B) on which these depositors could
   (C) that these depositors can
   (D) because these depositors can
   (E) for which these depositors could

259. <u>If a song is played on the radio often, a practice favored by popular radio stations, it</u> increases the chance that the singer will become famous.

   (A) If a song is played on the radio often, a practice favored by popular radio stations, it
   (B) If a song is played on the radio often, and favored by popular radio stations, it
   (C) A practice favored by popular radio stations, a song played on the radio often
   (D) A song played on the radio often, a practice favored by popular radio stations,
   (E) The playing of a song on the radio often, and a practice favored by popular radio stations,

260. Most Americans surveyed think that international environmental treaties are useless now but <u>that they will, or could,</u> be useful in the future.

   (A) they will, or could,
   (B) that they would, or could
   (C) treaties will be or could,
   (D) think that they will be or could
   (E) think that the treaties will be or could

261. Marine biologists believe that the sperm whale's head, from which hunters <u>are thought to have first extracted</u> oil, serves as an acoustic resonator for whale songs.

   (A) are thought to have first extracted
   (B) were thought first to extract
   (C) were thought at first to extract
   (D) are thought of as first extracting
   (E) were thought of as having extracted

Sentence Correction Guide - Questions

262. Contrary to popular opinion, the war on terrorism is <u>leading neither to better times for investing, more of a relaxed sense of national security, or</u> actually destroying the terrorists.

    (A) leading neither to better times for investing, more of a relaxed sense of national security, or

    (B) leading neither to better times for investing nor a more relaxed sense of national security, or

    (C) not leading to either better times for investing nor to more of a relaxed sense of national security, and neither is it

    (D) not leading to better times for investing, more of a relaxed sense of national security, and it is not

    (E) not leading to better times for investing or to a more relaxed sense of national security, nor is it

263. If additional sources of deuterium are found, <u>it will expand the amount that can be used as heavy water for nuclear reactors and reduce the cost of energy</u>, even if the sources are not immediately mined.

    (A) it will expand the amount that can be used as heavy water for nuclear reactors and reduce the cost of energy

    (B) that amount that is able to be used as heavy water for nuclear reactors will expand and the cost of energy will be reduced

    (C) it will cause an increase in the amount that is able to be used as heavy water for nuclear reactors and a reduction in the cost of energy

    (D) the amount that can be used as heavy water for nuclear reactors will increase and the cost of energy will drop

    (E) it will increase the amount of deuterium that can be used as heavy water for nuclear reactors and cause a drop in the cost of energy

264. Astronomical occurrences can be viewed in a religious light; <u>many people are known to rekindle their faith after the observation of a meteor shower.</u>

    (A) many people are known to rekindle their faith after the observation of a meteor shower

    (B) many people are known to have rekindled their faith once a meteor shower has been observed

    (C) there are many known people who have rekindled their faith once a meteor shower has been observed

    (D) after a meteor shower is observed, there are many known people who have rekindled their faith

    (E) rekindling their faith is known for many people after a meteor shower is observed

265. Following an inordinate number of post-surgery complications, medical investigators and insurance fraud agents concluded that many medical personnel work an excessive amount of overtime that has the potential of causing errors in decision-making.

   (A) overtime that has the potential of causing
   (B) overtime that has the potential to cause
   (C) overtime that potentially can cause
   (D) overtime, a practice that has the potential for causing
   (E) overtime, a practice that can, potentially, cause

266. Some analysts of the latest technological advances argue that technology moves forward not so much because of great sparks of ideas but because of smaller contributions, such as improved practices, better laboratories, and more knowledgeable designers.

   (A) because of great sparks of ideas but because of
   (B) because of great sparks of ideas as the results of
   (C) because of great sparks of ideas as because of
   (D) through great sparks of ideas but through
   (E) through great sparks of ideas but results from

267. Conquistadors began the destruction of South American cities, which was characterized by ornate gold decorations, large populations, and wonderful natural beauties.

   (A) which was characterized by ornate gold decorations, large populations
   (B) which was characterized by ornate gold decorations and large populations
   (C) which were characterized by ornate gold decorations, by large populations
   (D) being characterized by ornate gold decorations and large populations
   (E) characterized by ornate gold decorations, large populations

268. Although somewhat damaged, the librarians were able to read the cover of the aging tome.

   (A) Although somewhat damaged, the librarians were able to read
   (B) Although somewhat damaged, the librarians had read
   (C) Although it had been somewhat damaged, the librarians were able to read
   (D) Somewhat damaged though it had been, the librarians had been able to read
   (E) Damaged somewhat, the librarians were able to read

Sentence Correction Guide – Questions 153

269. At the end of the Second World War, the United States allocated huge sums of money to cover the <u>costs of reconstruction that it expected to undertake in Europe as a result of negotiations</u> with European governments.

    (A) costs of reconstruction that it expected to undertake in Europe as a result of negotiations
    (B) costly reconstruction it expected to undertake in Europe as a result from negotiations
    (C) costing reconstructions expected to be undertaken in Europe as a result of negotiating
    (D) negotiated costs in reconstruction it expected to undertake in Europe
    (E) costs expected to be undertaken in reconstruction in Europe from negotiating

270. <u>For all her asserted scorn of such books,</u> Jeanette had a bookcase full of romance novels.

    (A) For all her asserted scorn of such books,
    (B) Having always asserted scorn for such books,
    (C) All such books were, she asserted, scorned, and
    (D) Asserting that all such books were scorned,
    (E) In spite of assertions of scorning all such activities,

271. <u>The immolated monk, thought by some detectives to have occurred</u> around midnight, was a crucial factor in igniting the riots that ensued.

    (A) The immolated monk, thought by some detectives to have occurred
    (B) The immolated monk, which some detectives have thought to occur
    (C) Immolating the monk, occurred by some detectives at
    (D) The immolation of the monk, thought by some detectives to have occurred
    (E) The immolated monk, thought by some detectives to have been

272. By stealing atomic bomb secrets, the Rosenbergs readily demonstrated their desire <u>to be in sympathy with</u> the communist regime.

    (A) to be in sympathy with
    (B) to sympathize with
    (C) for sympathizing with
    (D) that they should, sympathize with
    (E) that they should have sympathy for

273. Standardized test scores of minorities are well below that of white students in spite of economic differences that are shrinking between the races.

    (A) well below that of white students in spite of economic differences that are shrinking
    (B) much below that of white students' despite economic differences shrinking
    (C) much below white students in spite of shrinking economic differences
    (D) well below those of white students in spite of shrinking economic differences
    (E) well below white students' despite their economic differences that are shrinking

274. The victories of the Canadian hockey teams were marked not so much by their brute effort as it was by their strategic planning.

    (A) as it was by
    (B) and also by
    (C) as by
    (D) and equally by
    (E) as there was

275. Plutonium and U235 result from the nuclear interchange of energies between U238 with neutrons to produce extreme radiation and high temperatures.

    (A) with neutrons to produce extreme radiation and high temperatures
    (B) with neutrons producing extreme radiation and high temperatures
    (C) and neutrons which has produced extreme radiation and high temperatures
    (D) and neutrons which have produced extreme radiation and high temperatures
    (E) and neutrons and are associated with extreme radiation and high temperatures produced by the interchange

276. It is common in the Helen Hayes Theater, as in almost every local theater, the opinion of administrators has played at least as large a part in deciding what to perform as has the desires of the public.

    (A) in almost every local theater, the opinion of administrators has played at least as large a part in deciding what to perform as has
    (B) in almost every local theater, that the opinion of administrators has played at least as large a part in deciding what to perform as has
    (C) it is in almost every local theater, that the opinion of administrators has played at least as large a part in deciding what to perform as have
    (D) is in almost every local theater, that the opinion of administrators have played at least as large a part in deciding what to perform as have
    (E) it is in almost every local theater, the opinion of administrators has played at least as large a part in deciding what to perform as has

Sentence Correction Guide – Questions

277. In disagreeing with the findings of the Warren Commission, the American public must take care to avoid moving the target of criticism from <u>government agencies collaborating in a coup d'etat to collaborating to overthrow foreign governments.</u>

    (A) government agencies collaborating in a coup d'etat to collaborating to overthrow foreign governments

    (B) government agencies collaborating in a coup d'etat to foreign governments being overthrown with collaboration

    (C) the collaboration of government agencies in a coup d'etat to the collaboration of the agencies in overthrowing foreign governments

    (D) collaboration of government agencies by coup d'etat with foreign governments, that are overthrown

    (E) a coup d'etat that government agencies collaborate in to collaboration that overthrows foreign governments

278. Despite Britain's obvious interest in using oil to power the Royal Navy, the creation of a national oil company lagged behind the Dutch and the Americans and <u>developed only after when oil well construction was supported by foreign speculators.</u>

    (A) developed only after when oil well construction was supported by foreign speculators

    (B) developed only after foreign speculators supported oil well construction

    (C) developed only after foreign speculators' support of oil well construction by foreign speculators

    (D) develops only at the time after the supporting of oil well construction by foreign speculators

    (E) developed only after there being foreign speculators' support of oil well construction

279. The chemicals that enter your body by smoking cigarettes not only gather in your lungs, thereby reducing the amount of air that you can absorb, <u>and also damage or destroy</u> sensitive tissue in your trachea and mouth.

    (A) and also damage or destroy

    (B) as well as damaging or destroying

    (C) but they also cause damage or destroy

    (D) but also damage or destroy

    (E) but also causing damage or destroying

280. There has been a drastic <u>decrease in crime caused by increasing the surveillance by undercover detectives of</u> drug dealers.

    (A) decrease in crime caused by increasing the surveillance by undercover detectives of

    (B) decrease in crime because of increased surveillance by undercover detectives of

(C) decreasing in crime because of increasing surveillance by undercover detectives to

(D) crime decrease caused by increasing surveillance by undercover detectives against

(E) crime decrease because of increased surveillance by undercover detectives to

281. Because many different cultures have different cultural norms, misunderstandings among different cultures are far greater as those among individuals from the same culture: slurping one's soup, in Japan a gesture of appreciation for the cook, is unforgivably rude in America.

(A) among different cultures are far greater as those among individuals from

(B) among different cultures are far greater than that among individuals from

(C) among different cultures are far greater than those among individuals of

(D) between different cultures are far more than that between individuals of

(E) between different cultures are greater by far than is that between individuals from

282. At a time when many English farmers had been virtually bankrupted by certain epidemics, they were further required to have destroyed animals with mad cow disease or foot and mouth disease.

(A) to have destroyed animals with mad cow disease or foot and mouth disease

(B) to have had destroyed animals with mad cow disease or foot and mouth disease

(C) either to have had destroyed animals with mad cow disease or foot and mouth disease

(D) to destroy animals with either mad cow disease or foot and mouth disease

(E) either to destroy animals with mad cow disease or foot and mouth disease

283. Producers of Broadway shows have never before been able to stage so extravagant productions of the kind they do today.

(A) so extravagant productions of the kind they do today

(B) so extravagant productions as they are today

(C) such extravagant productions as they do today

(D) such extravagant productions of the kind today's have

(E) so extravagant a production of the kind they can today

284. When it becomes more frequent to have parents who both earn substantial incomes, paying for children's college tuition will become easier.

(A) it becomes more frequent to have parents who both earn substantial incomes

(B) it becomes more frequent to have parents both earning substantial incomes

(C) it becomes more common that both parents should be earning substantial incomes

(D) it becomes more common for both parents to earn substantial incomes

(E) couples in which both of the parents earn substantial incomes become more common

Sentence Correction Guide – Questions

285. Like the wines from Germany, also an area with a temperate climate, wineries in upstate New York create rich, full-bodied wines.

    (A) Like the wines from Germany, also an area with a temperate climate, wineries in upstate New York create rich, full-bodied wines.

    (B) Wineries in upstate New York create rich, full-bodied wines similar to the wines from Germany, which, like upstate New York, is an area with a temperate climate.

    (C) Wineries in upstate New York create rich, full-bodied wines similar to Germany's, which, like upstate New York, is an area with a temperate climate.

    (D) Like Germany's wines, wineries in upstate New York, also an area with a temperate climate, create rich, full-bodied wines.

    (E) Similar to those from Germany, wineries in upstate New York, also an area with a temperate climate, create rich, full-bodied wines.

286. Many people discover a need for glasses in middle age, a consequence of sitting too close to the television screen for long periods of time.

    (A) a consequence of sitting too close to the television screen for long periods of time

    (B) a consequence from sitting for long periods of time too near to the television screen

    (C) a consequence which resulted from sitting too close to the television screen for long periods of time

    (D) affected from sitting too near to the television screen for long periods of time

    (E) affected because they sat too close to the television screen for long periods of time

287. The teacher lost control of her classroom as a result of poor discipline, a dull curriculum, as well as the destructive effects of student misbehavior that is persistent.

    (A) as well as the destructive effects of student misbehavior that is persistent

    (B) and the destructive effect of student misbehavior that is persistent

    (C) but persistent student misbehavior has had a destructive effect too

    (D) and the destructive effects of persistent student misbehavior

    (E) as well as the destructive effects of student misbehavior that persists

288. Touching on subjects like greed and corruption in corporate America and delivering a scathing condemnation of contemporary capitalism, the novel depicts one blue-collar man's attempts to succeed in the business world.

    (A) the novel depicts

    (B) the novel is going to depict

    (C) there will be a novel depicting

    (D) it is a novel that depicts

    (E) it will be a novel that depicts

289. During the internet boom in the 1990s, even a relatively small move in the tech market fooled many <u>investors having bought on rumor; they had to sell, and</u> the dumping of stock quickly revealed how over-valued many of the companies were.

   (A) investors having bought on rumor; they had to sell, and

   (B) investors who had bought on rumor; having had to sell,

   (C) investors who had bought on rumor; they had to sell, and

   (D) investors, those who had bought on rumor; these investors had to sell, and

   (E) investors, who, having bought on rumor and having to sell,

290. The ways children adapt to new situations tell psychologists more about <u>how they absorb information than</u> the children's I.Q.s.

   (A) how they absorb information than

   (B) how one absorbs information than

   (C) how children absorb information than do

   (D) absorbing information than

   (E) their information absorption than do

291. In a recent survey, *Physical Fitness Weekly* found that people exercising daily consider themselves <u>no healthier than do people exercising</u> three to five times a week.

   (A) no healthier than do people exercising

   (B) not any healthier than do people exercising

   (C) not any healthier than do people who exercise

   (D) no healthier than are people who are exercising

   (E) not as healthy as are people who exercise

292. <u>It may someday be feasible to try to retrieve organisms from tiny undersea vents</u>, but at the present time submersibles require such thick walls to withstand the high pressure that it is impossible.

   (A) It may someday be feasible to try to retrieve organisms from tiny undersea vents

   (B) Someday, it may be feasible to try and retrieve organisms from tiny undersea vents

   (C) Trying to retrieve organisms out of tiny undersea vents may someday be feasible

   (D) To try for the retrieval of organisms out of tiny undersea vents may someday be feasible

   (E) Retrieving organisms out of tiny undersea vents may be feasible to try someday

293. The great directors who create cult favorites are similar to <u>the world-class conductors directing</u> orchestras; both are critical in molding the talents of many individuals into a cohesive and beautiful form.

    (A) the world-class conductors directing
    (B) the world-class conductor which directs
    (C) world-class conductors who direct
    (D) ones to direct the world-class conductors
    (E) ones used in directing the world-class conductors

294. <u>To witness</u> the atrocious conditions suffered by abandoned children in the orphanages is to see the inhumanity of the government's ill-coceived policy.

    (A) To witness
    (B) Witnessing
    (C) Having witnessed
    (D) Once one witnesses
    (E) To have witnessed

295. <u>A male musician can find a career as a solo performer, an orchestra member, or a music teacher after he graduates from college with a degree in music, depending on his talent.</u>

    (A) A male musician can find a career as a solo performer, an orchestra member, or a music teacher after he graduates from college with a degree in music, depending on his talent.
    (B) After graduating from college with a degree in music, depending on his talent, a male musician can find a career as a solo performer, an orchestra member, or a music teacher.
    (C) After graduating from college with a degree in music, a male musician's talent will determine if he can find a career as a solo performer, an orchestra member, or a music teacher.
    (D) Talent determines whether a male musician, after graduating from college with a degree in music, can find a career as a solo performer, an orchestra member, or a music teacher.
    (E) The talent of a male musician, after graduating from college with a degree in music, will determine whether he can find a career as a solo performer, an orchestra member, or a music teacher.

296. Poor reading skills among students of inner-city schools have <u>not resulted from failures in teaching but</u> insufficiently supportive home environments.

    (A) not resulted from failures in teaching but
    (B) resulted not from failures in teaching but from
    (C) resulted from failures not in teaching but
    (D) resulted from failures not in teaching but have stemmed from
    (E) resulted not from failures in teaching as from

297. <u>The unsupervised party seeming</u> innocuous teenage fun, Judith Larkin, mother of two well-behaved daughters, thought nothing of allowing her children to attend it after the prom.

   (A) The unsupervised party seeming
   (B) As the unsupervised party was
   (C) In that the unsupervised party seemed
   (D) Since the unsupervised party was
   (E) Because the unsupervised party seemed to be

298. Since her husband began playing violin, Molly has become <u>much more expert in distinguishing between a tuned instrument and an out of tune one, a Stradivarius and</u> a student rental.

   (A) much more expert in distinguishing between a tuned instrument and an out of tune one, a Stradivarius and
   (B) far more expert in distinguishing a tuned instrument from an out of tune one, a Stradivarius from
   (C) much more expert when it comes to distinguishing a tuned instrument and an out of tune one, a Stradivarius from
   (D) far more expert in distinguishing a tuned instrument and an out of tune one, a Stradivarius and
   (E) far more the expert when it comes to distinguishing between a tuned instrument, an out of tune one, a Stradivarius, and

299. Although the music superstar agreed to a new contract, <u>she says that it must be posted on her public website so that both her new listeners and her old fans will know what is</u> going on behind the scenes.

   (A) she says that it must be posted on her public website so that both her new listeners and her old fans will know what is
   (B) she says it had to be posted on her public website so that both her new listeners and her old fans knows what is
   (C) she says that they would have to post the contract on her public website so that her new listeners and her old fans knew what was
   (D) she says that the contract would have to be posted on her public website so that both her new listeners and her old fans would know what was
   (E) saying that the contract had to be posted on her public website so that both new listeners and old fans would know what had been

300. With just a few quick slashes of the sword, <u>her opponents were defeated by the fencer, capitalizing on their slowness.</u>

   (A) her opponents were defeated by the fencer, capitalizing on their slowness
   (B) the fencer defeated her opponents, capitalizing on their slowness

(C) the fencer capitalized on the slowness of her opponents, defeating them

(D) the fencer defeated her opponents and also capitalized on their slowness

(E) her opponents and their slowness were defeated by the fencer

Chapter 5

Answer key

(1) E	(15) E	(29) B
(2) B	(16) D	(30) E
(3) D	(17) E	(31) B
(4) E	(18) C	(32) A
(5) D	(19) D	(33) C
(6) D	(20) C	(34) D
(7) D	(21) D	(35) A
(8) C	(22) C	(36) E
(9) D	(23) B	(37) A
(10) D	(24) B	(38) E
(11) D	(25) B	(39) E
(12) D	(26) B	(40) A
(13) E	(27) B	(41) C
(14) D	(28) B	(42) A

(43) E	(64) D	(85) C
(44) E	(65) C	(86) B
(45) D	(66) E	(87) C
(46) E	(67) E	(88) C
(47) D	(68) C	(89) C
(48) B	(69) C	(90) B
(49) E	(70) B	(91) C
(50) A	(71) D	(92) B
(51) E	(72) D	(93) C
(52) E	(73) A	(94) D
(53) D	(74) E	(95) D
(54) C	(75) C	(96) E
(55) D	(76) D	(97) A
(56) E	(77) C	(98) B
(57) E	(78) A	(99) D
(58) E	(79) B	(100) B
(59) D	(80) E	(101) B
(60) D	(81) B	(102) B
(61) C	(82) A	(103) C
(62) C	(83) C	(104) B
(63) C	(84) D	(105) A

Sentence Correction Guide - Answer key

(106) D	(127) E	(148) B
(107) A	(128) E	(149) A
(108) B	(129) D	(150) A
(109) A	(130) B	(151) A
(110) D	(131) D	(152) B
(111) C	(132) C	(153) A
(112) D	(133) A	(154) D
(113) E	(134) A	(155) A
(114) B	(135) E	(156) A
(115) B	(136) E	(157) A
(116) C	(137) B	(158) B
(117) A	(138) E	(159) C
(118) A	(139) B	(160) E
(119) A	(140) B	(161) A
(120) C	(141) B	(162) C
(121) C	(142) A	(163) C
(122) C	(143) D	(164) D
(123) D	(144) C	(165) A
(124) D	(145) A	(166) D
(125) B	(146) D	(167) D
(126) E	(147) E	(168) E

Sentence Correction Guide – Answer key

(169) E	(190) D	(211) C
(170) B	(191) E	(212) A
(171) E	(192) D	(213) B
(172) D	(193) B	(214) C
(173) A	(194) A	(215) A
(174) B	(195) C	(216) A
(175) A	(196) D	(217) C
(176) B	(197) A	(218) E
(177) C	(198) C	(219) D
(178) A	(199) E	(220) A
(179) C	(200) B	(221) B
(180) C	(201) D	(222) D
(181) A	(202) B	(223) B
(182) C	(203) C	(224) D
(183) C	(204) D	(225) C
(184) A	(205) B	(226) E
(185) D	(206) E	(227) E
(186) D	(207) A	(228) A
(187) E	(208) E	(229) D
(188) A	(209) B	(230) E
(189) A	(210) E	(231) B

Sentence Correction Guide – Answer key

(232) C	(255) D	(278) B
(233) D	(256) A	(279) D
(234) B	(257) A	(280) B
(235) A	(258) B	(281) C
(236) C	(259) A	(282) D
(237) B	(260) E	(283) C
(238) A	(261) A	(284) D
(239) D	(262) E	(285) B
(240) C	(263) D	(286) A
(241) D	(264) B	(287) D
(242) B	(265) E	(288) A
(243) A	(266) A	(289) C
(244) B	(267) E	(290) C
(245) E	(268) C	(291) A
(246) E	(269) A	(292) A
(247) D	(270) A	(293) C
(248) C	(271) D	(294) A
(249) E	(272) B	(295) D
(250) C	(273) D	(296) B
(251) A	(274) C	(297) E
(252) C	(275) E	(298) B
(253) A	(276) C	(299) A
(254) C	(277) C	(300) B

Chapter 6

Solutions

6.1 Subject-Verb agreement (SVA)

1. Concepts tested: SVA, Diction, Grammatical construction

   The intended meaning of the sentence:

   While it had been possible to consider, or entertain, the possibilities given in the draft proposal of the directors, the two options in the final bargaining round were not acceptable because the majority of the finance specified in the smaller details was dependent on output.

   Concept discussion:

   SVA: "None" and "Neither" are singular and will take the singular verb "was" but not the plural verb "were." Options A, B and C contain this error.

   Note: The following words are always singular when they're present in the subject as either adjective or pronoun: each, every, any, one, another, none, neither, either.

   Diction: English has many sets of words that have essentially the same meaning, but usage differs depending on whether the sentence involves two or more than two things.

   For example:

   For two – This is the *better* of the two options

   For more than two: This is the *best* of all options.

   "Neither" is used when two things are in discussion, whereas, "none" is used for more than two.

   In the given sentence, two "options" are being considered, and thus, "neither" is appropriate but "none" is not. Options A, B and D contain this error.

   Some other sets of words following the same rules:

For two	For more than two
Between	Among
Each other	One another
Either	Any

   Grammatical construction: Options present "because" and "because of": To join a clause, "because" should be used; for example: I am late because I missed my train. "Because of" should be used to join a noun or noun phrase; for example: I am late because of the train delay.

   In the given sentence, a clause is being joined - "the bulk of the finance stipulated in the fine print depended on output"; thus, "because" is correct but "because of" is not. If the sentence contained a noun phrase - "the bulk of the finance in the fine print," then "because of" would have been correct. Options A and D contain this error.

   The correct answer is option E.

2. Concepts tested: SVA, Pronouns mismatch, Tenses

   The intended meaning of the sentence:

Sentence Correction Guide – Solutions

The new government introduced reforms in its first budget to encourage foreign investment in the country; these reforms permit foreign companies to operate without paying taxes as long as they offer financial advice to their potential investors.

Concept discussion:

SVA and pronouns mismatch: The subject of the verb "have" is "the new government" (ask: who/what have introduced reforms? The new government). The subject "the new government is singular and will take the singular verb "has" and not the plural verb "have." Options A and C contain this error.

Similarly, the pronoun for the singular subject "government" needs to be the singular "its" and not the plural "their." Options C and D contain this error.

Also, the subject of the verb "permits" is "reforms in the budget" (ask: who/what permits companies? Reforms in the budget, not just the budget). Thus, the subject is plural and will take the plural verb "permit" and not the singular verb "permits." Options A and E contain this error.

Tenses: The action of introducing reforms began in the past and is continuing into the present and thus, should be denoted with the present perfect tense "has introduced." Using future tense "will" is incorrect because the action has already started and is continuing. Also, using the probability modal verb "might" for a definite action is incorrect. Options D and E contain this error.

The correct answer is option B.

3. Concepts tested: SVA, Meaning, Rhetorical Construction

   The intended meaning of the sentence:

   The sentence states that because parents disagree on the manner of disciplining their children, the teachers cannot teach well, as the children remain undisciplined and spoiled.

   Concept discussion:

   SVA: The subject of the verb "have/has made" is "disagreements" (ask: "who has made problems/what has made problems?") The subject "disagreements" is plural and will take the plural verb "have," but not the singular verb "has." Options A, B and C contain this error.

   Meaning: The intended meaning of the sentence is that teachers cannot teach the spoiled students because of the parents' disagreements about disciplining their children. Option E is incorrect because it suggests that the disagreements have made something problematic for teachers because they are teaching spoiled students (not that disagreements have made it difficult to teach spoiled students).

   Rhetorical Construction: The sentence needs a placeholder pronoun. The intended meaning must be conveyed in a clear and crisp, non-ambiguous way. Sometimes when the subject of some verb is difficult to represent directly, placeholder pronouns are used. For example: It seems crazy that she left this lucrative job.

   What seems crazy? That she left this lucrative job (The subject)

   Thus, "it" is holding the place, or representing, the subject "that she left this lucrative job."

Similarly, in the given sentence, "Parents' disagreements have made <something> problematic for the teachers."

Made what problematic? For the teachers to teach such spoiled students (the subject of "made something problematic")

So, we need the placeholder "it" between "made" and "problematic," i.e. "Parents' disagreements have made it problematic for the teachers to teach such students".

Options A, B and C contain this error.

Note: Using the placeholder "it" without strict need is to be avoided; such use creates ambiguity by introducing needless pronouns. For example:

I want it that the company get a new car for the directors. (Incorrect - "it" is an unnecessary placeholder)

I want the company to get a new car for the directors. (Correct)

The correct answer is option D.

4. Concepts tested: SVA, Comparisons

   The intended meaning of the sentence:

   Georgio's Café got a positive review in a travel guide, after which tourists outnumbered the regular customers at the café.

   Concept discussion:

   SVA: What was in excess? The number of tourists. "The number" is always taken as singular whereas, "a number" is taken as plural. Examples:

   The number of eagles *is* declining.

   A number of problems *have* been noticed.

   Using the plural verb "were" for the singular subject "the number" is incorrect. Option A contains this error.

   Comparisons: What is in excess compared to what? Tourists exceed the regular customers. Thus, a comparison must be clear and parallel. We can say either "the number of tourists is more than the number of regular customers" or "tourists are more plentiful than regular customers." However, we cannot say "the number of tourists is more than regular customers." Options C and D contain this error.

   Also, option B changes the meaning by saying "the number of tourists had an excess over...," thus, implying that the number of tourists had (eaten) more food.

   The correct answer is option E.

5. Concepts tested: SVA, Tenses

   The intended meaning of the sentence:

   The camp experiences for many ex-prisoners were so boring and tedious that they cannot even imagine, let alone remember, what being a prisoner in such a camp was like.

   Concept discussion:

SVA: What was monotonous and uneventful? 'The experiences of the captives' is plural and will take the plural verb "were," but not the singular verb "was." Option A contains this error.

Tenses: The sentence discusses a single event in the past, and thus, using the simple past tense "were" will suffice. There is no need for the past perfect tense "had been." The past perfect tense is used to denote the earlier action of two or more actions in the past. Using the past perfect tense in this sentence is incorrect. Option E contains this error.

The correct answer is option D.

6. Concepts tested: SVA, Pronoun mismatch, Idioms

   The intended meaning of the sentence:

   The USA gave Germany a lot of money based on the Marshall Plan; this money was used by Germany to build a modern industrial system.

   Concept discussion:

   SVA: What was used to build a modern industrial system? Huge sums of money, which is plural, and will take the plural verb "were" but not the singular verb "was." Options A and B contain this error.

   Pronoun mismatch: Using the singular pronoun "it" to refer to the plural noun "huge sums of money" is incorrect. Option E contains this error.

   Idioms: The correct expression is "under the auspices" and not "in the auspices." Option C contains this error.

   The correct answer is option D.

7. Concepts tested: SVA, Modifiers, Tense

   The intended meaning of the sentence:

   Newly married couples from the east coast of the United States have to concern themselves with deciding about the kind of mortgage they may need when they buy their first home.

   Concept discussion:

   SVA: The most important *decision* for couples is singular and will take the singular verb "concerns" and not the plural verb "concern." Option A and C contain this error.

   Modifiers: The decision to be made over the type of mortgages will occur at the time of buying the first house. Thus, the "buying" of a first house refers to the "point in time" the couples will make the decision. So, the best connector to use is "when" and not "while" to refer to "a point in time." Options B, and C contain this error.

   Tense: This scenario uses the simple present tense to illustrate a truth. Option E mixes in the past tense and is incorrect.

   The correct answer is option D.

8. Concepts tested: SVA, Diction

   The intended meaning of the sentence:

   The party currently in power has decided to hold onto power at any cost in the hope that inflation will dramatically decrease in the near future, thereby improving its chances of getting elected again. The party has arrived at this decision on the basis of results in local elections and popularity polls.

   Concept discussion:

   SVA: What/Who is determined to hang onto power? The ruling party, which is singular because it is a collective noun. The subject "ruling party" will take the singular verb "is" or "has" but not the plural verb "are" or "have." Options A, B and D contain this error.

   Diction: The usage of "chances" and "chance" is different. To suggest odds or probability, the typical diction is "chances": The chances of Team A winning are low (not the chance). To mean "fate" or to mean "opportunity," "chance" is used: Chance (fate) will determine the outcome between the teams. Or: There was no chance (opportunity) of escape.

   In the given sentence, since the probability of winning elections is being discussed, we need to use "chances" and not "chance." Options A and B contain this error.

   Also, using "being" with "determined" is incorrect; "to be determined" is a state of existence, i.e. either one is determined or one is not determined. States of existence cannot be used in the continuous tenses. For example:

   I am being a girl (incorrect); I am a girl (correct).

   Option E contains this error.

   The correct answer is option C.

9. Concepts tested: SVA, Parallelism

   The intended meaning of the sentence:

   Two children, one who uses crutches and the other who uses a wheelchair, are going to join the class on Monday.

   Concept discussion:

   SVA: The subject of the verb "join" is "two children." [Ask yourself "who joins the class on Monday? The children"] The subject "two children" is plural and will take the plural verb "join" and not the singular verb "joins." Options A, C and E contain this error.

   Parallelism: The modifier describing two children ("one...wheelchair") contains the conjunction "and," necessitating parallelism. "One" usually pairs with "the other" or with "another"; for example, "I need two books, one *on* geography and the other *on* history" or "I need two books, one *on* geography and another *on* history." Thus, "one" should be correctly paired with "the other" and not with "the other one." Also, since the sentence says "one with," the other half should say "the other with" to make it parallel. Options A, B and E contain this error.

   The correct answer is option D.

10. Concepts tested: SVA

    The intended meaning of the sentence:

    The sentence talks about a person's suitability for the school's basketball team. Three characteristics – talent, legs, and passion – make him well suited for the school's basketball team.

    Concept discussion:

    SVA with a compound subject: Using "and" to join these three things forms a compound subject, which is plural. Thus, the subject "athletic talent, long legs and his love of basketball" is plural and will take the plural verb "make" and not the singular verb "makes." Options A, B and C contain this error.

    Additive phrases: Using "as well as" creates an additive phrase, which is not part of the subject. For example: "The guru, as well as his disciples, is committed to celibacy" (not "are" because the subject is only "the guru." "As well as his disciples" is an additive phrase, not part of the subject.)

    Similarly, in option E, the subject is only "his love of basketball," which is singular. "As well as long legs and athletic talent" is an additive phrase, not part of the subject. Thus, the singular subject will take the singular verb "makes" and not the plural verb "make." Option E is incorrect.

    The correct answer is option D.

11. Concepts tested: SVA, Idioms

    The intended meaning of the sentence:

    The sentence intends to say that praise for Johnny Starstruck and the group following him is common, in spite of the fact that Americans connect his name with ritualistic murders.

    Concept discussion:

    SVA: Ask: what is/are common? We see that "praise" (for Johnny and others) is common. "Praise" is singular and will take the singular verb "is" and not the plural verb "are." Options A, B and C contain this error.

    Also, "statistics" is considered plural (when it means "trends"), and will take plural verb "show" and not the singular verb "shows." Options B, C and E contain this error.

    Note: When "statistics" means "a subject of mathematics," it is considered singular. For example: Statistics is a complex subject (not "are").

    Idioms: The verb "associate" is paired with "with" and not "to," i.e. "someone associates something with some other thing." Options C and E contain this error.

    The correct answer is option D.

12. Concepts tested: SVA, Concision

    The intended meaning of the sentence:

    The sentence talks about the role of an agency's attempts to decrease the gaps between the technology-rich and technology-poor cities around the space center. It states that the attempts have not been successful in decreasing the gaps significantly.

Concept discussion:

SVA: The subject of the sentence is "the GWS Agency's attempts," which is plural and will take the plural verb "have," but not the singular verb "has." Options A, B and C contain this error.

Concision: The phrase 'made a substantial decrease in the gap' is unnecessarily wordy. The verb *decreased* is preferable to the noun *a decrease*. Options C and E contain this error.

The correct answer is option D.

13. Concepts tested: SVA, Rhetorical construction, Redundancy

    The intended meaning of the sentence:

    The sentence talks about the impact of 'declining values' on currency trading while explaining the term 'bonds.' The sentence tells us that the declining values of bonds will make currency trading increase.

    Concept discussion:

    SVA: The sentence tests subject verb agreement. For agreement, the subject and verb must agree in number: singular subjects take singular verbs, whereas, plural subjects take plural verbs. The subject "declining values" is plural and will take the plural verb "are" but not the singular verb "is." Options A, B and C contain this error.

    Rhetorical construction: The use of "hedge against" in this sentence conveys the meaning that "investors hedge against the bonds"; thus, an acceptable construction would be "bonds, against which investors hedge..." but not "bonds which investors use to hedge against..." Options B, C and D contain this error.

    Redundancy: 'Bonds' themselves are *'financial vehicles'* and are not *'used as'* *'financial vehicles*; *'use as financial vehicles to hedge against'* is redundant. Options B and D contain this error.

    The correct answer is option E.

14. Concepts tested: SVA, Pronouns: mismatch and ambiguity, meaning-based parallelism

    The intended meaning of the sentence:

    The sentence means that the scorpion's sting is dangerous, causes red welts (swelling/bumps) to appear, and poses minor risk to infants who are vulnerable to the scorpion's venom.

    Concept discussion:

    SVA and Pronouns: What is the subject? It is 'sting' and not "Egyptian Scorpions." The subject 'sting' is singular and so must take singular verb 'is' and not plural verb 'are.' Also, the plural personal pronoun 'they' cannot refer to the subject 'sting' and needs to be replaced with singular personal pronoun 'it.' Using "its" before the "venom" will suggest that children are vulnerable to the "sting's venom." However, the venom is of the scorpions not of the sting, but even using "their" is incorrect because "their" can refer to "scorpions," "welts" or "infants," thus, causing a pronoun ambiguity error. Options A, B, C and E are eliminated.

Sentence Correction Guide – Solutions

Meaning-based parallelism: "posing minor risks" instead of "pose" becomes an effect of "red welts" but the meaning suggests that the sting causes red welts and (the sting) poses health risks. Options A and E contain this error.

The correct answer is option D.

15. <u>Concepts tested</u>: Meaning-based SVA, Meaning ambiguity

    <u>The intended meaning of the sentence</u>:

    The sentence means that a derivative of the <u>Echinacea</u> flower is effective in preventing colds and many small farmers out west grow the flower.

    <u>Concept discussion</u>:

    Meaning-based SVA: There are two meaning-based issues.

    (1) What is grown by the farmers? The flower, not the derivative. Thus, we must make "the North American Echinacea flower" the subject to attach it to the main verb and predicate "is grown by many small farmers out west." So, options A, B and C are eliminated.

    (2) What is effective in preventing colds? The derivative of the flower, not the flower itself. In option D, the subject of the "which" modifier is ambiguous; it could be 'the derivative' ("the flower has a derivative that is grown..."), or it could be "the flower that is grown." Also, the "which" modifier should have been preceded by a comma. Option D is eliminated. Option E conveys the correct meaning as the derivative is now used as an appositive/modifier and not as the subject of 'what is grown.' It correctly implies that the flower is grown and its derivative is effective in preventing colds.

    The correct answer is option E.

6.2 Parallelism

16. Concepts tested: Parallelism, Conjunctions

    The intended meaning of the sentence:

    African-Americans are arrested more readily by police officers because they belong to an ethnic minority, not because they usually commit crimes.

    Concept discussion:

    Parallelism and Conjunctions: The correct conjunction is "not X but Y."

    Using "although" will not work because "although" and "but" are redundant. Option B contains this error.

    When paired conjunctions are used, both the joined parts should be parallel. For example:

    Correct – John is either studying English or studying history.

    Correct – John is studying either English or history.

    Incorrect – John is either studying English or history.

    Similarly, in the given example, correct is "not because …but because …" Since the non-underlined part says "but because," we cannot insert "from" or "in that" after "not"; it'll break the parallelism. Options A and C contain this error.

    Option E is not parallel in the two clauses of "not X but Y." "X = because being significant perpetrators" whereas, Y = "because they are members of an ethnic minority"; However, option D's X and Y bits are parallel. Option E is incorrect.

    Note: This parallelism rule also applies to the following conjunctions:

    - not only X but also Y
    - neither X nor Y
    - either X or Y
    - from X to Y
    - between X and Y

    The X and Y parts should be parallel.

    The correct answer is option D.

17. Concepts tested: Parallelism, Diction, Meaning

    The intended meaning of the sentence:

    Now, even after a decade has passed since the Chernobyl disaster, certain physicists find that they have to simultaneously do three things: fight suspicion over the effects of the disaster, beg for more funds, and hire lawyers to defend themselves in court as a result of the Dresden case.

    Concept discussion:

    Parallelism: The use of the "and" necessitates parallelism. What is "and" joining? The sentence states that the scientists are doing simultaneous things – they find themselves fighting suspicion [one event]. The question is whether "begging for funds" and "having to hire lawyers" are the other two activities that "scientists find themselves doing" or are they dependent clauses on "fighting suspicion"? It seems unlikely that scientists are begging for funds and having to hire lawyers to fight suspicion. It is more likely that their simultaneous activities include: fighting suspicion, begging for funds and having to hire lawyers. Thus, these three actions should be parallel. Since "fighting" is not underlined, we have to make "beg" and have to hire" parallel to "fighting," i.e. they need to be "begging" and "having." Options A and B contain this error.

Diction: Affects-Effects: "Affect" is the verb form but "effect" is the noun form. We can use "affect" as an action but in the given sentence, we need the noun form "effect" because it is used as a noun, evidenced by the use of the article "the." [Articles (a, an, the) can only be applied to nouns].

The monsoon affects yields.

The effect of monsoons on yields is easily demonstrated.

Options B and C contain this error.

Meaning: Option D changes the meaning. By using "suspicion because of the effects," the sentence suggests that the suspicion is the result of the effects; however, the sentence intends to suggest that there is suspicion *about* the effects (not because of). So, option D is incorrect.

The correct answer is option E.

18. Concepts tested: Parallelism, Conjunctions, Concision

    The intended meaning of the sentence:

    The idea of a united Europe was proposed in 1962, then a charter was drawn up and a number of steps were taken to implement the idea; at that time, the idea seemed nearly impossible, but now it has been brought about.

    Concept discussion:

    Parallelism: Using "and" necessitates parallelism between the two actions of "proposing" and "drawing up" - "the idea was proposed" and the "charter drawn up" but not "proposed" and "had been drawn" or "drawing." Options A and B contain this error.

    Conjunctions: Various conjunctions such as "and," "but," "if" and "although" have been used to connect the first and the second half of the sentence. "But" and "although" can be used if there is a contrast between the first and the second half, while "and" can be used if there is no contrast.

    The first half is "idea was proposed and a charter drawn up," and the second half is "now it has been realized, what had seemed impossible." The two choices are - "something was conceptualized **and** has been actualized" or "something was conceptualized **but** has been actualized." There is nothing contradictory in the second half, and thus, we cannot use the contrast conjunctions "but" or "although." Also, "if" cannot be used because "if" is used to show conditions and results that may happen. However, there are no conditions or results. Options B, D and E contain this error.

    Note: Had the sentence been "something was conceptualized **but** it turned out to be different in actuality," then a contrast conjunction could have been used.

Concision: The sentence presents various forms of "put," i.e. "putting," "that put" and "to put." When providing reasons for a particular action, using "to verb" is the clearest, crispest structure.

For example: I went to the theatre to watch a movie.

"I went to the theatre for watching/for the watching of" will not convey the intended meaning in the crispest possible way.

Similarly, in the given sentence, "a number of tentative steps to put the concept into practice ..."

Options B and E contain this error.

The correct answer is option C.

19. Concepts tested: Parallelism, Comparisons, Pronoun mismatch

    The intended meaning of the sentence:

    In Finland, the influence of light engineering (unlike heavy engineering) is most apparent (visible) in its mobile phones.

    Concept discussion:

    Parallelism: Whenever comparisons are being made, parallelism is compulsory, especially in case of relative pronouns (who, which, that, where, when, etc) and prepositions (in, on, of, etc.)

    Examples:

    That she is the CEO at 30 is a *greater* landmark *than* that she is a woman.

    In no other movie did the actor cause *so* much sensation *as* in the latest one.

    Similarly, in the given sentence, repeating "in" is mandatory: Nowhere in Finland is engineering *more* apparent *than* in phones. Options A and B contain this error.

    Comparisons: In comparisons, "more" pairs with "than" but "so" or "as" pairs with "as." Pairing "so" (or "as") with "than" is incorrect. Option C contains this error.

    Pronoun mismatch: The pronoun is trying to refer to "Finland," which is singular and will take the singular pronoun "its" but not the plural pronoun "their." Options A, B and E contain this error.

    The correct answer is option D.

    With such comparison structures, it's necessary to remember what is being compared. All but (D) fail to make this clear.

20. Concepts tested: Parallelism, Conjunctions

    The intended meaning of the sentence:

    The sentence compares facilities available with two different apartment complexes – those living in the GW apartment can use the tennis courts and swimming pool, as long as they become members of the club, whereas, those living in AE apartments do not have such amenities but still have to pay higher rents than at GW apartments.

Sentence Correction Guide – Solutions

Concept discussion:

Parallelism: Since the options have conjunctions, parallelism is necessary. The non-underlined portion discusses the situation at AE apartments in the plural form – occupiers; thus, the part on the GW apartment should also be plural, i.e. "occupiers" and not "occupier." Options A, B and D contain this error.

Conjunctions: To join two clauses, a conjunction or a semicolon must be used (clause, conjunction + clause/ clause; clause). While options A, B and C use the conjunctions "while," "although," and "whereas" respectively, options D and E do not use a conjunction, causing a comma-splice error (joining two clauses with just a comma).

Options A and B contain this error.

The correct answer is option C.

21. Concepts tested: Parallelism, Pronoun mismatch

    The intended meaning of the sentence:

    The FDA has two requirements from a pharmaceutical company: 1) submit the number of casualties suffered by test subjects, and 2) provide the statistics to the public.

    Concept discussion:

    Parallelism: The conjunction "and" necessitates parallelism. We need to figure out what exactly the "and" is joining. The first part is "the company must report to the FDA certain things." The second part is that statistics should be released (by the company). So, to complete the sentence properly, we can say that the company must release the statistics to the public. Using "and that" is incorrect because there is no verb to which the "that clause" can refer; even if we assume that the "that" is referring to "report," the sentence remains nonsensical: "the company must report that the statistics be released to the public." Options A and B contain this error.

    Pronouns mismatch: Using the plural pronoun "their" to refer to the singular "company" is incorrect. The correct pronoun is "its." Options A, C and E contain this error.

    The correct answer is option D.

22. Concepts tested: Parallelism, Meaning

    The intended meaning of the sentence:

    Experiences in which a learner is completely immersed in a setting involving a language are important to teach students who cannot learn language in any other manner or cannot learn it even after months of being taught that language in a classroom setting.

    Concept discussion:

    Parallelism: The use of the conjunction "or" necessitates parallelism. Each item in the list must complete the sentence by itself and convey the intended meaning. Two settings in which the student is unlikely to learn the language are being discussed. Each setting must complete the sentence by itself. The sentence states that immersion experiences are important for students who cannot learn in other settings or (who cannot learn) during months of regular teaching.

Analysis of the options

- **(A)** "experiences are important for students who cannot learn language 1) in other settings OR 2) months of regular teaching" – In this structure, the second item does not complete the sentence. Even if we think that "in" is common for both, i.e. "experiences are important for students who cannot learn language in 1) other settings OR 2) (students who cannot learn in) months of regular teaching" – the second item is "students who cannot learn in months of regular teaching" is not correct because the correct preposition would be "during" for the duration of the months being discussed.

- **(B)** Contains the same error as option A.

- **(C)** "experiences are important for students who cannot learn language 1) in other settings OR 2) during months of regular teaching" – In this structure, parallelism is maintained as each item completes the list by itself. The original intended meaning is also conveyed.

- **(D)** Contains the same error as option A, but with the preposition "under" instead of with "in."

- **(E)** This option changes the meaning by using the double negative – "students unlikely not to learn"; this would mean students are likely to learn – different from the original meaning.

The correct answer is option C.

23. Concepts tested: Parallelism, Meaning clarity

    The intended meaning of the sentence:

    The sentence states that students learn the ability to distinguish between good and bad tones before they learn the ability to identify whether a violin is out of tune.

    Concept discussion:

    Parallelism: The sentence compares and distinguishes between two abilities that students learn, and states that one ability is acquired before the other ability. To convey the meaning in the crispest way, keeping the two abilities parallel would be ideal, i.e. one ability is learned long before the other ability is learned.

    In the given sentence, the first half is "Students can distinguish between good and bad tones"; thus, the second half should be (to make it parallel) "they can do something else," i.e. "they can identify that the instrument is out of tune." Options A, D and E contain an error regarding this.

    Meaning clarity: Since the first half and the second half of the sentence are talking about students' abilities, both need to mention students or refer to students. Thus, using "they" to refer to students is necessary, without which the meaning about whose ability is being talked about in the second half will remain ambiguous. Options A and E contain this error.

    The correct answer is option B.

24. Concepts tested: Parallelism, Conjunctions

    The intended meaning of the sentence:

The sentence reflects the belief of experts. According to them, senior citizens who have high cholesterol and (senior citizens) whose families are susceptible to developing cardiovascular disease are more likely to die at an age below that of their life expectancy.

Concept discussion:

Parallelism: Sentences involving multiple clauses and using conjunctions should make the clauses parallel by repeating the same or similar joiners. For example:

She argues <u>that</u> the agency acts with inhumane carelessness and **that** it should be shut down.

There are citizens <u>who</u> never pay their taxes but **whose** parents always did.

Similarly, in the sentence above, we need to repeat a joiner similar to "who" – "the senior citizens <u>who</u> have high cholesterol and **(whose)** families are susceptible to cardiovascular disease are more likely to die at an age below that of their life expectancy."

Options A, C and E contain this error.

Conjunctions: Using a conjunction between two clauses is necessary, i.e. "senior citizens who have high cholesterol **and** (senior citizens) whose families are susceptible to cardiovascular disease" need an "and" because these are two independent clauses describing senior citizens. Options D and E contain this error.

The correct answer is option B.

25. Concepts tested: Parallelism, Diction

    The intended meaning of the sentence:

    The sentence talks about the <u>consequences</u> of seriously mentally ill people not receiving medication. The consequences are: (1) They can grow unable to support themselves. (2) They can become irrational. (3) They can perhaps even threaten the safety of themselves or others.

    Concept discussion:

    Parallelism: The use of the conjunction "and" necessitates parallelism. Let's see the three things being joined by "and" and correctly determine their parallelism.

    The sentence:

    "If the mentally ill people do not receive medication, they can grow unable to support themselves, (they can) become irrational, and (they can) threaten their safety.

    So, "they can" has been made common, clear by the structure of the second item. Thus, the third item in the list needs to be parallel to the other two items in the list by completing the sentence properly with the common part "they can" . Using another verb ("may") will break the parallelism (they *can may* even threaten). Option C contains this error.

    Using "threatening" or the form "a threat" will also break the parallelism. Options A, D and E contain this error.

    Diction: We can use "as well as" only to join two items (for which we can also use "and"). However, for more than two items, we can use only "and" but not "as well as." Since the above sentence contains three consequences, we cannot use "as well as." Options D and E contain this error.

    The correct answer is option B.

26. Concepts tested: Parallelism

    The intended meaning of the sentence:

    The sentence lists the three things that were done as the journalist left to interview the convicted murderer: (1) she was advised of the man's short temper (2) she was told she should not anger him (3) she was given a tape recorder.

    Concept discussion:

    Parallelism: The use of the conjunction "and" necessitates parallelism. Let's see the three things being joined by "and" and correctly determine parallelism.

    The sentence:

    As she went to interview, she was: (1) advised of the man's short temper, (2) (she was) told she should not anger him, and (3) (she was) given a tape recorder.

    Thus, the part up to "she was" has been taken in a common way, and the three things that follow should be parallel in that they each should complete the sentence using "she was."

    For clear construction, all three things must be parallel with one another. The sentence can be made parallel in two ways:

    "She was advised of x, told y, and given z."

    OR

    "She was advised x, was told y, and was given z."

    However, the first construction is preferable for its concision.

    Analysis of the options

    Let's analyze each option to check what parts in common have been taken and read each of the three items with the common part to see whether the parts complete the sentence in a parallel way with the common part.

    (A) "As the journalist left to interview the convicted murderer, (she was) advised of the man's short temper, (she was) told she should not anger him, and (she was) **was** given a tape recorder." As can be seen from the above completed sentence, the use of "was" again in the third item breaks the parallel structure. Even if we assume that "was" was not taken in common, the sentence would be not parallel as follows: "As the journalist left to interview the convicted murderer, (she) was advised of the man's short temper, (she) **told** she should not anger him, and (she) **was** given a tape recorder."

    (B) "As the journalist left to interview the convicted murderer, **(she was)** advised of the man's short temper, **(she was)** told she should not anger him, and **(she was)** given a tape recorder." This option maintains the parallelism perfectly.

    (C) "As the journalist left to interview the convicted murderer, (she was) advised of the man's short temper, <u>and</u> **(she was) that** she should not anger him, <u>and</u> (she was) given a tape recorder." Using "and" twice for the items of the same list is incorrect. Also, taking "she was" as common does not complete the list. Even if we assume that "she was advised" has been taken in common, the list is still incomplete: "As the journalist left to interview the convicted murderer, **(she was advised)** of the man's short temper, <u>**and**</u> **(she was advised) that** she should not anger him, <u>**and**</u> **(she was advised) given** a tape recorder."

(D) "As the journalist left to interview the convicted murderer, **(she was advised that)** the man had a short temper, **(she was advised that)** she should not anger him, and **(she was advised that) given** a tape recorder." As can be seen from the above completed sentence, taking in common "she was advised that" makes the third item not parallel.

(E) "As the journalist left to interview the convicted murderer, **(she was advised)** that the man had a short temper, **(she was advised)** that she should not anger him, and **(she was advised) given** a tape recorder." Taking "she was advised" in common also breaks the parallel structure.

The correct answer is option B.

27. Concepts tested: Parallelism, Idioms

    The intended meaning of the sentence:

    The sentence states that the manager of a factory tried to convince disobedient workers that they should join forces to optimize production on the belt and not attempt to be in opposition.

    Concept discussion:

    Parallelism: This sentence makes a contrast comparison using the construction *x rather than y* or *x instead of y*; *x* and *y* must be parallel in either case. "Join" should be followed by "attempt" or "joining" should be followed by "attempting" to maintain parallelism in this case. Options A, D and E contain this error.

    Idioms: The correct usages of "convince" are *'convince somebody **of** something'* or *'convince somebody **to** do something,'* or *"convince somebody **that** something should be done."* *'Convince about'* or *'convince for'* is unidiomatic. Options A, C and D contain this error.

    The correct answer is option B.

28. Concepts tested: Parallelism, Meaning

    The intended meaning of the sentence:

    The sentence makes a point that the nine planets mentioned are thought to be a common phenomenon in the universe and <u>not</u> a development from a unique galactic phenomenon.

    Concept discussion:

    Parallelism: This sentence makes a contrast comparison using the construction *x rather than y* or *x instead of y*; *x* and *y* must be parallel in either case. The planets are *(x) a phenomenon* rather than *(y)*; here *y* should consist of an article and a noun to match *a phenomenon*; *(y)* can be "a type" but cannot be "developing," which is not parallel. Options A and D contain this error.

    Meaning: The verb *developed* is preferable to the awkward and wordy relative clause using the noun *development*; *incidental of* distorts the original meaning. The idiom *incidentally means accidentally from*, however, *'incidental of'* means *'following a consequence of'*; *a development that was incidental of . . .* expresses a meaning contrary to that expressed in the original sentence. The logic of this sentence requires the use of *incidentally from.* Option C contains this error.

Similarly, while *a development* may appear to parallel *a phenomenon*, *a development that was incidental of*... expresses a meaning contrary to that expressed in the original sentence. The verb *developed* is preferable to the noun *development*. Option E contains this error.

The correct answer is option B.

29. Concepts tested: Parallelism, Idioms, Redundancy

    The intended meaning of the sentence:

    The sentence intends to present the transition in Acme's work. It has moved away from traditional family programming and presently draws on the works of two kinds of entertainers: those who work for magazines and those who work in the movie industry.

    Concept discussion:

    Parallelism and Idioms: The sentence uses the structure 'both X and Y' to describe the entertainers. For the correct construction, X should be parallel with Y, that is, if it is "both those," it should be followed by "and those" or if it is "both who work" it should be followed by "and who work." Options A, C, D and E contain this parallelism error.

    Redundancy: Use of 'it' is redundant as the subject (Acme) has already been stated and doesn't need to be repeated using a pronoun. Option C contains this error.

    The correct answer is option B.

30. Concepts tested: Parallelism, Meaning

    The intended meaning of the sentence:

    The sentence means that the devastating earthquake did two things; namely it destroyed many buildings and led many to believe the city had become a permanent disaster zone.

    Concept discussion:

    Parallelism: Whenever there is a list of items mentioned in a sentence - for instance when someone or something did or caused multiple things - parallel structure is necessary. Since the earthquake did two things, both verbs need to be parallel in structure. The first action is 'destroyed' (i.e. the earthquake destroyed something), and the second action should be "led" so the two actions will be parallel. In light of this, options A, B and C are eliminated.

    Meaning: Using "as if" and "were," the subjunctive mood, to imply a hypothetical situation where there is none is incorrect. Options B and D contain this error.

    The correct answer is option E.

31. Concept tested: Parallelism

    The intended meaning of the sentence:

    The sentence means that the possibility of attack caused government officials to plan evacuation routes, build shelters, and offer pills to citizens so there will be fewer casualties in case of a leak of some harmful substances.

    Concept discussion:

Sentence Correction Guide – Solutions

Parallelism: Each item in the list needs to be parallel in structure. The three activities of the "officials" are to "plan, build and offer preventative medicine." Also, the parallel structure must be in the infinitive (to verb) form rather than the gerund form because the non-underlined part has "to," which cannot be changed. Thus, all options except B get eliminated.

The correct answer is option B.

32. Concepts tested: Parallelism, Meaning

    <u>The intended meaning of the sentence:</u>

    The sentence means that if one tries to mimic some of the pitch variations of a dolphin chattering it would sound the same as one who is intoxicated attempting to sing like a sick parakeet (a small bird). The noise would lack harmony and have apparent randomness; this implies that human vocal chords are completely incapable of reproducing these sounds.

    <u>Concept discussion:</u>

    Parallelism and meaning: This is a form of comparison where one action is similar to another action. Thus, both actions must take similar forms. "Trying to mimic…" is being compared to "attempting to sing…" and must be parallel. Also, the original meaning is that "trying" one activity is similar to "attempting" another activity. If "attempting" is removed, the meaning is changed, making the option illogical. Thus, options C, D and E are eliminated. Also, option B is eliminated because it is comparing a general action ("trying to do X") to a specific action ("an intoxicated person trying to do Y"). This is neither a parallel comparison nor a correct one.

    The correct answer is option A.

33. Concepts tested: Parallelism (ellipsis)

    <u>The intended meaning of the sentence:</u>

    The automobile dealers were compelled to reduce their stock, so they have cut down the prices and thus, now, these trucks sell.

    <u>Concept discussion:</u>

    Parallelism (ellipsis): Ellipsis is using parallel structure to eliminate some words but convey the correct meaning in the correct form. See examples below containing correct ellipses with eliminated words in brackets.

    I did not study earlier but now I do (study).

    I was not studying earlier but now I am (studying).

    What if the meaning suggests that the action has changed? In such a case, one cannot omit words but must use a full clause instead. See below.

    I did not study earlier but now I am studying (cannot stop at "am"; that would become "am study," which is certainly incorrect).

    I was not studying earlier but now I do study (cannot stop at "do"; that would become "do studying").

In the test example sentence given, words have been omitted, so we'll need to use the correct format, as given below.

The trucks have been/are priced to sell, and they do (sell). Since, the omitted word is "sell," using "do" would be appropriate with it.

All options except C contain this error.

The correct answer is option C.

34. Concepts tested: Parallelism in meaning

    The intended meaning of the sentence:

    Howard could not play the violin anymore, so he began teaching students to play the violin, and encouraged them to become as successful as he used to be.

    Concept discussion:

    Parallelism in meaning: If we use "imparted," it will be parallel to "taught," whereas, "imparting" will mean an effect of "taught." Are "imparting knowledge" and "teaching" two independent activities that Howard did? No, it was that Howard taught *by* imparting his knowledge to students. Thus, "impart" needs to be an effect of "taught." Using "imparted" will be incorrectly parallel with "taught." Options A and B contain this error.

    Also, if we use "encouraged," it will be parallel to "taught," whereas, "encouraging" will be parallel to "imparting," making that too an effect of "taught." Did Howard teach *by* imparting knowledge and *by* encouraging students? Or is it that Howard taught *by* imparting knowledge and, as an additional independent activity, he encouraged students? It seems more likely that "encouraging" is an additional activity that Howard did, beyond the "teaching." Thus, "encourage" cannot be parallel to "impart" or it will also be considered an effect of "taught." Options B, C and D contain this error.

    The correct answer is option D.

35. Concepts tested: Meaning-based parallelism, Conjunctions

    The intended meaning of the sentence:

    There is evidence that, under political pressure, NASA faked the first moon landing by doctoring (editing) TV transmissions by transposing a film of astronauts taken during gravity free training flights against a moon backdrop.

    Concept discussion:

    Meaning-based parallelism and Conjunctions: The options show choices between various forms of "transpose" – "transposed" or "transposing." "Transposed" is parallel to "faked"; opting for "transposed" would suggest that the NASA faked the landing and transposed something independently. However, NASA is not performing two independent activities (it faked something and transposed something else). Actually, NASA faked the landing by doctoring film footage. The "doctoring" WAS transposing a film against a backdrop. Option B contains this error.

    Also, using "and" between "doctoring" and "transposing" would suggest that these two are independent activities done to "fake" the moon landings; however, the "transposing" is dependent on the "doctoring"; thus, using "and" between them is incorrect. Option E contains this error.

Sentence Correction Guide – Solutions 189

Similarly, using "when" between "doctoring" and "transposing" would alter the meaning and make it incorrect. Option D contains this error.

Finally, "in 1968" is for "landing" not for "faking." That is, NASA did not fake "in 1968" but faked a landing "in 1968." Option C contains this error.

The correct answer is option A.

36. Concepts tested: Meaning-based parallelism, Conjunctions

    The intended meaning of the sentence:

    William said that he suspected the aides of taping a conversation and (suspected the aides of) using it to discredit the witness.

    Concept discussion:

    Meaning-based parallelism and Conjunctions: The options show choices between various forms of "use" – "used" or "using." "Used" is parallel to "suspected"; opting for "used" would suggest that the William suspected the surveillance and used it to discredit the witness. However, why would William suspect surveillance if he is eventually using it to do something? Either he used it, in which case he already knew that there was surveillance, or he did not use it, but the ones who taped the conversation used it, and William merely suspected it. Thus, the sensible sentence is that those who taped the conversation used it to discredit someone. Thus, "use" should be parallel to "taping" to convey the correct meaning. Options A, B and C contain this error.

    Redundancy: Using "they" to refer to "aides" is unnecessary; it is easily avoidable. The use of the past perfect "had had," too, is unnecessary. Options B and D contain this error.

    Ambiguity: The use of the conjunction "while" leaves things ambiguous. Who "used" the conversation? "While" can also mean simultaneous action; however, "taping" and "using" cannot happen at the same time. Option D contains this error.

    The correct answer is option E.

37. Concepts tested: Parallelism in meaning, Modifiers

    The intended meaning of the sentence:

    During the summer months of the year 1972, Kenyon is supposed to have travelled all over the continent, where he interviewed the natives and recorded his thoughts; this interviewing and recording led to the formulation of the theories upon which his final text was based.

    Concept discussion:

    Parallelism in meaning: There is a difference between independent and dependent actions.

    For example: She entered the café and ordered a coffee – entering the café and ordering the coffee are done independently of each other.

    Consider: The volcano exploded and blotted out the sun – the volcano exploded, but did the volcano blot out the sun? The volcano's exploding blotted out the sun. Thus, the volcano is not independently "blotting." Thus, we cannot make it parallel to "exploded."

The "blotting" happened because of "exploding"; such dependent actions are presented in "verb-ing" formats.

Similarly, in the given sentence:

In the summer of 72, Kenyon travelled all over the continent. He also interviewed the natives and recorded his thoughts. The "interviewing" and "recording" is part of his "travelling the length and breadth of the continent"; it is certainly not that Kenyon travelled all over the continent and independently interviewed and independently recorded. For such dependent actions, "verb-ing" structure is employed. We cannot make "interviewing" and "recording" parallel to "travelled." Option B contains this error.

Also, "formulation" of the theories happened as a result of "interviewing" and "recording." If we make "formulating" parallel to "interviewing" and "recording," we'd suggest that Kenyon's traveling led to interviewing, recording and (separately) formulating the theories. However, it is more likely that since Kenyon interviewed people and recorded his thoughts, he was able to formulate the theories. Thus, "formulating" is dependent on "interviewing" and "recording." Option C makes it parallel with conjunctions suggesting independent action, making it incorrect.

Modifiers: "Which" modifiers always refer to the noun right before. Thus, to refer to the preceding noun, one must use "which." For example:

The company is investing in its profits, which are up by five percent. (What is up by 5%? Profits, the noun right before "which.")

When "which" is not meant for the noun right before or there is no noun right before "which," then "which" cannot be used. For example:

The volcano exploded, which blotted out the sun.

In this case "blotted out the sun" is intended for "exploded," but "exploded" is not a noun, it is a verb. We cannot use "which" here. In such cases, we use "verb-ing" to imply that the second action is a result of the first action. Thus, the correct sentence would be:

"The volcano exploded, blotting out the sun."

However, sometimes, using the "verb-ing" structure is not possible. For example:

Jane hit John, which is unacceptable Jane hit John, being unacceptable.

Neither conveys the correct meaning. The way to correct it is to introduce a noun to which a modifier can refer:

Jane hit John, behavior that is unacceptable.

Another example: Pope began his translation of the Iliad, *a work* that took him 7 years to complete (not: Pope began his translation of the Iliad, which/that took him 7 years to complete).

Similarly, in the question sentence, we cannot use "which" or "that" directly, since it will refer to "thoughts" but cannot refer to "interviewing" and "recording," which are actions, not nouns. Thus, introducing the noun form "formulation" with a modifier "that" after it would work - Kenyon travelled all over, interviewing and recording, (thereby leading to) the formulation of the theories that ...

The correct answer is option A.

38. <u>Concepts tested</u>: Parallelism, Modifiers

    <u>The intended meaning of the sentence</u>:

    The new Xerox machine can do a lot more than just copy documents; it can also resize, lighten, and collate documents.

    <u>Concept discussion</u>:

    Parallelism: Comparisons necessitate parallelism.

    Examples:

    I *sing* better than I *dance*.

    I am better at *singing* than *dancing*.

    The two actions being compared are "doing something" and "copying something" [What's more than what else? The Xerox *does* more than *copy*.] Thus, those two actions need to be parallel. Using "copying" will be incorrect because all options have either "does" or "has," with which "copy" will be parallel. Options A, B and C contain this error.

    Modifiers: The adverb "simply" is modifying "copy"; adverbs are placed before the verb, except "enough," which is always placed after.

    Examples:

    She is not simply singing but dancing, too!

    I have seen enough of the world.

    Placing "simply" after "copy" will make the structure incorrect. Option D contains this error.

    The correct answer is option E.

6.3 Comparison

39. **Concepts tested**: Comparisons, Parallelism

    The intended meaning of the sentence:

    Aggressive teenagers annoy adults by wearing provocative clothing and by not heeding rules.

    Concept discussion:

    Comparisons: "As" always pairs with "as," whereas, "more" or "less" pairs with "than."

    Correct – She is *as* intelligent *as* John.

    Correct – She is *more* intelligent *than* John.

    Incorrect – She is *as* intelligent *than* John.

    Incorrect – She is *more* intelligent *as* John.

    In the given sentence, the non-underlined part contains "as" [as much by...]; thus, we have to choose options with "as" to make "as much ... as." Options A, B and C do not offer this.

    Parallelism: Comparisons necessitate parallelism.

    For the given sentence:

    Parallel – Teens anger adults as much *by wearing* ... as *by disregarding*

    Parallel – Teens anger adults as much *by their clothing* ... as *by their disregard*

    Not parallel – Teens anger adults as much *by wearing* ... as *by their disregard*

    Option D contains this error.

    The correct answer is option E.

40. **Concepts tested**: Comparisons, Diction

    The intended meaning of the sentence:

    John H. McWhorter, who is recognized as an authority on this subject, has claimed that African-Americans don't do well in school because of social pressure that is put on them, in a very subtle way, to fail.

    Concept discussion:

    Comparisons: "More" or "less" must always be paired with "than," without which the comparison is incorrect. Options B and C contain this error.

    Diction: While both "no less than" and "not less than" are acceptable and convey the intended meaning, standard English accepts only "no less/more than" but not "not less/more than...," which is considered colloquial (slang). Options D and E contain this error.

    The correct answer is option A.

41. **Concepts tested**: Comparisons, Pronoun mismatch

    The intended meaning of the sentence:

The final calculations contained an error that could have been found by comparing estimates with the estimates of the previous years.

Concept discussion:

Comparisons: To compare similar things (estimates to estimates), "compared with" can be used, but not "compared to." For example: Compared with the BMW, the Mercedes is cheaper [comparing one car to another car – similar things]. "Compared to" can be used to compare incomparable things; for example: He compared her to the sun [comparing a person to the sun – dissimilar things]. Options A, D and E contain this error.

Pronoun mismatch: Using the plural pronoun "they" for the singular noun "someone" is incorrect. Option B contains this error.

The correct answer is option C.

42. Concepts tested: Comparison, Parallelism

    The intended meaning of the sentence:

    Harry's workload includes the audit; it is at least as great as John's workload, and could be even greater than John's workload. Harry's work involves either finding questions or solving questions.

    Concept discussion:

    Comparison: When dual comparison is used (i.e. both positive degree "as great as" and comparative degree "greater than"), each comparison should be complete by itself. Using "greater" without "than" or using "as" without "as" is incorrect. Options C, D and E contain this error

    Parallelism: When paired conjunctions are used, both the joined parts should be parallel.

    For example:

    Correct – John is either studying English or studying history

    Correct – John is studying either English or history

    Incorrect – John is either studying English or history.

    Similarly, in the given example, correct is either "classified as either question finding or question solving" or "classified either as question finding or as question solving." However, since the non-underlined part says "or question solving," we cannot insert "as" after "either"; it'll break the parallelism. Options B and C contain this error.

    Note: This parallelism rule also applies to the following conjunctions:

    - not only X but also Y
    - neither X nor Y
    - not X but Y
    - from X to Y
    - between X and Y

    The X and Y parts should be parallel.

    The correct answer is option A.

43. Concepts tested: Comparisons

    The intended meaning of the sentence:

    By 2010, the average expenditure of an American family on food is expected to be eight times the expenditure of a comparable Sudanese family on food.

    Concept discussion:

    Comparisons: In comparisons, the two subjects being compared should be parallel and logically comparable. What is expected to be eight times the size of something else? The average expenditure of an American family on food, which can be compared with the average expenditure of another family on food. However, we cannot compare "average food expenditure of a family" simply with another family ("Sudanese family"). Options A, B and C contain this error.

    The two correct ways of comparing are:

    (A) The average expenditure of an American family on food with *that* of a Sudanese family [that of = expenditure of]

    (B) The average expenditure of an American family on food with a Sudanese family's (expenditure)

    Consider: The cart's wheel is broken [the wheel belongs to the cart, represented by apostrophe "s"].

    The wheel of the cart is broken [the wheel belongs to the cart, represented by "of"].

    Both the sentences given above are correct. However, the following is incorrect:

    The wheel of the cart's is broken ["of" + apostrophe "s"].

    When denoting possession, either "of" or apostrophe "s" should be used, but never both. Option D contains this error.

    The correct answer is option E.

44. Concepts tested: Comparison, SVA, Conciseness

    The intended meaning of the sentence:

    Dalmatians are liked by children, but owners with limited amounts of money state that Dalmatians are twice as costly to maintain as Alsatians.

    Concept discussion:

    Comparison: The sentence intends to compare the maintenance costs of Dalmatians and Alsatians, but not to compare Dalmatians to Alsatians. Comparing maintenance costs of Dalmatians to Alsatians (not maintenance costs of Alsatians) is illogical. Option A contains this error.

    SVA: When the subject of the verb "cost" is "Dalmatians" (plural), the plural verb "cost" is correct; however, when the subject is "keeping Dalmatians" (singular), the plural verb "cost" is incorrect and the singular verb "costs" is needed. [Ask yourself: What costs twice as much? Not just Dalmatians; keeping Dalmatians (the maintenance of Dalmatians)]. Options C and D contain this error.

    Conciseness: Consider: John is taller than Jane. There is no need to say "John is taller than Jane *is*." It is redundant. Similarly, stating "D costs twice as much to keep as A" is sufficient. Using "do" or "keeping" again is redundant: "D costs twice as much to keep as A does" is unnecessary. Option B contains this error.

The correct answer is option E.

45. Concepts tested: Comparisons, Diction

    The intended meaning of the sentence:

    Dewey industry's sale did not cause many dire consequences; however, in contrast, the sale of US Fox, made worse by the Carolina closures, will have dire consequences.

    Concept discussion:

    Comparisons: The sentence intends to compare the selling of two companies and suggests that unlike the sale of one company, the sale of another company will have negative consequences. Using "unlike" or "like" involves comparison; such comparison must be parallel and logical. Also, the correct format for the comparison of subjects is "Unlike/Like subject 1..., subject 2..." Thus, the two subjects being compared should be placed next to each other in the format given and must be parallel. For example:

    "**Unlike** *John's batting, Jake's batting* is outstanding."

    "**Like** *in India,* which is a tropical country, *in Malaysia,* the rains are torrential."

    So, the above sentence should also place logical and parallel subjects in the given format, i.e. it should be either: "Unlike sale 1...sale 2...," or "Unlike one company..., another company..." Any other structure would be unacceptable. Only option D maintains this parallelism: Unlike the Dewey Industries sell-off [sale 1], the sale of US Fox [sale 2] ...." All other options compare incorrect items. Option E places "unlike" incorrectly, which is placed either at the beginning or right after the first subject (Unlike X, Y ...; Y, unlike X...), but is extremely awkward in its order.

    Diction: For comparisons, the use of "like" or "unlike" is better than "compared to" or "differing from." Options A and C contain this error.

    The correct answer is option D.

46. Concepts tested: Comparisons, Awkwardness, SVA

    The intended meaning of the sentence:

    A car has new variations; the various speeds of the new variations are below the speeds of the Toyota models, even though there is not much difference in their engine sizes.

    Concept discussion:

    Comparison: The sentence is discussing the speeds of two models of cars. Comparing logically comparable elements – the speeds of these other models to the speeds of Toyota models – is necessary. To compare the speeds of models of a car simply to Toyota models is incorrect. Options A and B contain this error.

    Furthermore, since the sentence includes the plural "speeds" for the first subject, the second subject should also compare the plural "speeds," but not the singular "speed."

    Correct – Lions are better than tigers/A lion is better than a tiger.

    Incorrect – Lions are better than a tiger.

    Option C contains this error.

Awkwardness: "Diminishing differences in engine size" is crisper and less awkward than "differences in engine size diminishing," because the adjective "diminishing" is meant to describe the plural noun "differences," and is, thus, best placed next to its noun. Options B, C and D contain this error.

SVA: What/Who is well below the Toyota models? The speeds of the variations of the car, which is plural and will take the plural verb "are," but not the singular verb "is." Option B contains this error.

The correct answer is option E.

47. Concepts tested: Comparisons, Parallelism, Pronoun mismatch

    The intended meaning of the sentence:

    An Apex insurance policy judges buyers on their driving competency; this policy is different from a normal first car insurance policy, which judges buyers on the length of their driving experience.

    Concept discussion:

    Comparisons and Parallelism: Using "unlike" or "like" involves comparison; such comparison must be parallel and logical. Also, the correct format for comparison of subjects is "Unlike/Like subject 1..., subject 2..." Thus, the two subjects being compared should be placed next to each other in the format given and must be parallel. So, the above sentence should also place logical and parallel subjects in the given format, i.e. it should be either "Unlike a normal insurance policy..., an Apex insurance policy..." , or "Unlike with a normal insurance policy..., with an Apex insurance policy..." Any other structure would be unacceptable. Comparing "normal insurance *policy*" with "an apex insurance policy *buyer(s)*" is incorrect. Options A, C and E contain this error.

    Also, option B is incorrect because it inserts "with" in the second part ("with an Apex insurance policy"), making it not parallel with the first part ("a normal insurance policy").

    Pronoun mismatch: "Buyers" is plural and will take the plural pronoun "their," whereas, the singular pronoun "his or her" is used for the singular noun "buyer." Option B contains this error.

    The correct answer is option D.

48. Concepts tested: Comparisons, Meaning, Awkwardness

    The intended meaning of the sentence:

    The French are different from Americans in that the French linger over their meals while Americans eat so quickly that they have a type of meal called "fast food."

    Concept discussion:

    Comparisons: Whenever we use "like/unlike," we compare two subjects; in such structure parallelism is necessary between the two subjects being compared. For example: Like *Batman*, *Superman* is a classic superhero.

    Like *that of Batman*, *Superman's cape* is classic. [that of Batman = Batman's cape]

    In this question, the second subject is "Americans" - a group of people - which can be compared to another group of people - the French. However, some options contain "that

Sentence Correction Guide – Solutions

of the French" as their first subject; "that of the French" may refer to something singular belonging to the French, like "the style of the French," but "that of the French" cannot be compared to "Americans." Option A contains this error.

Meaning: To refer to the noun right before, the best structure is "who" (in the case of people, but for nouns that do not refer to people, use "which"). Using "verb-ing" is not as effective as using "who." Options C and D contain this error.

Awkwardness: To show dissimilarity between two nouns, the crispest and clearest construction is using "unlike"; using "dissimilar to" or "lacking similarity" is awkward and wordy. Options D and E contain this error.

The correct answer is option B.

49. Concepts tested: Comparisons, Awkwardness, Idioms

    The intended meaning of the sentence:

    Both factories and old-fashioned glass-blowers can make glass objects. The ones that are mass-produced in factories have a value similar to the ones made individually by remaining glass-blowers.

    Concept discussion:

    Comparisons: The sentence intends to convey that glass vessels created by factories (on a large scale) are nearly as valuable as the ones made by glass blowers. Thus, the comparison involves glass vessels made in a factory and vessels made by glass blowers (the skilled artisans who blow melted glass). Using the singular pronoun "that" to refer to the plural "vessels of glass blowers" is incorrect. We need to use the plural pronoun "those." Options A, B and D contain this error.

    Awkwardness: Using "vessels of glass blowers that remain" is awkward and ambiguous compared to "vessels of remaining glass blowers." Options A and B contain this error.

    Idioms: Something is "of value" and not "in value." Better construction would be not using "value" as a noun at all. Options C and D contain this error.

    The correct answer is option E.

50. Concepts tested: Comparisons, Meaning

    The intended meaning of the sentence:

    The PTA has decided that other drugs should be discussed in health class, just as alcohol is, to prevent students from getting addicted by making them aware of the dangers.

    Concept discussion:

    Comparisons and meaning: The sentence intends to compare two actions, but not two nouns; that is, the sentence does not intend to compare alcohol to drugs, but intends to draw a similarity between the action taken to prevent alcohol addiction to the action that should be taken to prevent addiction to other drugs – "*the way* alcohol is discussed in health class is *the way* other drugs should be dealt with." To compare such actions, we can use "just as." "Like" and "similar to" are used to compare nouns – Like John, Jane is a teacher; Jane is similar to John in that they are both teachers. "While" is used to denote two actions as simultaneous – While I was walking, I was talking on the phone. All options except A contain these types of errors.

The correct answer is option A.

51. Concepts tested: Comparisons, Pronoun mismatch, SVA

    The intended meaning of the sentence:

    The American School of Ethical Culture has always embraced the philosophy of non-violence, much the same as its sister schools in England (which also have embraced the philosophy of non-violence).

    Concept discussion:

    Comparisons: Whenever we use "like/unlike," we compare two subjects; in such structure parallelism is necessary between the two subjects being compared. For example:

    Like *Pele*, *Messi* is a classic soccer player.

    Like *that of Pele*, *Messi's dribbling* is classic. [that of Pele = Messi's dribbling]

    In this question, the second subject is "American School of Ethical Culture" – a school – which can be compared to other schools. However, some options contain "that of schools in England" as their first subject; "that of schools" can refer to something singular belonging to the schools, like "philosophy of schools," but "that of schools" cannot be compared to "the American School." Options B and D contain this error.

    Pronoun mismatch: "the American School" is a school, which is singular. Thus, using the plural pronoun "their" is incorrect. "The American School" will take the singular pronoun "its." Options A and B contain this error.

    SVA: "The American School" is a school, which is singular, and will take the singular verb "has" and not the plural verb "have." Option C contains this error.

    The correct answer is option E.

52. Concepts tested: Comparisons, Meaning

    The intended meaning of the sentence:

    The sentence discusses an event that happens during gladiator matches, in which a prisoner is given a short sword against ten soldiers with horses and whips; this uneven match can drive the prisoner into a manic frenzy (adrenaline-fueled survival mechanism of the body); this manic frenzy is comparable to a bull's rage that increases when the bull is pierced with swords.

    Concept discussion:

    Comparisons: Using "like" and "just as" compares different things.

    If we use "like" we will end up comparing the prisoner to a bull or a bull's rage. If we use "just as," we'll compare the prisoner being driven into manic frenzy to the bull's rage increasing. Comparing a prisoner to a bull seems illogical since the similarity has been drawn using the rage of the bull, which seems comparable to the frenzy of the prisoner. Options A, B and C contain this error.

    Meaning: Option D illogically suggests that the bull itself is piercing its hide with swords to increase its rage.

    The correct answer is option E.

Sentence Correction Guide – Solutions

53. Concepts tested: Comparison, Parallelism

    The intended meaning of the sentence:

    The sentence presents the scenario in which the chorus divides the women into sopranos and altos. In such a scenario, the chorus will be able to sing songs that are many times more complicated than the songs that can be sung by the chorus now.

    Concept discussion:

    Comparison: The sentence compares two elements and, for a valid comparison, the two elements being compared must be parallel. The sentence states that "after dividing, the chorus will sing songs more complicated ..." "More" must always pair with "than." Options A and B contain an error with this.

    Parallelism: Comparison should be parallel. The comparison is between the songs that will be sung after division of the chorus and the songs that are sung before the division of the chorus.

    The structure is: After division, the chorus will sing songs more complicated than songs that are sung now (i.e. before division).

    Thus, to refer to "songs" in the second half of the comparison, we can use plural "those" but not the singular "that." Option D contains this error.

    Also, "singing" is not parallel to "sing songs" and does not have someone doing the action. "Those that can be sung" does not need a person doing the action, and keeps the simple structure intact. Option E contains this error.

    The correct answer is option D.

54. Concepts tested: Comparison

    The intended meaning of the sentence:

    The sentence intends to say that **colonies of** Portugal, France, and Germany **are different from** the **colonies of** England because the colonies of England are still affected by the former imperial power in modern days.

    Concept discussion:

    Comparison: For a correct comparison, the entities being compared must be logically and grammatically parallel. In this case, colonies of one must be compared with colonies of the other. The non-underlined portion already contains the word "colonies" in both the subjects being compared. Thus, using "those of" or "that of" is illogical because it has no referent. Options A, B and D contain this error.

    Also, using "dissimilar to" will be awkward. Better is "unlike." Option E contains this error.

    The correct answer is option C.

55. Concepts tested: Comparison, Modifiers

    The intended meaning of the sentence:

    The sentence presents the finding of a survey. The survey shows the difference in the psychological stability of children raised in a family with two parents and those raised in a family with one parent.

Concept discussion:

Comparison: As a rule, the elements being compared must be grammatically and logically parallel. Also, the comparison must be unambiguous. The sentence compares children raised in two types of families – Children are better **in** *type 1 family* than **in** *type 2 family*. Since the non-underlined part ends at "in," we need to choose an option that is parallel to the type 1 family, i.e. "a family with two parents." We cannot introduce words like "of," "that" or "those." Such constructions would break the parallelism. Options B, C and E contain this error.

Modifier: We can use "where" to refer to actual, physical places – Minnesota is a state where winters are harsh. However, to refer to theoretical concepts, situations, phenomena, metaphorical places, we use "in which." For "families," too, we need to use "in which," not "where." Options A and B contain this error.

The correct answer is option D.

56. Concepts tested: Parallelism in comparison, Meaning, Pronoun errors

    The intended meaning of the sentence:

    The sentence intends to compare the U.S.'s percentage of the defense budget spent on development of an anti-missile shield (AMD) with the People's Democratic Republic of North Korea (PDRNK)'s percentage of its defense budget on nuclear missile technology (NMT), and states that the U.S. spends a greater percentage.

    That is,

    % of the U.S. defense budget spent on AMD > % of North Korea's defense budget spent on NMT

    Concept discussion:

    Parallelism in comparison: The structure used to draw the comparison is: *In the U.S., a larger amount is spent on AMD than is spent in PDRNK on NMT.*

    Analysis of the options

    (A) This option is **incorrect** because the structure of the sentence is ambiguous. It could be interpreted as saying that the US is spending its defense budget on AMD and on NMT in North Korea – a larger % is spent on AMD than is spent on NMT in North Korea. However, this does not make sense. Why would the U.S. spend money on its AMD and on North Korea's NMT?

    (B) This option is **incorrect** because 'they' is missing an antecedent; that is, there is no noun that 'they' can refer to.

    (C) This option is **incorrect** because the structure is not parallel in its comparison. The U.S. part discusses the percentage of spending whereas, the North Korea part discusses merely spending.

    (D) This option is **incorrect** because the U.S. 'spends X ... than PDRNK spending...' is not parallel. Also, without a helping verb, 'PDRNK spending' is ungrammatical.

    (E) This option is **correct** because the structure is parallel. The U.S. spends a larger percentage of X on developing its AMS than PDRNK spends on NMT.

    The correct answer is option E.

Sentence Correction Guide – Solutions 201

57. <u>Concepts tested</u>: Comparison-parallelism

<u>The intended meaning of the sentence</u>:

The sentence means that while by the end of the nineteenth century five western countries had developed a railroad system, only one in the east had developed the same.

<u>Concept discussion</u>:

Comparison-parallelism: The comparison is not between the Western and Eastern countries, but rather between 'Western countries building a rail system' and 'Eastern ones building such a system.' Thus, we would need to use a verb after the Eastern countries to compare with the "had developed" in the first subject. Options A and B are eliminated because they do not use such a verb. Options C and D are eliminated because they use an incorrect verb to compare with "had developed." If you say 'five X had,' then you have to follow it by saying, 'but only one Y had,' not "was" or "did." The simple past 'did' suggests "five of the Western European countries *had* developed a railroad system but only one in the East *did (developed)*," making it incorrect. Option E corrects the structure by stating "five of the Western European countries *had* developed a railroad system but only one in the East *had (developed one)*."

The correct answer is option E.

58. <u>Concepts tested</u>: Comparison-format and logic, Meaning, Diction

<u>The intended meaning of the sentence</u>:

The sentence intends to compare the number of young men in the Chinese army with the number of students in colleges in India. It states that the Chinese army consists of several million young men. This number is equal to the number of students in colleges in India.

<u>Concept discussion</u>:

Comparison and Meaning: As a rule, the elements being compared must be grammatically and logically parallel. Also, the comparison must be unambiguous, and the original intended meaning must be maintained.

Enrollment: 'Enrollment of' implies 'the act of registering.' We cannot compare "men" in the army to the "enrollment," as such a comparison is faulty. Options A and D contain this error.

Equivalent/Equal: Using these words would lead to a comparison between men in the army to students in colleges – the army has millions of men, equal/equivalent to those people in colleges. However, the sentence intends to compare "the number of men" in the army to "the number of students" in colleges, but not the actual people themselves. Options B and C contain this error.

Diction: Equal can mean number, but it does not have to. An example of "equal" as "number": "We have an equal number of pets." (you and I have the same number of pets). To talk about number, the word "number" must be mentioned, without which there can be ambiguity; for example: "People are created equal" - not number, but quality. Option C contains this error.

"Equivalent" is used to mean "the same in quality" or "a replacement of," but does not have to mean equal in number. Example: "The top five European companies are equivalent to the top nine American companies." Obviously, they are not equal in number, but they are "equivalent," as in interchangeable or balanced. It could also mean the same number, but you would need to say "the equivalent number." Options A and B contain this error. Using "as much as" and "as many as" automatically compares the number of one to that of another. You cannot use these to mean that things are equal/equivalent in quality.

The correct answer is option E.

59. Concepts tested: Comparison: Logic and format, SVA, Awkwardness

    The intended meaning of the sentence:

    There are no gasoline taxes set by state or local authorities in New Jersey, a situation that is different from other states in the tri-state area (where gasoline taxes must be set by local or state authorities).

    Concept discussion:

    Comparison: logic and format: Using "unlike" or "like" involves comparison; such comparison must be parallel and logical. Also, the correct format for the comparison of subjects is "Unlike/Like subject 1..., subject 2..." .Thus, the two subjects being compared should be placed next to each other in the format given and must be parallel. For example: "**Unlike** *John's batting*, *Jake's batting* is excellent," or "**Like** *in India*, which is a tropical country, *in Malaysia* the rains are torrential." So, the above sentence should also place logical and parallel subjects in the given format, i.e. it should be either "Unlike in other states..., in New Jersey...," or "Unlike other states..., New Jersey..." Any other structure would be unacceptable. Options A and B contain this kind of error.

    SVA: The subject "taxes" is plural and will take the plural verb "have" and not the singular verb "has." Option E contains this error.

    Awkwardness: Option C is structured awkwardly because of its use of "no such one," which has no clear referent.

    The correct answer is option D.

60. Concepts tested: Comparisons – structure, ambiguity

    The intended meaning of the sentence:

    It is known that *Time* magazine has a higher number of women and African American employees relative to total workforce than does any other major magazine.

    Concept discussion:

    Comparison structure: When comparing a single entity with a group or with another entity from a group, using "other" is necessary. For example:

    "She is taller than any girl in the class." [She is being compared with girls in the class; thus, she is a girl in the class; is she taller than herself?]

    Such constructions make illogical meaning. Thus, in such situations, using "other" to exclude the first subject of comparison is necessary; she is taller than any other girl in the class.

    Similarly, in the given sentence, we need to ensure that *Time* magazine is excluded from the group of magazines with which it is being compared; using "other" magazines is necessary. Otherwise *Time* magazine might remain a part of the group "major magazines," creating an illogical construction like the one discussed in the example above. Options A and B contain this error.

Also, using the comparative form of the adjective and "more" is incorrect. Either the comparative adjective or "more" should be used.

Correct: This is *more important than* that.

Correct: This is *better than* that.

Incorrect: This is *more better than* that.

Option C contains this error.

Ambiguity: Consider the example:

John likes Jane more than Mary.

Does it mean that John likes Jane more than Mary likes Jane, or that John likes Jane more than he likes Mary?

Such structures are ambiguous and need additions to make them clearer.

Correct – John likes Jane more than Mary does (John and Mary are being compared).

Correct – John likes Jane more than he likes Mary (Jane and Mary are being compared).

In the original question, too, it is possible to see some ambiguity...

Does *Time* have more women and African Americans than it has other magazines [comparing women and African Americans, and magazines], or does *Time* have more women and African Americans than do other magazines [comparing *Time* magazine and other magazines]?

To remove ambiguity, we need to use one of the above structures. We need to use a helping verb ("does/do") to show the correct comparison between *Time* magazine and other magazines. Options A and E contain this error.

The correct answer is option D.

61. Concepts tested: Comparison structure, Redundancy

    The intended meaning of the sentence:

    The sentence discusses a US Census finding that college graduates have a greater inclination towards owning houses than owning apartments.

    Concept discussion:

    Comparisons – structure: In comparisons, "more" always pairs with "than," whereas, "as" pairs with "as." Any other pairing is incorrect. Option A contains this error.

    Redundancy: Also, comparison necessitates parallelism. To compare by simply stating that "X is more likely to do Y activity than Z activity" is sufficient. Spelling it out with such details as "X is more likely to do Y activity than X is likely to do Z activity" is redundant and needless. It would have been necessary if the meaning were ambiguous. Since the meaning is clear, removing the redundant part would make the sentence crisp and parallel. Additionally, using the plural pronouns "they" or "them" to refer to graduates will introduce ambiguity because of the plural noun "houses." Options B, D and E contain this error.

Using the placeholder "it" without strict need is to be avoided; such use creates ambiguity by introducing needless pronouns. For example:

I want it that the company get a new car for the directors (Incorrect; needless placeholder "it")

I want the company to get a new car for the directors. (Correct)

Similarly, in the given sentence, the use of "it" as a placeholder is unnecessary because the other options are conveying the correct meaning without it. Options D and E contain this error.

The correct answer is option C.

Sentence Correction Guide – Solutions

6.4 Modifiers

62. <u>Concepts tested</u>: Modifiers, Meaning

    <u>The intended meaning of the sentence:</u>

    More and more prevalent and wretched (unfortunate) panhandlers (beggars) are asking for money on the streets; it seems that money is hard to get in the deteriorating economy.

    <u>Concept discussion:</u>

    Modifiers: "Wretched" [meaning: unfortunate] is an adjective and will describe "panhandlers," whereas, "wretchedly" is an adverb and will describe "prevalent." Does the sentence seem to indicate that the beggars are unfortunate or that the beggars are unfortunately prevalent? What is unfortunate? The beggars are unfortunate; their being present is not unfortunate. Thus, we need to use "wretched" to describe "panhandlers." Options D and E contain this error.

    Similarly, "increasing" is an adjective and will describe "panhandlers," whereas, "increasingly" is an adverb and will describe "prevalent." Does the sentence seem to indicate that the beggars are more and more or that the beggars are more and more prevalent? The sentence suggests that beggars are more and more prevalent. Thus, to describe "prevalent," we need to use "increasingly." Options A and B contain this error.

    Meaning: What seems to be hard to come by? Money or streets? Money seems hard to come by, because of which there are more and more panhandlers. Thus, we need to place the noun "money" next to the clause "seems to be ..." to make the meaning clear. If we don't place "money" correctly, the clause "seems hard to come by" will refer to "streets." Options D and E contain this error.

    The correct answer is option C.

63. <u>Concepts tested</u>: Modifiers, Meaning

    <u>The intended meaning of the sentence:</u>

    Jane was upset by the litter around her neighborhood, and so she suggested a cleanup activity after school as a substitute for detention (detention = punishment for breaking school rules). Instead of having detention, students would clean up the neighborhood.

    <u>Concept discussion:</u>

    Modifiers: Who was upset by the litter around her neighborhood? The idea, Jane, or after school cleanup? Jane was upset. Thus, the subject of the modifier "upset ...neighborhood" is "Jane" and the sentence must begin with "Jane" after the modifier to conform to the rules of modifiers. Options A, B and E contain this error.

    Meaning: The sentence implies that since Jane was upset by the litter, she wanted the schools to set up an after-school cleanup program in which children would be made to clean up the litter instead of being sent to detention. Thus, to convey this correctly, we need to say "substitute cleanup for detention" or "cleanup as a substitute for detention." If we say "detention be substituted as cleanup," it is idiomatically incorrect and suggests that instead of cleanup the students should be in detention, the reverse of the intended meaning. Option D contains this error.

Note: Whenever you are confused with which noun should go in X and Y in the idiom, "substitute X for Y," just use the word "replace" instead of "substitute" and "with" instead of "for" and the intended meaning will become clear.

Substitute detention for cleanup = replace detention with cleanup [So, detention gets chucked out, while cleanup gets instituted]

The correct answer is option C.

64. Concepts tested: Modifiers, Meaning

    The intended meaning of the sentence:

    Annabelle smokes a lot, a cigarette pack a day; this habit has caused serious damage to her lungs that might even be fatal.

    Concept discussion:

    Modifiers and Meaning: The modifiers "serious and potentially fatal" is describing "damage" and not "lungs" and thus, must be placed right before "damage" and not after it."

    Consider:

    John has a fast, red car in the garage. OR John has a car, fast and red in the garage.

    The second style is awkward and ambiguous.

    Options B, C and E contain this error.

    Serious-seriously: "Serious" is an adjective and will modify "damage," whereas, "seriously" is an adverb and will modify "fatal." Does the sentence intend to say "serious damage" or "seriously fatal damage"? "Fatal" is a pretty extreme word, meaning "causing death." It's an absolute word, that is, we can't say "very fatal" or "less fatal." It's either "fatal" or not. Similarly, we cannot use "seriously fatal" because nothing can be "seriously" or "slightly fatal." It's more likely that the sentence implies that the smoking did "serious [damage] and potentially fatal damage)." Options A and B contain this error.

    Also, when "damage" is used as a noun, it is followed by the preposition "to"; for example: your loud music has done damage to my ears.

    When "damage" is used as a verb, it cannot take the preposition; for example: your loud music damaged my ears.

    Option C uses the verb form of "damage" but the non-underlined part contains the preposition "to," making it incorrect.

    The correct answer is option D.

65. Concepts tested: Modifiers, Meaning

    The intended meaning of the sentence:

    The Europeans were unchallenged (had no real opponents) because of their 16th century weapons; early Native Americans feared the white men because of the white men's weapons, thought of as thunder sticks of death pointed at them (Native Americans).

    Concept discussion:

    Modifiers and meaning: Who was unchallenged as a result of having European firearms? The white men or the early Native Americans? It has to be "the white men" [Caucasians

Sentence Correction Guide – Solutions

or Europeans] that had European firearms. Thus, the sentence must have "white men" after the modifier "unchallenged ... firearms." Options A and B contain an error with this.

Also, who feared the thunder sticks of death pointed at them? The Native Americans. Thus, to refer to "Native Americans" we can use "who" (modifier meant for "nouns referring to people"). Using "it" is incorrect because there is no singular noun for "it" to refer to. Options D and E contain this error.

The correct answer is option C.

66. Concepts tested: Modifiers, Pronouns

    The intended meaning of the sentence:

    Some painkillers such as Oxycodone have been proven to be addictive; this nature of such drugs might limit their potential to reduce pain.

    Concept discussion:

    Modifiers: Consider an example: Jane hit John, which is unacceptable.

    What is unacceptable? John? Jane? No, neither. That Jane hit John is unacceptable. However, "which" or "that" modifiers cannot refer to the verb "hit" or to "the fact that Jane hit John." Modifiers have to refer to nouns actually present in the sentence. In such a scenario, a noun to imply "the fact that Jane hit John" can be introduced to which the modifiers can refer.

    Correct – Jane hit John, behavior that is unacceptable.

    Correct – Jane hit John, violence that is unacceptable.

    Similarly, in the given sentence, what may limit the drugs' potential? Patients? Drugs? No, the fact that they are shown to be addictive. "Which" (or "that") modifiers always refer to nouns. However, the modifier is currently trying to refer to an absent noun ("the quality of being addictive"). Thus, we cannot use "which" or "that" directly; a noun that describes the thing to which the modifier is trying to refer will have to be introduced. The options present the noun "effect" to refer to "the fact that some drugs have been shown to be addictive" for which the modifier can be used. Options A, B and C contain an error with this.

    Pronouns: Using the plural pronoun "their" to refer to the noun "drugs" can create ambiguity given the presence of another plural noun ("patients"). Options A, B and D contain this error.

    The correct answer is option E.

67. Concepts tested: Modifiers, Awkwardness

    The intended meaning of the sentence:

    Fencing is a tantalizing sport (teases the senses), and it is not appreciated as it should be; in fencing, two opponents fight a pitched and very fast battle using electrically connected swords and vests made of metal.

    Concept discussion:

Modifiers: To indicate time, "when" is the best subordinator. If it were referring to a place, "where" would have been used. "In which" is used for metaphorical indications.

When – She was born in an <u>age</u> *when* jazz was at its peak [it's a real, actual "age"]

In which – The book proposes the concept of an <u>age</u> *in which* the human race is split into two species [it's a metaphorical, unreal "age"]

Where – Minnesota is a state where winters are harsh [it's a real place]

In which – Democracy is a state in which people get complete control [it's not a real "place"]

"In which" is also used for abstract nouns such as "phenomenon," "situation," etc.

In the given sentence, we're trying to refer to a characteristic of the sport, not a place or a time. Thus, "in which" is appropriate but not "where" or "when." Options A, B and D contain this error.

Awkwardness: Option C is wordy and awkward compared to option E. Also, using "that has" refers to "battle" rather than to "sport"; however, "battle" does not have swords, but the sport does. Option D contains this error.

The correct answer is option E.

68. Concepts tested: Modifiers, Conjunctions

    The intended meaning of the sentence:

    The festival continued throughout the summer and attracted many spectators. Many concerts were held during the week but most of them happened on the weekends because that's when people are free to attend and forget their poor lives and listen to music.

    Concept discussion:

    Modifiers: The clause "people were free to forget their poor lives and listen to music" is being joined to the first half of the sentence; for this joining, an appropriate subordinator must be used. Since we're talking about a time when people were free, "when" is the best subordinator. If it were referring to a place, "where" would have been used. "In which" is used for metaphorical indications, but not for real, actual times.

    In the given sentence, since the "weekend" is a real time, we can use "when" but not "in which" or "that." Options A, D and E contain this error.

    Conjunctions: To indicate a contrast, a contrast conjunction must be used [but, though, even though, although]. There is a contrast in the two fragments "with a number of concerts being held midweek" and "the majority taking place on the weekend." Simply put, the two fragments are "many held during the week" but "most held on weekends." Since there is a contrast, using "and" is inappropriate. Option B contains this error.

    The correct answer is option C.

69. Concepts tested: Modifiers, Meaning

    The intended meaning of the sentence:

    When he returned from England, he was twenty; to save taxes, his father gave him control of two companies, which he used to build a fortune.

    Concept discussion:

Modifiers: "At the age of twenty ...England" is a modifier describing "him" and thus, after the modifier, despite the presence of an appositive phrase "albeit to save taxes" [appositive phrases are pieces of extra information set off by commas], the sentence must begin with "he" to keep the subject of the modifier as the immediate noun after the modifier for maximum clarity (as dictated by modifier rules). Starting the sentence with "his father" will erroneously suggest that "At the age of twenty ...England" is a modifier describing "his father." Options A, B and D contain this error.

Meaning: The phrase "albeit to save taxes" is meant to explain why his father gave him control of two companies, but not why he built a fortune. Thus, its placement should be closer to "gave companies" but not to "founded a fortune" to convey the intended meaning. Option E contains this error.

The correct answer is option C.

70. Concepts tested: Modifiers, Meaning

    The intended meaning of the sentence:

    The correct answer can usually be found if one follows the correct procedures, by following the elimination technique.

    Concept discussion:

    Modifiers: Using "verb-ing" at the beginning of a sentence makes a modifier ("employing ...technique"), necessitating a correct subject for the modifier (who's employing the technique? Someone, but not "the answer"). Since the subject of the modifier is not present after the modifier, using modifiers is incorrect. Option A and E contain this error.

    Meaning: The sentence implies that the answer can be found "if" certain techniques are followed. "Unless" means "if ...not," and to convey the correct meaning with "unless" we will need to use "not," too, i.e. – "Unless the correct procedures are followed...The answer can*not* be found." Not using "not" will alter the meaning and make it incorrect. Thus, option D is incorrect.

    Option C radically changes the meaning by suggesting that the answer to procedures can be found, rather than suggesting that answer can be found using procedures. Option C is incorrect. Only option B keeps the meaning intact.

    The correct answer is option B.

71. Concepts tested: Modifiers, SVA, Idioms

    The intended meaning of the sentence:

    A breakfast cereal called Cap'n Crunch contains more vitamins than any other breakfast cereal does, and those vitamins are better quality-wise than vitamins in other cereals on the market.

    Concept discussion:

    Modifiers: What has more vitamins than other breakfast cereals have? Cap'n Crunch, not vitamins. "As well as ...cereals have" is a modifier whose subject is "Cap'n Crunch" but not "the vitamins." Thus, after the modifier the sentence must begin with the word

"Cap'n Crunch" to enhance clarity and conform to the correct rules of modifiers. Options A and E contain an error with this.

SVA: What contains better quality vitamins? Cap'n Crunch, the breakfast cereal, does. Thus, the subject is "Cap'n Crunch," which is singular, and will take the singular verb "contains" but not the plural verb "contain." Options B and C contain this error.

Idioms: Both "in the market" and "on the market" are idiomatically correct. "On the market" refers to the general act of being available for sale: There is nothing better available on the market. "In the market" refers to being in an actual physical market place – I am in the market right now – or to being available to purchase something – If you have a good house, I am in the market for it. In the given sentence, either "in" or "on" will be acceptable.

The correct answer is option D.

72. Concepts tested: Modifiers, Pronouns, Rhetorical Construction

    The intended meaning of the sentence:

    An alleged recruit of the KGB, PD remains under a cloud (under suspicion) despite his denials about the absurdity (ridiculousness) of his taking a small amount of money as a bribe.

    Concept discussion:

    Modifiers: The modifier "Allegedly recruited…" refers to "Pointdexter" and not to "a cloud"; thus, after the modifier the sentence must begin with the word "Pointdexter" to enhance clarity and conform to the correct rules of modifiers. Options A, C and E contain an error with this.

    Pronouns: Pronoun before a gerund (verbing) should be in the possessive form (his) and not objective form (him). Take, for example: I hate him and his singing (not "him singing"). Options B and C contain this error.

    Rhetorical Construction: Using an article before nouns is recommended. "Absurdity" is a noun that needs the article "the." Options A and C contain this error.

    The correct answer is option D.

73. Concepts tested: Modifier, Diction, Concision, Awkwardness

    The intended meaning of the sentence:

    Even though the drug Diatoxin causes allergic reactions, since alternatives are not available, the doctors have to prescribe it, but they are doing so in small dosages.

    Concept discussion:

    Placement of the correct subject after the modifier: The modifiers "Despite the prevalence …Diatoxin" and "for lack …treatment" refer to the "doctors"; thus, after these modifiers the sentence must begin with the word "doctors" to enhance clarity and conform to the correct rules of modifiers and associated phrases. Option E contains this error.

    Diction: "prescribe" versus "proscribe": "Prescribe" means to "order the use of" (something that the doctors do) whereas, "proscribe" means to "prohibit" or "forbid," which goes against the intended meaning of the given sentence. Options B and C contain this error.

Concision: The best structure for the second modifier is "for lack of any alternative treatment" since it suits the structure of "Despite the prevalence ...Diatoxin"; using verb-ing "lacking..." or "requiring..." does not go with the noun phrase "Despite the prevalence ...Diatoxin"; similarly, using a sentence instead of just a modifier ("because any alternative treatment is lacking") clashes with the previous modifier. Options B, C and D contain this error.

The correct answer is option A.

74. Concepts tested: Modifiers, Tenses, Concision

    The intended meaning of the sentence:

    Studies indicate that a child born into a family having members with a criminal past involving violence might end up committing a violent crime as well.

    Concept discussion:

    Modifiers: To show belonging or possession, "whose" is used – that is, "family whose members..." (members belonging to the family). "Where" is restricted to actual places:

    Minnesota is the town where I learned to ski.

    "In which" can be used for intangible nouns – El Nino is a phenomenon in which the warm and cold currents move in a specific manner – or can be used to imply "inside something" – the drawer in which I kept my certificates is locked.

    In this case, "in which" could be used to imply "members in the family" but the best construction would be "family whose members." Options B and D contain this error.

    Tenses: "Might" suggests possibility, as does the word "probably." Using them together is redundant and incorrect. With words denoting probability, such as "it is likely that," "it is possible that," "it is doubtful that," we cannot use "can," "may" or "might" but can use only "will" to prevent "double probability."

    Incorrect – It is *doubtful* that he *may* come.

    Correct – It is *doubtful* that he *will* come.

    Incorrect – It is *possible* that he *may* come.

    Correct – It is *possible* that he *will* come.

    Options C and D contain this error.

    Concision: "for those offenses that involve violence" is lengthier and more awkward than "offenses involving violence." Options A and C contain this error.

    The correct answer is option E.

75. Concepts tested: Modifiers

    The intended meaning of the sentence:

    Hendry is known throughout the world as a pioneer in the commercial uses of the internet, but very few people know that he is also an expert drummer and a member of a particular band.

Concept discussion:

Modifiers: Who is known throughout the world as a pioneer in the commercial uses of the Internet? Hendry is, but not "very few people." "Known throughout ... of the Internet" is a modifier whose subject is "Hendry" but not "very few people." Thus, after the modifier, the sentence must begin with the word "Hendry" to enhance clarity and conform to the correct rules of modifiers. Options A, B and D contain this error.

Similarly, "The Whiplash" is the name of the band of which Hendry is a member; the name of the band is presented as a modifier; thus, the subject "a successful Jazz band" must be next to its modifier "The Whiplash." Options B and E contain this error.

The correct answer is option C.

76. Concepts tested: Modifiers, Meaning

    The intended meaning of the sentence:

    A housewife may appear happy and content, but is not always so; her unhappiness is known to people who know the housewife closely.

    Concept discussion:

    Modifiers: "seems content" refers to "the housewife" and not to "housewife's unhappiness"; thus, "she seems content" should be placed next to "housewife" and not next to "housewife's unhappiness." Options A, B and C contain this error.

    Meaning: The sentence presents a clear contrast – the housewife seems content but is not. Thus, using a contrast conjunction is necessary to convey the intended meaning. Option E does not use any contrast indicator at all.

    The correct answer is option D.

77. Concepts tested: Modifiers, Tenses, Redundancy

    The intended meaning of the sentence:

    Rogue generals have created a new form of torture to extract information from people who are unwilling to share it; the new form has been created using the methods of Country X's agents.

    Concept discussion:

    Modifiers: The modifier "Using/Employing the methods…" refers to "rogue generals" and not to "a new form of torture" [ask "who's using the methods/who's employing the methods? The rogue generals are using the method, not the new form of torture"]; thus, after the modifier, the sentence must begin with the word "rogue generals" to enhance clarity and conform to the correct rules of modifiers. Options A, D and E contain this error.

    Tenses: Using the future tense twice is incorrect and awkward; for example: I will return your book when you will come back from your vacation. The second "will" is unnecessary. Similarly, in option B, "will" has been used twice, making it awkward.

    Redundancy: Using "employed" after "using" is redundant. Option A contains this error. Also, using "there was" as a subject when the actual subject is "rogue generals" is needless and redundant. Option D contains this error.

    The correct answer is option C.

Sentence Correction Guide – Solutions

78. Concepts tested: Modifiers

    The intended meaning of the sentence:

    The sentence describes Fanny, a high school student who is fanatically devoted to modern art. Fanny has toured five museums and touring the enormous Museum of Modern Art was remarkable.

    Concept discussion:

    Modifiers: Placement of the correct subject after the modifier - The modifiers "A high school student …" refers to "Fanny"; thus, after the modifier the sentence must begin with the word "Fanny" to enhance clarity and conform to the correct rules of modifiers and associated phrases. Starting with any other noun, such as "five museums," would suggest that the museums are a high school student devoted to modern art. All options except A contain this error.

    Remarkable-remarkably: "Remarkable" is an adjective, while "remarkably" is an adverb. Adjectives modify only nouns, whereas, adverbs can modify verbs, adjectives or other adverbs.

    If we use "remarkable," it will modify the noun "museum," making the phrase "remarkable museum." However, the meaning does not imply that the museum is remarkable. The meaning implies that Fanny has toured five museums, and even surprisingly (toured) a very large one (which might be difficult to tour given its size). Thus, the "remarkableness" is for "touring something enormous" and not for the museum itself. Thus, "remarkable" needs to modify "toured," which is a verb. So, we need to use the adverb form "remarkably," making the sentence "remarkably (touring) the enormous Museum of Modern Art (a huge museum that probably is difficult to tour because of its size, thus, making the whole action "remarkable")." All options except A contain this error.

    The correct answer is option A.

79. Concepts tested: Modifiers, Idioms, Meaning

    The intended meaning of the sentence:

    The sentence describes the confusion of many people about a certain diet (the Atkins Diet). Though this diet permits such seemingly less healthy foods as bacon, it forbids bread. The sentence uses a modifier to introduce information about the diet.

    Concept discussion:

    Modifiers: "Which" modifiers always refer to the noun right before. Thus, to refer to the preceding noun, one must use "which." For example: The company is investing in its profits, which are up by five percent. (What is up by 5%? Profits, the noun right before "which.")

    When "which" is not meant for the noun right before or there is no noun right before "which," then "which" cannot be used. For example:

    The volcano exploded, which blotted out the sun.

    In this case "blotted out the sun" is intended for "exploded," but "exploded" is not a noun, but a verb. We cannot use "which" here. In such cases, we use "verb-ing" to imply that the second action is a result of the first action. Thus, the correct sentence would be: The sun exploded, blotting out the sun.

In the above sentence, "permits certain foods..." is intended for "Atkins Diet," which is a noun. Thus, using "which" would be the best possible construction for it. Using "verb-ing" will not necessarily refer to "Atkins Diet." Options D and E contain this error.

Seeming-seemingly: "Seeming" is a verb, while "seemingly" is an adverb. Adverbs can modify verbs, adjectives or other adverbs. We need to modify the adjective "healthy," and the way to do that is with the adverb "seemingly." The meaning implies that what might appear to be healthy foods may not actually be healthy.

Options A, C and E contain this error.

Idioms: "Like" is used for comparisons while "such as" is used to illustrate examples.

Like: Fruits, like vegetables, contain fiber. ("vegetables" are not examples of "fruits")

Such as: Fruits such as oranges and limes contain vitamin C. ("oranges and limes" are examples of "fruits") Options C and E contain this error.

The correct answer is option B.

80. Concepts tested: Modifiers, Meaning, SVA

    The intended meaning of the sentence:

    The sentence states that at some earlier point in time, the Communists did not allow rallies that had an intention of spreading the principles of democracy (since communists would not agree with democratic ideas), but now those democratic ideas are slowly being allowed by the new generation of Communists.

    Concept discussion:

    Modifiers: The relative pronoun 'which' usually refers to the noun/noun phrase that comes before it. It is always important to understand whether the pronoun modifies the correct noun by asking the question who or what to understand the subject and then ensure that it is placed correctly to avoid any inconsistency in meaning. Option A is eliminated.

    Meaning: Changing the subject from 'rallies' to 'organizing rallies' would alter the original meaning. It would incorrectly mean that 'organizing rallies' is prohibited. Option C is eliminated.

    SVA: The subject of the sentence is "rallies" and will take the plural verb "are" and not "is." Option B is eliminated.

    Pronoun ambiguity: Using the pronoun 'they' creates ambiguity because it can refer to both the leaders and the rallies. Option D is incorrect.

    The correct answer is option E.

81. Concepts tested: Modifiers, Meaning-based parallelism

    The intended meaning of the sentence:

    The sentence means that historic buildings were riddled with bullets, shattered by bombs, and hidden in alleys (lanes). Because of this, tourists ignored these buildings, and travelled to some other places instead.

Sentence Correction Guide – Solutions

Concept discussion:

Modifiers: Always ensure that modifiers are placed close to the subject. In this sentence, what was riddled with bullets? The buildings and not the tourists! So, options C, D and E are eliminated.

Meaning-based parallelism: Using the present participle 'traveling' will refer to the part of the sentence before or to the buildings but not to the tourists. However, the original meaning is that tourists traveled to more well-known places. Thus, to ensure that "traveling" refers to "tourists," using the modifier "who" would be best. So, option A is eliminated.

The correct answer is option B.

82. Concepts tested: Modifiers

    The intended meaning of the sentence:

    Besides offering certain listed benefits, the practice of karate can provide other benefits if practiced regularly.

    The benefits are offered by "the practice of karate" and not just by "karate."

    Concept discussion:

    Modifiers: Always ensure that the modifier and the subject of the modifier are placed as close together as possible so that there is no ambiguity of meaning. To understand the subject, ask the question "who" or "what" of the verb or the modifier. For instance, in this sentence, if we ask "what offers such physiological rewards as toned muscles?" the answer is 'the practice of Karate,' which becomes the subject.

    Options C and D are eliminated because they use "body" as the subject of the modifier (Besides offering…muscles). Similarly, even options B and E have "one" and "results of karate" as the subject of the modifier (Besides offering…muscles), making them incorrect.

    The correct answer is option A.

83. Concepts tested: Modifiers, Tenses

    The intended meaning of the sentence:

    The Smiths have a surprisingly obedient cat that heeds commands like "come" or "sit," commands that dogs have been known to follow but not cats.

    Concept discussion:

    Modifiers: Who/What is surprisingly obedient? The Smiths or the cat? The cat is surprisingly obedient. Thus, the sentence must place "the cat" after the modifier "surprisingly obedient" to conform to the rules of modifiers. Options A and B contain this error.

    Tenses: To make a correct statement, we need a proper verb for the subject "cat"; using "following" will not make a sentence: …the cat …following instructions…" Option E contains this error.

    This is a general statement about the Smiths' cat, evidenced by the word "usually" and "respond." Thus, we need to use simple present tense "follows" for a generalization and not the present perfect tense "has followed." Option D contains this error.

The correct answer is option C.

84. Concepts tested: Modifiers, Meaning

    The intended meaning of the sentence:

    Hitler, the most infamous leader of Germany, was responsible for slaughtering 6 million Jews.

    Concept discussion:

    Modifiers: Who's Germany's most infamous leader? Hitler or his policies? Hitler is Germany's most infamous leader. Thus, the sentence must place "Hitler" and not "Hitler's policies" next to the modifier "Germany's most infamous leader" to conform to the rules of modifiers. Options A, B and C contain this error.

    Meaning: Who is responsible for the slaughter of 6 million Jews? Hitler or his policies? Hitler is responsible for the slaughter of 6 million Jews. Thus, suggesting that his "policies" caused the slaughter is incorrect. Option E contains this error.

    The correct answer is option D.

85. Concepts tested: Modifiers, Meaning, SVA

    The intended meaning of the sentence:

    The miners were reluctant to accept the company's new policy of unionization because they thought that the policy was only a publicity stunt and that it did not show any commitment to contract negotiation or to subsequent increases in salary.

    Concept discussion:

    Modifiers: Eventual-Eventually: "Eventual" is an adjective, while "eventually" is an adverb. Adjectives modify only nouns whereas, adverbs can modify verbs, adjectives or other adverbs.

    If we use "eventual," it will modify the noun "increases (in salary)," making the sentence "eventual increases in salary." There is no verb, adjective or adverb for "eventually" to modify. Thus, "eventual" is correct. Options A and B contain this error.

    Meaning: Option D changes the meaning. The sentence implies that the miners are wary of the contract because it did *not* reflect any commitment to contract negotiation or to subsequent increases in salary; however, option D suggests that they are reluctant because it *does* reflect commitment. Why would miners be reluctant to accept the contract if it did reflect the things they wanted it to? So, option D is incorrect.

    SVA: What was the commitment (not) reflected in the contract? It is 'negotiation and increases in salary,' which is plural and will take the plural verb "were" and not the singular verb "was." Option E contains this error.

    The correct answer is option C.

6.5 Pronouns

86. <u>Concepts tested</u>: Pronouns, Modifiers

<u>The intended meaning of the sentence:</u>

The country's economy is in good shape, even though income from the country's oil fields has hardly increased over the past two decades.

<u>Concept discussion:</u>

Pronouns: For the sake of absolute clarity, pronouns cannot be used for nouns that are not actually present in the sentence.

In the given sentence, the singular pronoun "its" is trying to refer to the "country" {its oil field = whose oil field? The country's oil field}. However, in the sentence, the actual noun "country" itself is not present [in "country's economy," the noun is "economy" and "country's" is merely an adjective]. Thus, we cannot use a pronoun to refer to "country." All options except B contain this error.

Modifiers: Using modifiers in this sentence is unacceptable because a modifier should always be followed by its subject. [A modifier is a sentence fragment (never a full sentence) that describes a particular noun]:

Correct – The son of Rita, John is a graduate of Harvard.

Incorrect –John is a graduate of Harvard, the son of Rita.

Correct – Despite being quite intelligent, John sometimes makes foolish decisions.

Incorrect – Despite being quite intelligent, foolish decisions are sometimes made by John.

Similarly, in the given sentence, "income barely increasing in oil fields" or "there being barely any increase in its oil fields" are modifiers describing the noun "the country," which should immediately follow the modifier. However, the modifiers are followed by "careful budgeting," which is not correct for the modifiers. Thus, we cannot use modifiers but have to use a conjunction ("although" or "even though") and make two independent statements instead. Options D and E contain this error.

The correct answer is option B.

87. <u>Concepts tested</u>: Pronoun mismatch, Parallelism

<u>The intended meaning of the sentence:</u>

A researcher spent three years studying one small species of seabird to understand the bird's social organization, mating rituals, and foods of choice.

<u>Concept discussion:</u>

Pronoun mismatch: The noun "the puffin" is singular (as evidenced by the use of the modifier "one of the smaller species") and thus, will take the singular pronoun "its" and not the plural pronoun "their." Options A and B contain this error.

Also, option E does not use the pronoun at all, but a pronoun is needed to explain that it's the puffin's organization, rituals, and foods that are being studied.

Parallelism: The use of the conjunction "and" necessitates parallelism in the list of things that are being learned by Ms Kardon about the puffin: 1) social organization, 2) mating rituals, and 3) preferred foods. Using "foods that are preferred" is not only unnecessarily wordy but also not parallel. Options A and E contain this error.

Also, using the preposition "about" for the third item in the list in option D is incorrect. Either all three things should have "about" or only the first item should have "about."

The correct answer is option C.

88. Concepts tested: Pronoun ambiguity, SVA, Diction

    The intended meaning of the sentence:

    Over the past six months, the percentage of investment has risen sharply, though the rise could well be just short term and the percentage of investment may possibly decline in the near future.

    Concept discussion:

    Pronoun ambiguity: Using the pronoun "it" to refer to any singular noun is ambiguous because of multiple singular nouns ("percentage" and "investment"). Instead, a pronoun should be avoided altogether and a noun should be used for maximum clarity. Options A, B and D contain this error.

    SVA: The subject of the verb "have risen" is "percentage of investments" [ask: what has risen? The percentage of investments, not just investments]. Thus, the singular subject "percentage of investments" will take the singular verb "has" and not the plural verb "have." Option A and E contain this error.

    Diction: To refer to cumulative investments, using the singular "percentage" is better than the plural "percentages." The sentence does not imply that many different groups of investment are present, each group with its own percent; rather, many investments have increased, and those investments are in a group, in which the percentage has gone up – similar to a collective noun [a bunch of investments; a group of investments]. Option E contains this error.

    The correct answer is option C.

89. Concepts tested: Pronoun Ambiguity, SVA

    The intended meaning of the sentence:

    The sentence states that doctors are reluctant to prescribe powerful painkillers since the misuse of these painkillers as addictive drugs is a danger for many patients.

    Concept discussion:

    Pronoun Ambiguity: Using a pronoun to refer to painkillers will create ambiguity because there is another possible pronoun antecedent ("doctors"). Thus, using pronouns would be incorrect. Options A, B and E contain this error.

    SVA: The subject in the sentence is "the abuse (of drugs)," which is singular and will take the singular verb "is" and not the plural verb "are." Option D contains this error.

    The correct answer is option C.

90. Concepts tested: Pronoun ambiguity, Awkwardness

    The intended meaning of the sentence:

The sentence presents multiple contrasts. A manufacturer announced a rise in earnings but a drop in revenue, when, in fact, the manufacturer had expected the revenue to possibly rise.

'Whereas' is used to show the contrast between the actual outcome (decrease) and the expectation (rise) regarding the level of revenue.

Concept discussion:

Pronoun ambiguity: Some options have used forms of the pronoun "it" (it, its) twice in the options, causing ambiguity. Such options imply that 'something' might have expected 'something else' to rise. We know from our understanding that it was 'revenue' that might have been expected to rise, but the introduction of another 'it' with no clear antecedent makes the construction ambiguous, leading to flawed construction. In some cases, 'it' seems to be used as a placeholder (meaning that in this case 'it' is not referring to any particular 'noun.' For example: It is raining.), however, the second 'it' seems to refer to the noun, revenue. This leads to ambiguous and imprecise construction. Options A and C contain this error.

Awkwardness: Using "would" or "should" along with "expectation" is unnecessarily wordy. Also, using "there" without any clear referent is also awkward. Options C and E contain this error.

The correct answer is option B.

91. Concepts tested: Pronoun ambiguity, mismatch

    The intended meaning of the sentence:

    This sentence means that employers must inform employees of their (employees') legal right to holidays and overtime pay.

    Concept discussion:

    Pronoun ambiguity and agreement: In the various options, the subjects change from "employers" to "employer" and objects change from "employees" to "employee"; the pronouns also vary. In the sentence, the pronoun (their) is intended for the "employee(s)" and must agree with that noun in number without ambiguity. In options A, B and D, the nouns (employee or employees) and pronouns do not match in number, i.e. either the noun is plural and pronoun singular or vice versa. Thus, options A, B and D are eliminated. Option E is eliminated because it contains pronoun ambiguity (using the pronoun 'they,' which can refer to either of the plural nouns, i.e. employers or employees).

    The correct answer is option C.

92. Concepts tested: Pronouns mismatch, Modifiers, Idioms

    The intended meaning of the sentence:

    Research has found that children who are born in a family having schizophrenics are highly likely to become schizophrenics too.

    Concept discussion:

    Pronoun mismatch: The non-underlined portion contains the plural pronoun "their," meant to refer to the noun "children." Thus, using the singular noun "a child" is incorrect. Options A and C contain this error.

Modifiers: "Families" is a collective noun of people but not places. For "families," using the modifier "where" is incorrect; "where" should be used to denote actual places. For families, we can use "whose" or "in which." Options D and E contain this error.

Idioms: "Likely" should be followed by "to + verb" and not by "verb."

Incorrect – She will *likely study* tomorrow.

Correct – She is *likely to study* tomorrow.

Options A, C and E contain this error.

The correct answer is option B.

93. Concepts tested: Pronouns mismatch, Idioms, Conjunctions

    The intended meaning of the sentence:

    The union (though not happily) agreed to impose a surcharge on some repayments, which upset the members so much that they marched in protest in front of headquarters.

    Concept discussion:

    Pronoun mismatch: The noun "union" is a collective noun, and is therefore, singular. It will take the singular pronoun "its" but not the plural pronoun "their." Option A contains this error.

    Idioms: "Surcharge" is followed by "on" but not by "to" or "in." Options B and E contain this error.

    Conjunctions: The sentence intends to convey that the reluctant acceptance of the surcharge by the unions angered the members. Thus, the actions happened in a similar time frame. For such actions, the conjunction "when" is suitable to indicate that something happened at a time (and probably as a result of) another action – when the union agreed, the members were angered. Using "if" is incorrect because "if" is used to denote condition and results of things yet to happen; if the sentence were "if the unions agree, the members will be angered," "if" could have been used. However, since the events are already in the past, using "when" is best. Option D contains this error.

    The correct answer is option C.

94. Concepts tested: Pronoun mismatch, Tenses, Parallelism in meaning

    The intended meaning of the sentence:

    Even though the board decided to publish its report before the interim figures were announced, because of an emerging crisis over debt control, it has changed its mind about its decision and set up a meeting next month.

    Concept discussion:

    Pronoun mismatch: The noun "the board" is singular (as it is a collective noun), and the pronoun "its" in the non-underlined part reinforces this. Using the plural pronoun "they" to refer to the "board" is incorrect. Options A and B contain this error.

    Tenses: The past perfect tense "had been announced" can only be used for the earlier action of two actions in the past. "Announcing" happens after "publishing" and "reconsidering" and thus, cannot take the past perfect tense but should take the simple past tense "were announced." Option C contains this error.

Sentence Correction Guide – Solutions 221

Parallelism in meaning: Consider: The teacher entered the room and started the lessons.

Is it that because the teacher entered, she started the lessons? We cannot say so. The two actions simply happened in that natural order. Thus, we cannot make "started" an effect of "entered," and thus, cannot say "the teacher entered the room, starting the lessons," but need to keep it as "The teacher entered the room and (then) started the lessons."

Similarly, in the given sentence, the action of "reconsidering" happens independently before the action of "calling for a meeting." Using "calling" in the "verb-ing" format would suggest that the "calling" is a dependent action of "reconsidering," that the "calling" is an effect of "reconsidering." However, the "reconsider" is connected to "publish." The board published its figures before something; now it is reconsidering its position and has called for a meeting because of the crisis. Thus, the "calling" is because of the crisis and not necessarily because of "reconsider." For this reason, we need to make it parallel (independent) and not dependent. We cannot say "the board reconsidered, calling a meeting because of the crisis" but need to say "the board reconsidered and (then) called a meeting because of the crisis." Option E contains this error.

The correct answer is option D.

95. Concepts tested: Pronoun mismatch, Conjunctions, Modifiers

    The intended meaning of the sentence:

    A bird that is related to the common sparrow is found throughout southern Africa; it builds a nest from mud that is a perfectly rounded ball-like structure; its wings flash so rapidly that a special film is needed to capture the scene in motion.

    Concept discussion:

    Pronoun mismatch: The non-underlined part of the sentence uses the plural pronoun "them" to refer to the "relation of the common sparrow"; thus, using the singular noun "a relative of the common sparrow" will not match the plural pronoun "them," but the plural noun "relations of the common sparrow" will. Options B and C contain this error.

    Also, using the correct plural noun but using the incorrect singular pronoun "its" will also cause a mismatch. Options A and E contain this error.

    Conjunctions: "So" always pairs with "that" to denote intensity of some thing; for example: The bus was *so* crowded *that* I could not get on. Since the non-underlined part already contains "that," we have to use "so" to make "so fast that" and correctly show the intensity that the sentence intends to convey. Options A and C contain an error with this.

    Modifiers: Either "relations of the common sparrow" or "a perfectly rounded mud nest" could be the correct subject of the modifier "found throughout southern Africa." So, we cannot eliminate any option on the basis of that.

    The correct answer is option D.

96. Concepts tested: Pronoun mismatch, Meaning, Awkwardness

    The intended meaning of the sentence:

    The sentence intends to show a contrast in the money that came in the beginning of the show with the tip received by the average singer at the end of the show.

Concept discussion:

Pronoun mismatch: Using the plural pronoun "their" to refer to the singular noun "singer" is incorrect. All options except E contain this error.

Meaning: Options C and D imply that the singers themselves decreased their tips, whereas, the original intended meaning is simply that the money brought in by the shows contrasted between beginning and end, as they brought lots of money in the beginning but had a decline in tips for the singers at the end. Options C and D contain this error.

Awkwardness: Using "what" twice with no clear referent makes option B awkward.

The correct answer is option E.

97. Concepts tested: Pronoun mismatch, Diction

    The intended meaning of the sentence:

    The sentence talks about an exhibit that consisted of hundreds of paintings. Further, it tells us that each painting was a tiny etched landscape inside its own ceramic work of pottery.

    Concept discussion:

    Pronoun mismatch: Words such as 'each' and 'every' are always singular, even if you are referring to multiple elements. You would say, for example: each boy in the class is wearing a sweater. Despite the fact that you are referring to multiple boys, you are still emphasizing each one of them and thus, a singular verb/pronoun needs to be used. In the above sentence, the singular pronoun "its" needs to be used for "each" or "every." Options D and E contain this error.

    "All" is plural and needs the plural pronoun "their." Option C contains this error.

    The underlined part of the original sentence acts as a modifier, or a phrase in apposition (*Apposition is a grammatical construction in which two elements, normally noun phrases, are placed side by side, with one element serving to identify the other in a different way. The two elements are said to be in apposition.*), describing paintings in the exhibit. The modifier correctly uses the singular for all three terms: *painting, landscape,* and *its* all agree. However, in option B the plural "all paintings" does not agree with the singular "a tiny landscape," which, in turn, does not agree with "their." Option B is, thus, incorrect.

    The correct answer is option A.

6.6 Meaning

98. <u>Concepts tested</u>: Meaning

<u>The intended meaning of the sentence</u>:

Bush is well-funded by a band of Texan oil tycoons and is one of the most popular of the Republican front runners; it is no coincidence that he is announcing his candidacy now.

<u>Concept discussion</u>:

Meaning: What is not a coincidence? The fact that Bush is announcing his candidacy at a particular time. Thus, the sentence must correctly provide a subject for the predicate "is certainly no coincidence." Using "Bush" as a subject will not work because the meaning does not suggest that "Bush is certainly no coincidence." Using "candidacy" as the subject will also not work. The correct subject is "the action/time of Bush's announcing his candidacy." Using "this" to refer to "announcing his candidacy at this time" is grammatically incorrect because "this" is a pronoun that can refer only to a noun. For example:

Correct – I like the book you gave me. This/It is nice [referring to the noun "book"]

Incorrect – The girl was singing. This relaxed her. [What relaxed her? That she was singing – not a noun but a clause] Thus, we cannot use a pronoun.

"This" is best used as an adjective for a noun. For example: The girl was singing. This action relaxed her. [Functioning as an adjective for the noun "action"]

In the given sentence, using only "this" to refer to "Bush announcing his candidacy" is incorrect because "this" cannot refer to clauses. Options A, C and D contain this error.

Option E is incorrect because it changes the meaning by suggesting that Bush will announce when it is not a coincidence, implying that he hasn't already announced. However, the original sentence implied that the candidacy has already been announced at a time that is not a coincidence. Only option B conveys this meaning.

The correct answer is option B.

99. <u>Concepts tested</u>: Meaning, Redundancy

<u>The intended meaning of the sentence</u>:

In ancient Egypt, the first sacrifice was to be done when the moon rose and peeked over the top of the Gaza Pyramid; however, later, in subsequent years, this ritual was changed.

<u>Concept discussion</u>:

Meaning: "Rise" indicates a completed action, whereas, "rising" indicates continuity. In this case, since we're discussing actions in continuity (a sacrifice was done when the moon was rising/not when the moon rose), we need to use "the rising." Options B, C and E contain this error.

Redundancy: "Topmost tip" is redundant; either "topmost point" or "tip" would do the job. Options A, B and E contain this error.

The correct answer is option D.

100. Concepts tested: Meaning, Tenses

    The intended meaning of the sentence:

    There was a hurricane in the region that is continuing to ravage the region; this hurricane destroyed some vehicles and damaged some other vehicles, vehicles that had been stolen from the army camp nearby

    Concept discussion::

    Meaning: "And" is inclusive while "or" is selective. In the given sentence, we need "damaged *or* destroyed" but not "damaged *and* destroyed" because the vehicles can be either damaged *or* destroyed but cannot be damaged after being destroyed. Options A and E contain this error.

    Tenses: The sentence discusses events in the past – damaged, destroyed, stolen, etc. Of these, "stealing" happened before the "getting damaged/destroyed." Thus, the earlier of the two actions in the past should take the past perfect tense "had been stolen" and not simple past tense "were stolen" or present tense "are stolen." Options A, C and D contain this error.

    The correct answer is option B.

101. Concepts tested: Meaning, Redundancy

    The intended meaning of the sentence:

    Candidates who are physically-challenged or are sick would be at a disadvantage against other candidates, and so, such candidates are exempted from sitting for an entry exam, but other candidates have to.

    Concept discussion:

    Meaning: The sentence does not intend to compare candidates who are physically-challenged or sick to other candidates. If it intended to compare two groups of candidates, it would have said "Unlike sick/challenged candidates, *other* candidates have to..."; however, the sentence instead says "Unlike sick/challenged candidates, *candidates* have to..." "sick/challenged candidates" cannot be compared to "candidates" since the "sick/challenged candidates" are included in the group of "candidates." Thus, it cannot be a comparison. Options A and C contain this error.

    What the sentence intends to say is that "*except for* a certain group of candidates, every other candidate has to take an exam." Thus, the meaning required is that of exception or exemption and so we need to use words such as "other than" or "apart from." Using "unless" is incorrect because "unless" conveys "if ... not"; for example:

    Unless you study, you will fail = If you do not study, you will fail.

    The sentence does not intend to say that "if certain candidates are disadvantaged if they participate, all candidates have to take an exam" because it would not exempt the "sick/challenged candidates" from taking the exam. Thus, option E is incorrect.

    Redundancy: "Obligatory" means "compulsory" and "required" also implies that something "must" be done. Using "obligatory" and "required" together are redundant. Option D contains this error.

    The correct answer is option B.

Sentence Correction Guide – Solutions

102. Concepts tested: Meaning, Pronoun mismatch

The intended meaning of the sentence:

A shocking thing transpired on a trek; the Indian Agency, which is supposed to protect the natives, gave in to the will of the pioneers who wanted an Indian boy hanged for stealing a lump of bread.

Concept discussion:

Meaning: The issue is about the "demand." Who is demanding that the Indian boy be hanged? The sentence suggests that the pioneers are demanding that the Indian boy be hanged (since the agency is surrendering to the pioneers' will, implying that pioneers would be demanding something.) Thus, to refer to pioneers, we need to use "who" because "who" refers to the "person" noun right before it. If we use "demanding," it would end up being an effect of the entire sentence before, or even referring to the Indian Agency.

Also, using "and" is incorrect because it suggests that the Agency did two independent activities – gave in to the pioneers and (separately) gave in to their demands. However, the Agency gave into the pioneers, who demanded certain things (dependent actions). Option E contains this error.

Pronoun: The pioneers are demanding that who hangs the Indian boy? The sentence suggests that the pioneers are demanding that the Indian Agency hang the Indian boy for stealing a lump of bread. To refer to the "Indian Agency," we need a singular pronoun "it" and not plural "them." Option A and D contain this error.

The correct answer is option B.

103. Concepts tested: Meaning, Rhetorical Construction, Redundancy

The intended meaning of the sentence:

Robert Hunter of The Interstate Insurance Committee claimed that there is a correlation between high premiums and poor credit ratings, but this claim was denied by the Federal Association of Insurers.

Concept discussion:

Meaning clarity: We need to ensure that the intended meaning comes across in the right option. If more than one option conveys the intended meaning, the grammatically better one becomes the right choice.

Redundancy: Using two contrast conjunctions ("although" and "but") to join two sentences is redundant.

Analysis of the options

(A) This option is **incorrect** because it does not provide complete meaning. It merely suggests that when Robert did something ... has been denied. It should have stated "When Robert claimed something, the claim was denied."

(B) This option is **incorrect** because it tries to unsuccessfully change the meaning. It suggests that the claim was denied on the basis of "why Robert claimed..."

(C) This option is **correct** because it accurately conveys the intended meaning that the Association denied Robert's claim that ...

(D) This option is **incorrect** because it is incomplete. It uses the conjunction "when," but does not provide two clauses, an error that is also present in option A. Also, the use of the "which" modifier is incorrect because it refers to the noun right before, i.e. credit ratings; however, not "credit ratings" but "Robert's claim" has been denied.

(E) This option is **incorrect** because it uses two contrast conjunctions ("although" and "but") involving redundancy. Also, "this" is used as a pronoun in this option, but it lacks a clear referent, making it ambiguous. Such ambiguity is best avoided.

The correct answer is option C.

104. Concepts tested: Meaning, Tenses

    The intended meaning of the sentence:

    It might be true that, if more people die due to fatal car accidents caused by production (and availability) of faster cars, society would be better off overall; this is contrary to popular opinion (that it might be bad for society if such a thing happened).

    Concept discussion:

    Meaning: The sentence intends to convey that something popularly thought of as not beneficial might be beneficial; the matter under discussion is that when faster cars are produced, more people die in fatal car accidents. Thus, we need to convey this meaning correctly. Saying "increasing fatal accidents" will suggest that it is deliberate and not just a consequence. For example: Increasing the water intake of plants will eventually cause a water shortage [this suggests that "if someone increases water intake, something will happen].

    Increased water intake will eventually cause a water shortage [this suggests that if water intake increases (by itself, or not deliberately), something will happen].

    Similarly, in the given sentence, we need to suggest that "if the number of accidents increased (by itself, not deliberately), society would benefit." Thus, we need to use "increased" and not "increasing" for "fatal accidents." Options A and C contain this error.

    Tenses: Using the simple past tense "increased" or the past perfect tense "had increased," as in options D and E, is incorrect because it would suggest that the increase happened in the past and is no longer valid. However, the sentence is in the present tense ("may be," "would be"), and thus, we need to keep the rest in the present tense. Options D and E contain this error.

    The correct answer is option B.

105. Concepts tested: Meaning, Modifiers, Tenses

    The intended meaning of the sentence:

    Isabelle loved her husband (who is now dead), so much that she made copies of many of the diaries from the collection that she was forced to sell.

    Concept discussion:

    Meaning: We need to figure out whether she made 50 copies or copied 50 diaries. Making 50 copies seems needless; more likely is that the collection of diaries had 50 diaries (volumes), all of which she made copies of, so as not to lose her husband's collection.

Options suggesting that 50 copies were made are incorrect. Options B and C contain this error.

Modifiers: The word "first" intends to modify "making copies," as in, she first made copies, and then sold the collection. Thus, the best placement for it is before the verb it modifies, i.e. before "made copies." Options B and E contain this error. Option D, too, is incorrect because it eliminates the word "first" altogether and does not use its equivalent either, like option E (beforehand), thereby not conveying the original intended meaning.

Tenses: The entire sentence is in the past tense (loved, sold, etc.); thus, we need to put the underlined verb "made/copied" also in the past tense, without which the sentence would be incorrect. Option E contains this error.

The correct answer is option A.

106. Concepts tested: Meaning ambiguity, Comparisons

    The intended meaning of the sentence:

    The sentence discusses the speed of eye movements, and states that the speed is higher when a person is dreaming than it is when a person is awake.

    Concept discussion:

    Meaning-ambiguity and Comparisons: The sentence intends to convey that eye movements are more rapid during the dream phase than the phase in which the person is awake. Using the word "waking" is ambiguous because it could mean the actual act of "waking" (up) or mean the time a person is awake. Using "awake" is clearer. Options A, C and E contain this error.

    Also, we need to clearly compare the two phases of differing eye movements. If "rapidly" is not correctly placed before "during dreams," it will modify something else. In option B, the incorrect placement implies that "dreaming" itself is more rapid.

    Only option D correctly compares eye movement during dreams with eye movement during the period of being awake.

    The correct answer is option D.

107. Concepts tested: Meaning

    The intended meaning of the sentence:

    The sentence discusses the singer Marian Corey, who has a cold and possibly a persistent cough, the combination of which might negatively affect her voice, for which she is famous.

    Concept discussion:

    Meaning: We need to figure out whether to use "with" or "that." Each has a separate meaning.

    If we use "with," the sentence becomes "Marian has developed a cold with coughing," implying that the cold developed due to coughing or that both things have developed simultaneously. However, the original sentence says that the cold, if combined with something else like coughing, is likely to strain her voice, indicating that the two have not developed simultaneously as of now. Thus, it seems unlikely that "with" is the correct meaning.

If we use "that," the sentence becomes "Marian has developed a cold that, with coughing (if coughing were to happen), could strain her voice..." This structure keeps the hypothetical combination intact. Options C, D and E contain an error with this.

Option B also changes the meaning to suggest that the cold was developed due to coughing.

The correct answer is option A.

108. Concepts tested: Meaning, Concision, Ambiguity

    The intended meaning of the sentence:

    The sentence intends to say that because hospitals are increasing the number of work hours of doctors, the frequency of surgical errors is increasing, leading to an increase in the already big cost of malpractice lawsuits, costs which the hospitals have to bear.

    Concept discussion:

    Meaning: Significant – significantly: Using the adjective form "significant" will not refer to "affecting" but will refer to either the noun "doctors" or to "hospitals." However, the meaning suggests that the "affecting" is significant. Thus, we need the adverb form "significantly" to refer to "affecting." Options D and E contain this error.

    Also, the sentence suggests that the surgical errors are already a substantial burden on the hospitals, and these costs will be increased by the increase in the frequency of surgical errors. Using "and" to connect "affecting the frequency of errors" and "costs hospitals" would suggest that these two activities are independent, which they are not. Options D and E contain this error.

    Option C uses "with," creating ambiguity because "with" may or may not be related to the previous clause.

    Concision: "Are a cost" is needlessly lengthier than the verb form "cost." Option A contains this error.

    Ambiguity: Some options use "surgical errors frequency" while others use "frequency of surgical errors." Certain constructions create ambiguity. For example: "moderate alcohol consumption" – what is moderate? Alcohol or consumption? Such a construction is considered ambiguous and "moderate consumption of alcohol" would be better, as it is clear and unambiguous.

    Similarly, is the expression "surgical frequency of errors" or "frequency of surgical errors"? Using "frequency of surgical errors" eliminates ambiguity. Options C and E contain an error with this.

    The correct answer is option B.

109. Concepts tested: Meaning, Tenses, Diction

    The intended meaning of the sentence:

    The sentence intends to describe when Henry dreams about his dead wife. When he does so, he sees her as she was in her youth.

    Concept discussion:

Sentence Correction Guide – Solutions

Meaning: The sentence intends to say that in Henry's dreams, Henry sees his wife as she used to be in her youth. Thus, she is being imagined as she used to be. Using "she was" is necessary again to complete the meaning. Simply saying, "Henry sees her as in her youth" will not convey the correct meaning. Options C and E contain this error.

Tenses: Using the past perfect tense to describe just a single event in the past is incorrect. The past perfect tense is used when there are multiple events in the past, and the earliest event takes the past perfect. For example: I had written three books before I was ten years old. (Two actions, of which "writing" happened earlier than "becoming ten.")

However, for just a single event in the past, using the simple past tense is adequate. For example: I wrote three books by the age of ten. (only one event in the past)

When I see John, I think of his brother who died in the war. (only one event, thus, "died," not "had died")

Similarly, in the given sentence, using the simple past tense (was) is adequate, since there is just one action in the past, and using the past perfect tense (had been) is unnecessary. Option B contains this error.

Diction: Using "as if" and "as though" indicate hypothetical situations; however, in the given sentence "as she was in her youth" is not hypothetical. Thus, using "as if" and "as though" instead of just "as" is incorrect. Options C and E contain this error.

Also, "during" is best used for "durations." For example: I learned French during my vacations.

However, using "during" for "youth" is inappropriate because "youth" is a state; one can be in a state or not be in a state. So, "during her youth" is awkward and "in her youth" is correct. Options D and E contain this error.

The correct answer is option A.

110. Concepts tested: Meaning, Pronouns, Subjunctive

The intended meaning of the sentence:

The newly-formed Soviet communist state was defeated by the Polish general, Jozef Pilsudski, and the general demanded that the state move back its borders east of Vilnius.

Concept discussion:

Meaning: The issue is about the "demand." Who is demanding that which country push back borders? The sentence suggests that Jozef is demanding that the newly-formed Soviet Communist state push back its borders (since Jozef routed the state in a surprising victory.) Thus, to refer to Jozef, we need to use "who" because "who" refers to the "person" noun right before it. If we use "demanding," it would end up being an effect of the entire sentence that came before or even referring to the state.

For example: The owner came and yelled at the staff, demanding that work be done.

The "demanding" will never refer to "staff" (noun right before), but will refer to "owner." Options A and B contain this error.

Pronoun: Who is demanding that which country push back borders? The sentence suggests that Jozef is demanding that the newly-formed Soviet communist state push back its borders. To refer to the "state," we need the singular pronoun "it" and not the plural "them." Option E contains this error.

Subjunctive: Certain verbs (demand, suggest, recommend, insist) are followed by a slightly different form of the third-person singular.

For example: I demand that he tell me the truth.

There is no "s" on the third-person form in such sentences.

The correct answer is option D.

111. Concepts tested: Meaning, Idioms

    The intended meaning of the sentence:

    The sentence intends to state that unless a condition *(that internal networks involve identical operating systems)* is satisfied, all legacy multi-system networks need software emulators to communicate.

    Concept discussion:

    Meaning: We need to convey that "if networks do not have identical systems with the same protocol, all systems need emulators to communicate." Thus, we need to use either "if" or "unless." Any other conjunction would not convey the conditional nature of the sentence. Conjunctions such as "as well as," "in addition to," "together with" are not meant to join conditional clauses, but are for additive information. 'Except for' is often used as a preposition and is followed by a noun or a noun phrase to mean 'not including' or 'excluding.' All options except C contain this error.

    Idioms: 'Between identical operating systems with the same identification protocol' is unidiomatic; similarly, 'between identical operating systems, whose...' is unidiomatic. The correct idiom is "between X and Y." Options D and E contain this error.

    The correct answer is option C.

112. Concepts tested: Meaning, Parallelism

    The intended meaning of the sentence:

    The sentence intends to describe two observations that have been calculated: first, every three minutes a human being will be struck by a vehicle; second, each minute two animals can be expected to die from such collisions.

    Concept discussion:

    Meaning: Using "should" is inappropriate in this sentence because it would suggest that the Department of Motor Vehicles (DMV) wants one human being to die – the DMV calculated that one person should die every 3 minutes. However, this sounds absurd and contradictory to what the rest of the sentence indicates – that the death is the average of accident deaths. Options A, B and E contain this error.

    Parallelism: The non-underlined part, *each minute two animals...*, necessitates parallelism. Thus, the correct answer should begin with "every three minutes." Options A, B and C contain this parallelism error.

    The correct answer is option D.

113. Concepts tested: Meaning, Parallelism

    The intended meaning of the sentence:

Sentence Correction Guide – Solutions

New engines show the potential of high power and performance without costly maintenance and consumption of particular fuel that were needed by earlier models.

Concept discussion:

Meaning: The intended meaning is that the newer model does not need some costly things that the earlier model did. You are presented with various options for the costly "things." Will "requirements of earlier models" be costly or will "maintenance and fuel consumption of earlier models" be costly? Using "requirements" as costly is not as logical as "maintenance and fuel consumption" itself being costly. All options except E contain this error.

Parallelism: The use of the conjunction "and" necessitates parallelism between "maintenance" and "consumption." Options A, B and C contain this parallelism error.

The correct answer is option E.

6.7 Rhetorical construction

114. Concepts tested: Rhetorical construction, Clarity, Conjunctions

The intended meaning of the sentence:

Good communicators can understand a conversation by understanding the tone of the speaker and the body language, even though they may not understand the language.

Concept discussion:

Rhetorical construction and Clarity: Using "the person" to refer to "a savvy communicator" is awkward because it is not entirely clear that "the person" is necessarily referring to "a savvy communicator." Options C and D contain this error.

Also, the sentence is intended as a generalized statement about "good communicators." For such generalizations, plural forms are always better.

Consider:

(1) A girl is likely to get married sooner.
(2) Girls are likely to get married sooner.

Sentence 2 sounds more like a generalization than sentence 1. Thus, for making generalized or universal statements, using plural forms is correct. Options C and E contain this error.

Conjunctions: When a conjunction such as "though," "even though" or "although" is used, two complete clauses must be present. Using a modifier and a clause with such conjunctions is incorrect.

Incorrect – Though not knowing the game, he joined the team.

Correct –Though he did not know the game, he joined the team.

Correct –Despite not knowing the game, he joined the team.

The correct answer is option B.

115. Concepts tested: Rhetorical construction, Concision

The intended meaning of the sentence:

Deer damage plants; this damage can be prevented if human hair is spread around the garden.

Concept discussion:

Rhetorical construction and Concision: What can be prevented if human hair is spread? Damage by deer can be prevented. To make the most concise and the clearest construction, it is best to turn the underlined part into a subject for the predicate "can be prevented..." Making the underlined part into a clause – "when deer damage..." or "deer damage plants..." – adds to wordiness by introducing pronouns and subordinates and takes away concise clarity. Options A, D and E contain this error.

Also, what can be prevented? The fact that deer damage something can be prevented, or the actual damage can be prevented? The "fact" cannot be prevented, but the actual "damage" can be prevented. Thus, option C has an incorrect subject for the predicate.

The correct answer is option B.

116. <u>Concepts tested</u>: Rhetorical construction, Parallelism

<u>The intended meaning of the sentence</u>:

Books that are meant to be added to the high school curriculum should not contain profanity or lewdness and they should be educational.

<u>Concept discussion</u>:

Rhetorical construction: Using "in them" in the given structure will create an awkward redundant structure.

Consider: The movie contains various subplots in it.

In the example, the subject is "the movie" and it "contains" something; using "in it" to refer to things that the "movie contains" is redundant and awkward.

Similarly, in the given sentence, the subject is "books" that "contain" something; using "in them" to refer to things that "the book contains" gives us this sentence: "The books should not contain profanity or lewdness in them." This is incorrect. Options A, B and E contain this error.

Parallelism: Option D is not parallel in "without containing X or Y." Also, after using "without," using "nor" creates a double negative; better would be "without containing <u>profanity</u> *or* <u>lewdness</u>" to make it parallel and clear. Option D is incorrect.

The correct answer is option C.

117. <u>Concepts tested</u>: Rhetorical Construction, Concision, Modifiers

<u>The intended meaning of the sentence</u>:

The sentence talks about Mary's actions. It seems like sometimes Mary does certain things, things that look like they are done only to prevent her husband from having a good time when he's out with his friends.

<u>Concept discussion</u>:

Rhetorical Construction: The intended meaning must be conveyed in a clear, crisp, and non-ambiguous way. Sometimes when the subject of some verb is difficult to represent directly, placeholder pronouns are used. For example:

It seems crazy that she left this lucrative job.

What seems crazy? That she left this lucrative job. (the subject)

Thus, "it" is "holding place/representing" the subject "that she left this lucrative job."

Similarly, in the given sentence, "Mary does things only to make <something> inconvenient for her husband."

Make what inconvenient? For her husband to have a good time.

So, we need the placeholder "it" between "make" and "inconvenient," i.e. "Mary does things only to make it inconvenient for her husband to have a good time..."

Options B, D and E contain this error.

<u>Note</u>: Using the placeholder "it" without strict need is to be avoided; such use creates ambiguity by introducing needless pronouns. For example:

I want it that the company get a new car for the directors. (Incorrect; Needless placeholder "it")

I want the company to get a new car for the directors. (Correct)

Concision: The sentence presents various forms of "make," i.e. "making" and "to make." To provide reasons for a particular action, using a "to verb" is the clearest, crispest structure.

For example: I went to the theatre to watch a movie.

"I went to the theatre for watching/for the watching of" will not convey the intended meaning in the crispest possible way.

Similarly, in the given sentence, "Mary does things only to make something inconvenient …"

Options C, D and E contain this error.

Modifiers: Inconvenient-inconveniently – The sentence intends to say that Mary makes something inconvenient for her husband. Thus, we need to use "inconvenient" to refer to Mary's actions. Using "inconveniently" will refer to the husband's action or not clearly refer to Mary's. Options D and E contain this error.

The correct answer is option A.

118. Concepts tested: Rhetorical construction, SVA, Active/ Passive, Concision

    The intended meaning of the sentence:

    The sentence intends to say that in every ten households in the United States, seven households have at least two televisions.

    Concept discussion:

    Rhetorical construction: This is a question of order of relevance. Who or what is the subject here? It's 'seven households.' Knowing the subject makes this question very easy. The actor/agent usually comes first and that is the case here. Also, the sentence uses the expression 'out of,' which indicates the source or derivation of something. In other words, it means 'from.' Options B and E break this order.

    SVA: The subject of the sentence is "seven households," which is plural, and will take the plural verb "own" and not the singular verb "owns." Options B and D contain this error.

    Active/ Passive: The use of passive voice makes the sentence complex and wordy. Options C and E contain this error.

    Concision: Using "every" is unnecessary. All options except A contain this error.

    The correct answer is option A.

119. Concepts tested: Rhetorical construction, Diction

    The intended meaning of the sentence:

    Those who are actors on Broadway have to also be singers and dancers simultaneously.

    Concept discussion:

    Rhetorical construction: Since the sentence discusses "actors" in general, we need to maintain the construction by using the plural form "singers" and "dancers." Using the singular form would make the sentence rhetorically incorrect. Options C, D and E contain this error.

Diction: As-like: In comparisons, "as" and "like" are equivalent but follow different structures, as follows:

Like Jane, John is a teacher.

John is a teacher, as *is* Jane.

John teaches, as *does* Jane.

While the meaning remains the same, the structure differs. In "like" phrases, nouns are used, but no verbs, whereas, in "as" clauses, verbs (is, am, does, do, did, etc.) are necessary.

Separately, "as" can also be used in non-comparison scenarios to mean "in the role/function of." Examples:

Jane works as a receptionist.

Ledger acts as the Joker in *Batman Returns*.

In the given sentence, there is no comparison happening and the meaning required is "in the role/function of"; that is, "actors have to *perform* (in the function of) as dancers.

Using "like" is incorrect in this situation. Options B and C contain this error.

The correct answer is option A.

6.8 Redundancy

120. Concepts tested: Redundancy, Diction, Awkwardness

The intended meaning of the sentence:

The store profits have not risen much, hardly a fraction; still, because of careful accounting and purchasing at discounted prices, the store has remained in the possession of the family and not been sold off.

Concept discussion:

Redundancy: Using "fraction" and "barely" together is redundant as they both mean the same thing. Options A and B contain this error.

Diction: "Raise" and "rise" differ in meaning. "Rise" happens automatically, as in, "the sun rises (by itself), whereas, "raise" is done by someone and does not happen by itself – "he raised the flag (the flag did not rise by itself). "Profits" will rise unless some action is indicated as a measure taken to "raise" profits. In this case, since the sentence is discussing the general trend of profits, it should be "rise." If the sentence discussed some measures or intervention, "raise" could have worked – for example, cost-cutting raised the profits. However, no such implication has been made about the profits in this statement; thus, using "raise" is incorrect. Option E contains this error.

Awkwardness: Option D is awkward because of its use of "there being," without which the sentence could have been constructed, as it is in option C. Thus, option D is incorrect.

The correct answer is option C.

121. Concepts tested: Redundancy

The intended meaning of the sentence:

At the end of a long meeting on a stock reissue, the spokesman expressed that he was doubtful that the money could be raised before the deadline.

Concept discussion:

Redundancy: "meeting on something" already means "getting together and discussing something"; using "meeting" with "discuss" or "converse" is redundant. Options A, B and D contain this error.

Similarly, using "lengthy/long" and "protracted" together is redundant, as they both mean the same thing. Option A contains this error.

Also, using "doubts" with "misgivings" is also redundant because they both mean the same thing. Options A, B and E contain this error.

The correct answer is option C.

Sentence Correction Guide – Solutions   237

6.9 Grammatical construction

122. Concepts tested: Grammatical construction, Conjunctions, Meaning

The intended meaning of the sentence:

Elvis Presley was famous as the King of Rock and Roll; millions of his fans mourned his death.

Concept discussion:

Grammatical construction: A clause must have a single subject. A sentence containing two subjects with just one predicate is ungrammatical. "Mourned his death" is a predicate for which the subject is "millions of fans," but the subject "Elvis Presley" has no predicate. The modifier "known by ..." cannot act as a predicate. The sentence is essentially – Elvis, known for stuff, millions of fans mourned his death. The correct sentence would have been "Elvis was known ... and millions mourned his death." Option A contains this error.

Conjunctions: The first half of the sentence discusses the fact that Elvis Presley was famous as the King of Rock and Roll, while the second half discusses the fact that his fans mourned his death. There is no contrast between these two halves, and so we cannot use the contrast conjunction "but." Option D contains this error.

Also, we cannot say for sure that *because* Elvis was famous as the King of Rock and Roll, his fans mourned his death. It could be just that he was perceived as a nice artist or as a nice human being and so they mourned his death. Since the sentence presents no clue to the causality of the second statement, we cannot use such a conjunction that suggests that the first half is a cause of the second half. Using "so" would suggest this, making it incorrect. Option E contains this error.

Meaning: The sentence suggests that Elvis was famous as the King of Rock and Roll. For this, we can state that he was famous for being the king. To use "becoming" would suggest that he was famous for the action of becoming king, rather than for being king itself.

For example – He is famous for being a great doctor/ He is famous for becoming a great doctor.

Why would someone become famous for "becoming" something? It is more likely that someone is famous for being something. Option B contains this error.

The correct answer is option C.

123. Concepts tested: Grammatical construction, Meaning

The intended meaning of the sentence:

The device is very complex; even though it has an operating manual in English, users complain that the wording is too fancy to be understood by laymen.

Concept discussion:

Grammatical construction: When a conjunction such as "even though" or "while" is used, using two clauses (sentences) becomes necessary.

For example: While/Even though I don't like eating cheese, I will make a pizza.

Using only one clause is not grammatically correct – While/Even though I don't like eating cheese.

"Which" or "that" are modifiers that are not part of the main sentence, and, without the modifiers, there should be a full sentence.

For example: Harvard, *which is a great school*, takes all kinds of students.

The sentence is "Harvard takes all kinds of students" and the modifier "which is a great school" describes "Harvard." Without this modifier, the sentence would be complete. However, simply using a modifier instead of a clause will not create a grammatical sentence.

For example: Harvard, *which is a great school*.

This is not a complete sentence because the main verb for the subject "Harvard" is missing.

It could be corrected as "Harvard is a great school."

Thus, "which" or "that" modifiers cannot be used to replace actual sentences.

Back to the point of conjunctions such as "even though" or "while" requiring two clauses – when such conjunctions are used, two clauses are needed, and clauses cannot be "which" or "that" modifiers.

For example: Even though it takes all kinds of students, Harvard, which is a great school.

This is incorrect because there aren't two clauses.

Correct – Even though it takes all kinds of students, Harvard is a great school.

Similarly, in the given sentence, two clauses are required because of the use of "even though" or "while." A "that" modifier has been used instead of a clause ("users complain that even though [clause 1] it comes with a manual, which is in English and has complex wording" [modifier, not clause 2, as it should be]). To correct it, we need to turn the modifier into a clause as follows: "users complain that even though [clause 1] it comes with a manual, which is in English, it has complex wording" [clause 2, as it should be].

Options A, B and E contain this error.

Meaning: The sentence intends to convey that users find the manual too complex even though it has a manual in English. The sentence never intended to show that some users complain while others say something else. Option C suggests that some users find something wrong, while others find some other thing wrong. Option C is incorrect.

The correct answer is option D.

124. Concepts tested: Grammatical construction, Meaning

The intended meaning of the sentence:

The number of petty crimes because of children skipping school is increasing; given this, a law is going to be introduced. This law says that children between 12 and 16 years old who skip school need to be kept at home by their parents.

Concept discussion:

Grammatical construction: Certain verbs have specific structures that need to be maintained. Verbs such as "require," "recommend," "order" have one of the following two structures:

(1) Verb + that + subject + bare infinitive: Example: The doctor recommended that she take her medicine (not takes) [Bare infinitive = infinitive form of the verb without "to"]. Also, in this structure, insertion of "should" or "would" or any other auxiliary is not permitted.

(2) Verb + object + infinitive + object: Example: The doctor ordered her to take her medicine.

Thus, the given sentence can follow one of the following structures:

(1) ... a law requiring that parents ... keep children at home

(2) ... a law requiring parents ... to keep children at home

No other structure is acceptable.

Options A and E use "that" but also use "will be kept" instead of just "be kept," making them incorrect.

Option C uses "which" instead of "that," making it incorrect.

Meaning: The sentence intends to convey that parents of such children will need to keep them (the children) at home, not that parents need to be kept at home. Such incorrect meaning is conveyed in options A, B and E [...parents of children ...be kept at home]. Thus, options A, B and E are incorrect.

The correct answer is option D.

125. Concepts tested: Grammatical construction, Idioms, Diction

The intended meaning of the sentence:

The handbook specifies that every recruit has to select one course of action over another and that the recruit must use his initiative and skills to survive some struggle/ordeal.

Concept discussion:

Grammatical construction: The non-underlined part after the underlined part uses "and that" implying that "that" should have been used beforehand. Options A, C and E contain this error.

Idioms: "Responsible" can be followed by "to" or "for" depending on the context.

To discuss the actual responsibility, "for" is used - He is responsible for the laptop (his responsibility is the laptop).

To discuss to whom the person is responsible, "to" is used - He is responsible to the CEO [the CEO can hold him accountable and the person is responsible to the CEO, but for what responsibility we don't know, because the sentence does not specify].

In the given sentence, we need "for" because "selecting an action" is the actual responsibility, not the person to whom the recruit is responsible. Options A, C, and D contain this error.

Diction: "Each" pairs with "other," whereas, "one" pairs with "another." In this case, since all options have "one," we can only use "another" but not "other." Options D and E contain this error.

The correct answer is option B.

126. <u>Concepts tested</u>: Grammatical construction, Diction

<u>The intended meaning of the sentence</u>:

The market fluctuated to quite an extent in the course of 24 hours, but such a thing has almost never happened in the history of the US, even if the 1926 stock crisis is considered.

<u>Concept discussion</u>:

Grammatical construction: In certain sentence structure, inversion is used. Normally, the subject precedes the verb, or, in other words, the verb follows the subject. In inversion sentences, the verb precedes the subject.

Such inversions are required in:

Questions: Did he call? [Normal – He did call.]

Comparative time expressions – rarely, scarcely, seldom: Seldom has he seen something so weird. [Normal – He has never seen anything so weird.]

Succession time expressions – no sooner, barely: No sooner had he gotten up than the doorbell rang. [Normal: As soon as he got up, the doorbell rang.]

In the given sentence, too, since the sentence begins with "rarely," inversion is necessary.

Normal: The market has fluctuated.

Inverted – has the market fluctuated

Options A and B contain this error.

Diction: To indicate an extreme extent, the correct phrase is "to such an extent/to such a degree." Using plural "extents" or "degrees" is incorrect, as is using "many." All options except E contain this error.

The correct answer is option E.

127. <u>Concepts tested</u>: Grammatical construction, Idioms, Conjunctions, Diction

<u>The intended meaning of the sentence</u>:

It is established that Socrates used mind-altering drugs; however, if it is suggested that his expressed ideas can be attributed to the drugs, it implies that he was just a tool in their creation. {Thus, his ideas cannot be attributed merely to drugs.}

<u>Concept discussion</u>:

Grammatical construction: The conjunction "but" is joining two clauses "It's an …drugs" and "in attributing …creation." However, the second clause is incomplete because it does not have a proper subject for the verb "implies."

"In verb-ing" will not make a proper sentence; for example, "In ditching the player effectively implies he is not necessary to the team" is not a sentence. However, "to verb" or "verb-ing" can make a sentence: "Ditching the player effectively implies he is not necessary to the team," or "To ditch the player effectively implies he is not necessary to the team."

Similarly, in the given sentence, we can use either "attributing" or "to attribute" but not "in attributing" to make a proper clause.

Sentence Correction Guide – Solutions

Incorrect: In attributing his ideas to drugs effectively (in effect) implies he is merely a tool.

Correct: Attributing his ideas to drugs effectively (in effect) implies he is merely a tool.

Correct: To attribute his ideas to drugs effectively (in effect) implies he is merely a tool.

Options A and C contain this error.

Idioms: "Attribute" is always followed by "to" and never "for"; for example: The climatic conditions cannot be attributed only to winds. Option D contains this error.

Conjunctions: Using "while" for contrast is not ideal; "while" is best used for simultaneous actions – I was talking on the phone while walking. To indicate contrast, "but" is better. Option B contains this error.

Diction: "Affect" is the verb form but "effect" is the noun form. We can use "affect" as an action, but in the given sentence we need the noun form "effect" because "in effect" is a phrase that means "effectively/producing an effect." Option B contains this error.

Examples:

The monsoon affects yields.

The effect of monsoons on yields is easily demonstrated.

Passing this law in effect/effectively implies that criminals are being welcomed.

"In effect" also means "in (to) operation" – This law will come in effect in January.

The correct answer is option E.

128. Concepts tested: Grammatical construction, Idioms, Pronoun structure

The intended meaning of the sentence:

Housing cooperative committees have enforced a new contract, according to which tenants cannot accept sub-tenants (tenants of tenants) when the original tenants are out of town taking a holiday, i.e. tenants can no longer sublet their apartments.

Concept discussion:

Grammatical construction: In perfect tenses (past, present and future), the main verb is always the past participle form: examples – eaten (not ate), sung (not sang), broken (not broke), begun (not began). So, in the given sentence, since the tense is present perfect "have begun," we need the past participle form of the main verb "to begin," that is "begun" and not the simple past tense "began." Options A and D contain this error.

Idioms: "prohibit" is always followed by "from verb-ing" and not by "to verb." In the given example, it should be "prohibit tenants from accepting" and not "prohibit tenants to accept." Options B, C and D contain this error.

Also, "begin" should be followed by "to verb" rather than by "verb-ing" because the latter is considered informal and slang. In the given sentence, it should be "have begun to prohibit" rather than "have begun prohibiting." Options C and D contain this error.

Pronoun structure: Pronoun before a gerund (verb-ing) should be in the possessive form (my, your, his, its, their, our) and not objective form (me, you, him, it, them, us). Take for example:

I hate him and his singing (not "him singing"). In the given sentence, it should be "their taking a holiday" and not "them taking a holiday." Options A and B contain this error.

The correct answer is option E.

129. Concepts tested: Grammatical Construction, Tenses

    The intended meaning of the sentence:

    Elementary school teachers have not been paying adequate attention to the field of math because they prefer topics that can be explained with hands-on activities (practical teaching).

    Concept discussion:

    Grammatical Construction: Every sentence must have a subject and a verb to be grammatical. Mere nouns, phrases, or modifiers do not make sentences.

    Not a sentence: John, who is a graduate of Harvard.

    Sentence: John *is* a graduate of Harvard. ["is" is the main verb]

    Not a sentence: Math, which has been neglected by teachers, who prefer something else [both "which" and "who" parts are modifiers and will not be part of the main sentence, thus, cannot contribute verbs towards the main sentence].

    Sentence: Math has been neglected by teachers, who prefer something else.

    Sentence: Teachers prefer something else to math, which has been neglected.

    Options A, B and C contain this error.

    Tenses: We have to determine whether to use the simple past "was" or the present perfect "has been." Since the sentence is talking about an action that started in the past and continues into the present, we need the present perfect. To talk about a specific point in the past, simple past "was" can be used; for example: I was born in 1988. Options A, B and E contain this error.

    The correct answer is option D.

130. Concepts tested: Parallelism, Ambiguity

    The intended meaning of the sentence:

    The general belief today is that women have acquired equal treatment with men, but sociologists state that even now the gap is as wide and terrible as it was ten years ago, as can be seen from the statistics of post grad education and of median income.

    Concept discussion:

    Parallelism: The second half of the sentence discusses a comparison "as drastic a gap as …" Thus, parallelism is necessary. The easiest to figure out is whether to use 'of' at the end of the option. To say "he is as melodramatic of a man as any I have seen" is inappropriate; instead, "he is as melodramatic a man as any I have seen" is sufficient. Options A and E contain this error.

    Also, the paired conjunction "both X and Y" necessitates parallelism; the X and Y parts needs to be parallel. Option C contains this error.

    Ambiguity: Also, using the word "statistics" before the conjunction "both X and Y" is better to avoid ambiguity. If we place it after "both X and Y," it may create confusion that statistics is only referring to Y, i.e. median income statistics (but not postgraduate

Sentence Correction Guide – Solutions

education statistics). If placed before, it will have to refer to both. Options C and D contain this error.

The correct answer is option B.

131. Concepts tested: Pronouns, Concision

    The intended meaning of the sentence:

    The sentence intends to describe a survey conducted on men that revealed that 30 percent of them had had homosexual experiences which ranged from an isolated incident to something permanent.

    Concept discussion:

    Pronouns: Using pronouns "they" or "them" to refer to "men" can create ambiguity because of the presence of other plural nouns such as "experiences." Thus, pronouns must be avoided in this case. Options A, C and E contain this error.

    Concision: "from an isolated incident to a permanent lifestyle" in the non-underlined part is describing "homosexual experiences." It is not an independent part, and thus, should not be separated using "and" or another clause. Using "ranging" to describe "homosexual experiences" will keep the meaning intact in a concise manner. Options A, C and E contain this error.

    The correct answer is option D.

132. Concepts tested: Grammatical construction, Verb tense, Conjunctions

    The intended meaning of the sentence:

    The sentence intends to say that America's nuclear arsenal has expanded but, at the same time, India's and Pakistan's nuclear arsenals have also expanded.

    Concept discussion:

    Grammatical construction: The given structure is 'X has happened (America's nuclear arsenal has expanded), but Y & Z have also happened' (India's and Pakistan's nuclear arsenals have also expanded). A verb must be used after the conjunction, too, because without one, the sentence will be incomplete. Options A, B and D contain this error.

    Tenses: The first part uses the present perfect tense (has expanded). Using the past tense (did) leads to a tense inconsistency. The correct structure would be: 'X has happened, but Y & Z have also happened.' Option E contains this error.

    Conjunctions: The options present a choice between "and" and "but." "But" is used for contrasts. The sentence intends to say that America's nuclear arsenal has expanded (a situation that is threatening and negative for other countries) but at the same time India's and Pakistan's nuclear arsenals have also expanded (thus, alleviating India's and Pakistan's worries, or perhaps increasing the worry for all remaining countries). So, "but" is appropriate. Options B and D contain this error.

    The correct answer is option C.

133. Concepts tested: Grammatical Construction, SVA

    The intended meaning of the sentence:

The sentence intends to state that given the decline in memory with age, for a correct experiment, a group tested for memory loss caused by drugs must be compared with a control group.

Concept discussion:

Grammatical construction: Certain phrases have specific structures that need to be maintained. Phrases such as "it is important," "it is necessary," "it is imperative" have the following structure:

Phrase + that + subject + bare infinitive: Example: It is important that this work **be** finished by midnight (not "is") [Bare infinitive = infinitive form of the verb without "to"]. Also, in this structure, the insertion of "should" or "would" or any other auxiliary is not permitted.

In the given sentence, the structure needs to be "... **it is important that** a group (subject) ... be (bare infinitive) compared with a control group."

Using "are," "should" or "to" before "be compared" would break the grammatical structure.

All options except A contain this error.

SVA: Using the plural verbs "are compared" or "are to be compared" for the singular subject "a group" is incorrect. Options B and D contain this error.

The correct answer is option A.

134. Concepts tested: Grammatical Construction, Concision

   The intended meaning of the sentence:

   The sentence talks about a condition required by most MBA programs. The majority of MBA programs make it mandatory for potential applicants to complete their undergraduate work before applying.

   Concept discussion:

   Grammatical Construction: Certain verbs have specific structures that need to be maintained. Verbs such as "require," "recommend," "order," and "mandate" have one of the following two structures:

   (1) Verb + that + subject + bare infinitive: Example: The doctor recommended that she take her medicine (not take) [Bare infinitive = infinitive form of the verb without "to"]. Also, in this structure, insertion of "should" or "would" or any other auxiliary is not permitted.

   (2) Verb + object + infinitive + object: Example: The doctor ordered her to take her medicine.

   Similarly, in this case, the sentence can be:

   "Programs mandate that applicants be finished with their degrees."

   OR

   "Programs mandate applicants to finish their degrees"

   Options B and C contain this error.

Sentence Correction Guide – Solutions

Concision: Using "have a mandate" when "mandate" can be directly used as a verb is unnecessarily wordy. Options D and E contain this error.

The correct answer is option A.

135. Concepts tested: Grammatical construction, Logic

    The intended meaning of the sentence:

    The CEO of a company has proposed a new policy in which employees can retain their pensions for any length of time, or employees can cash the pensions in when they retire.

    Concept discussion:

    Grammatical construction: Certain verbs have specific structures that need to be maintained. Verbs such as "require," "recommend," "order" have one of the following two structures:

    (1) Verb + that + subject + bare infinitive: Example: The teacher recommended that she study her notes (not "studies") [Bare infinitive = infinitive form of the verb without "to"]. Also, in this structure, insertion of "should" or "would" or any other auxiliary is not permitted. Option A contains this error.

    (2) Verb + object + infinitive + object: Example: The teacher ordered her to study her notes.

    In the given sentence, the verb "require" will also need one of these two structures. Some options present the word "that" while others present "to"; however, some options do not present such a structure at all. Options C and D contain this error.

    Logic: In Option B, what is being retained? The answer is pensions. In the second part of the sentence, however, what is the subject of the verb "be allowed"? Logically, we know it is meant to be "employees," but this option only provides "all pensions" as a possible subject, which is, of course, not correct.

    The correct answer is option E.

136. Concepts tested: Grammatical construction

    The intended meaning of the sentence:

    The sentence describes the President's order to the intelligent agencies in light of the attack on the World Trade Center. The order is to prepare a list of America's most wanted terrorists.

    Concept discussion:

    Grammatical construction: Certain verbs have specific structures that need to be maintained. Verbs such as "require," "recommend," and "order" have one of the following two structures:

    (1) Verb + that + subject + bare infinitive: Example: The parent recommended that the child go to bed early. (not "goes") [Bare infinitive = infinitive form of the verb without "to"] Also, in this structure, insertion of "should" or "would" or any other auxiliary is not permitted.

    (2) Verb + object + infinitive + object: Example: The parent ordered the child to go to bed early.

In the given sentence, the verb "order" will also need one of these two structures. Since no option presents the word "that" after "order," we cannot use the first structure discussed above. It needs to be the second structure, i.e. followed by "to + verb" after "order." Only option E does this. Every other option contains an error with this.

The correct answer is option E.

Sentence Correction Guide – Solutions 247

6.10 Concision

137. <u>Concepts tested</u>: Concision, Redundancy, Awkwardness

    <u>The intended meaning of the sentence</u>:

    Even though Saul had fought against abortion when he was a teenager, he eventually became a supporter of family planning (he became the head of the Planned Parenthood Association).

    (Planned parenting refers to using methods of birth control, and using the option of abortion if necessary to help with family planning.)

    <u>Concept discussion</u>:

    Concision and Redundancy: The use of the word "teenager" automatically refers to a specific set of years; using "in the years" or "the time of" with "teenager" is redundant. Also, using "as a teenager" is most appropriate because that is the typical idiomatic way. For example: She was always cranky *as a baby* but she is no longer that way *as an adult*. Options C, D and E contain this error.

    Redundancy: Using "while" with another contrast conjunction ("although") is redundant. Option A contains this error.

    Awkwardness: To say "being a teenager" is awkward; it is a state of existence, but not a continuous activity. One cannot say "I am being a teenager." Options A and E contain this error.

    The correct answer is option B.

138. <u>Concepts tested</u>: Concision, Idioms, Pronouns

    <u>The intended meaning of the sentence</u>:

    The sentence describes why the UN arms inspectors are reviewing Iraq's arsenal of weapons. The reason is to determine whether the requirements set by the Security Council are being met by Iraq.

    <u>Concept discussion</u>:

    Concision: The sentence presents various forms of "determine," i.e. "for the determination of," "for the determining of," "determining" and "to determine." When providing reasons for a particular action, using a "to verb" is the clearest, crispest structure.

    For example: I went to the theatre to watch a movie.

    "I went to the theatre for watching/for the watching of" will not convey the intended meaning in the crispest possible way.

    Similarly, in the given sentence, "the inspectors are reviewing Iraq's arsenal to determine whether..."

    All options except D contain this error.

    Idioms: Using "whether" automatically implies "yes or no." Thus, "whether" and "or not" are incorrect. Options B and C contain this error.

    Pronouns: Using the plural pronoun "they" to refer to the singular noun "arsenal" is incorrect. In fact, the intended meaning can be conveyed without using pronouns at all.

Thus, pronouns can be avoided, especially since they often create ambiguity. Options A and B contain this error.

The correct answer is option E.

139. Concepts tested: Concision, Meaning, Active/Passive Voice

    The intended meaning of the sentence:

    In spite of the costly set up initially, the electrification led to increased work efficiency while cutting energy costs in half.

    Concept discussion:

    Concision and Meaning: Using "the electrification of lighting" is essential because it conveys the correct meaning; "lighting electrification" may sound concise but does not convey the proper meaning. For example: "moderate alcohol consumption" is concise but ambiguous: what is moderate – alcohol or consumption? The clearer version would be "moderate consumption of alcohol." Options D and E contain this error.

    Active/Passive Voice: Generally, everything else being equal, active voice is preferred to passive voice. Using "costs were cut" is unnecessary when the active/direct version "cutting costs" is available. Options A, C and D contain this error.

    The correct answer is option B.

140. Concepts tested: Concision, Awkwardness

    The intended meaning of the sentence:

    Historians and philosophers regard 'Plato's work' as the ultimate work of political philosophy and describe it as a paradigm of political discourse that cannot be surpassed.

    Concept discussion:

    Concision and Awkwardness: This question has to do with efficiency of language. We need the clearest and most concise, but least awkward, way of describing Plato's work.

    Analysis of the options

    A. This option is **incorrect** because 'it was' makes the sentence unnecessarily wordy. The construction is incorrect in using a sentence after the comma, making a comma splice error.

    B. This option is **correct** because the unnecessary words have been omitted for clarity and concision. The descriptive modifier 'the one paradigm...' is placed directly after the comma, leading to a clear construction.

    C. This option is **incorrect** because the use of 'for' (meaning "because") changes the intended meaning, suggesting that historians and philosophers argued because Plato's work was the one paradigm of political discourse. However, no such meaning was suggested originally.

    D. This option is **incorrect** because this option changes the meaning by its use of 'a paradigm' rather than 'the paradigm.' 'A paradigm' implies that there were others and that this was not the trendsetter it is made out to be in the first half of the sentence. Also, using "there was" is awkward because it is unnecessary.

    E. This option is **incorrect** because the use of *'as being'* is unnecessary and awkward.

The correct answer is option B.

6.11 Idioms

141. Concepts tested: Idioms, Parallelism

The intended meaning of the sentence:

Schools policies do not stop a teacher from scolding a student or from calling the student's parents based only on another child's accusations. The teachers are allowed to do so.

Concept discussion:

Idioms: "Forbid" can be used in one of the following ways:

- **(A)** Forbid someone from verb-ing – I forbid him from watching TV.
- **(B)** Forbid someone to verb – I forbid him to watch TV.
- **(C)** Forbid something [noun] – The rules forbid smoking on train.

Using "that" or verb-ing" directly after "forbid" is incorrect. Options C and E contain this error.

Parallelism: The use of the conjunction "or" necessitates parallelism. Parallel structure would be either "forbid a teacher from scolding...or calling..." or "forbid a teacher to scold...or to call..." Any mismatch will break the parallelism. Option A contains this error. If option D had used "the" before "calling" and turned it into a noun ("the calling" like "the scolding") as well, it could have been considered further. So, option D is also incorrect.

The correct answer is option B.

142. Concepts tested: Idioms, Comparison

The intended meaning of the sentence:

Lawyers can make highly persuasive arguments, because of which juries find it difficult to differentiate between the innocent and the guilty; DNA testing helps in such circumstances by preventing innocent people from being convicted.

Concept discussion:

Idioms: "Distinguish" can be used in one of the following two ways:

(1) Distinguish between X and Y – It's difficult to *distinguish between* human cells *and* those of rats.

(2) Distinguish X from Y – It's difficult to *distinguish* human cells *from* those of rats.

No other structure is correct. Options B, D and E contain an error with this.

Note: The word "differentiate" also follows the same idiomatic structure as "distinguish."

Comparison: While both options A and C are idiomatic, option C contains an incorrect comparison. The juries find it difficult to separate "the innocent" from "the guilty." Using "that of" is incorrect because there is nothing for it to refer to. If the sentence were "juries find it difficult to separate the behavior of the innocent from that (behavior) of the guilty," "that of" could have been used. Option C is incorrect.

The correct answer is option A.

143. Concepts tested: Idioms, Pronoun mismatch

The intended meaning of the sentence:

The music pieces that were performed in the latest concert demonstrate that the musicians have combined styles of music from the Middle East with styles of music from Russia.

Concept discussion:

Idioms: "Combined" pairs with "with"; for example: To get yellow, combine blue with green. The preposition "to" or use of the word "and" is incorrect. Options A, B and E contain this error.

Note: Even "correlate" and "connect" pair with "with."

Pronoun mismatch: Using the singular pronoun "that" to refer to the plural noun "styles of music" is incorrect. "Those" will correctly refer to the noun "styles." Options A, B and C contain this error.

The correct answer is option D.

144. Concepts tested: Idioms, Rhetorical Construction

The intended meaning of the sentence:

Initially, the two proposals look very similar, but if one reads the details, one can find that between the corollaries (a derivative statement), concepts on expanding production have been put forth.

Concept discussion:

Idioms: The idiom is "sandwiched between" and not "sandwiched among"; it means "hidden/ squeezed between." Example: I was sandwiched between a sweaty person and a sleeping person on the train ride home. Options B and D contain this error.

Rhetorical construction: The second half of the non-underlined part "how production could be expanded" refers to "concepts" that have been propounded. Thus, "concepts" should immediately precede the clause "how production could be expanded" to make the clearest construction. If the verb "propounded" is put before the clause "how production could be expanded," clarity is less. Options A, D and E contain this error.

The correct answer is option C.

145. Concepts tested: Idioms, Diction

The intended meaning of the sentence:

Even though many of the ideas were derived from looking at the work of colleagues in the field, the Senate still wanted to conduct its own independent verification.

Concept discussion:

Idioms: "Access": when used as a noun, it should be followed by the preposition "to"; for example: I have access to the codes. However, when "access" is used in the gerund form (verb-ing), it cannot take any preposition (to, into, in). Options C, D and E contain this error.

Diction: "Much" and "many" differ in their use; "much" is used for uncountable things whereas, "many" is used for countable things. Countable nouns are those that can be actually counted – one star, two stars, three stars…so on and so forth: Thus, "stars" are considered countable. Uncountable nouns cannot be counted (and thus, cannot be made plural) – one rice, two rice…cannot be done. Thus, "rice" is considered uncountable.

Note: sometimes the phrase "as much as" [or even "much as"] is used to indicate contrast; for example: "As much as I like being with you, I have to leave now." In such a situation, "as much as" cannot be substituted by "as many as."

In the given sentence, a contrast is being indicated – "As much as those ideas were derived from accessing the work of colleagues, the Senate insisted on …."

To denote contrast, we will have to use "as much as" and not "as many as." Option B contains this error.

Note:

Countable nouns	Uncountable nouns
Fewer	Less
Many	Much
Number	Amount

The correct answer is option A.

146. Concepts tested: Idioms, Tenses

    The intended meaning of the sentence:

    According to the committee's latest proposal, the money allotted to research on hereditary diseases will be increased to adhere to the wishes of the specifications in the will; this will keep the criticism of the fund trustees at bay.

    Concept discussion:

    Idioms: "Research" can be followed by either "on" or "into." However, "abide" can be followed by "by" but not "to" or "with." "Abide by" is used to mean "follow/adhere to" – The members abide by all the rules of the group. Options A, B and C contain this error.

    Also, "ward" is followed by "off" to mean "keep something away" – Sage is burned to ward off evil, according to ancient traditions. No other preposition can be used instead of "off." Options B and C contain this error.

    Tenses: The sentence intends to convey that something is being done to prevent criticism. Thus, the budget is being increased. We need to use the passive form to imply that it is being done, i.e. "budget will be increased" or "the budget has *been* increased." Not using the passive form will imply it happened on its own – "the budget increased." Option E contains this error.

    The correct answer is option D.

147. Concepts tested: Idioms, Awkwardness

    The intended meaning of the sentence:

    Buffalo squirrels, which have human-like cries and red fur, are very common in Southeast Asia, but are native to South Africa and were brought to India by British colonialists, who had them as pets.

Sentence Correction Guide – Solutions

Concept discussion:

Idioms: "Common" is followed by "in" to mean "available plentifully/found commonly in some place/time": Mangoes are common in India in the summer. "Common to" is used to mean "always present in all": for example: this feature is common to all applications on this platform. "Common to" in such a context is incorrect since we intend to suggest that the squirrels are commonly found in Southeast Asia. Options B and D contain this error.

Also, "native of" means "citizen of/belongs to": Chris is a native of Russia but he moved to the UK. "Native to" means "originated in/indigenous to": The plant neem is native to/indigenous to India. In the given context, we need to state that the squirrel is actually indigenous to South Africa but was introduced elsewhere by the British. Thus, we need "native to" and not "native of." Option C contains this error.

Awkwardness: Using "having" for "red fur" is awkward because "having" can also mean "eating" [I am having my dinner late today]. Also, "having" could end up applying to both "red fur" and "human-like cries," making it ambiguous and more awkward. Without "having," the intended meaning is conveyed. Options A and C contain this error.

The correct answer is option E.

148. Concepts tested: Idioms, Conciseness and clarity

    The intended meaning of the sentence:

    Chemists at the Carnegie Research Center seem to have discovered super glue that belongs to a type never seen before.

    Concept discussion:

    Idioms: Believe is/to be: "Believe" can be followed by both "is" and "to be" but when "who" believes is not present, using "to be" is necessary: For example,

    The scientists have discovered an insect believed to be the pollinator of the night orchids.

    In the given sentence, both "is" and "to be" will work.

    However, we need the preposition "of"; the sentence implies that the glue *belongs to* a type not seen yet, but not that the glue itself is a type not seen yet. Thus, to show the possession we need to say "the glue is of a type never seen before." Options A, D and E contain this error.

    Conciseness and clarity: Using the pronoun "it" to refer to "glue" when another pronoun ("one") has already been used is needless and awkward. Without "it," the sentence is concise and clear. Option C contains this error.

    The correct answer is option B.

149. Concepts tested: Idioms, Active/Passive voice, Rhetorical Construction

    The intended meaning of the sentence:

    Books that discuss the wilderness of Canada portray grizzly bears as extremely wild animals that roar fiercely from the tops of the mountains. In truth, the bears are not really that ferocious, and are actually playful and sociable, and will attack only if they or their cubs are in danger.

Concept discussion:

Idioms: "Portray" should always be followed by "as," and not by "to be" or any other structure; for example:

The media portrayed him as a cruel dictator.

Options D and E contain this error.

Note: The same rule also applies for "regard," view" and "think"; these too must be followed by "as."

Active/Passive – The active construction "books portray bears as..." is better than the passive construction "bears are portrayed in books as...." Option C contains this error.

Rhetorical Construction: Using a preposition in the subject is unnecessary. "Books" is the subject of the verb "portray." Using "in" with "books" is unnecessary because it does not form a proper subject, but instead becomes a prepositional phrase, which is ideally used as a modifier.

Correct: In books, bears are portrayed as savage.

Correct: Books portray bears as savage.

Incorrect: In books portray bears as savage.

Option B contains this error.

The correct answer is option A.

150. Concepts tested: Idioms, Tenses

The intended meaning of the sentence:

A NATO spokesman made an announcement that emphasized that the UN mandate (rule) that makes a distinction between Serb councils and Albanian exile councils; Serb councils had been democratically elected before they were disbanded (dispersed/scattered), whereas, Albanian councils are exiles returning from Macedonia.

Concept discussion:

Idioms: Idiomatically, "distinguish" can be used in one of the following two ways:

(A) distinguish X from Y: Scientists distinguish humans from primates in many ways.

(B) distinguish between X and Y: Scientists distinguish between humans and primates in many ways.

No other style is acceptable. In the given sentence, X is "Serb councils" while Y is "Albanian councils."

Options B and E do not use any of the above two acceptable structures, and thus, are incorrect.

Option D uses "between X from Y" instead of "between X and Y," making it incorrect.

Note: The above two idiom structures are also exactly applicable for "differentiate." The phrase "make a distinction" works with the second idiom structure.

Tenses: The sentence states that Serbian councils were (first) democratically elected and (then) disbanded. Thus, it is clear that they no longer actually exist as councils. So, we cannot use anything other than past tense for "elected": either "had been elected" or

Sentence Correction Guide – Solutions

"were" elected are correct, but not "have been elected" since they no longer exist. Option C contains this error.

The correct answer is option A.

151. <u>Concepts tested</u>: Idioms, Diction, Awkwardness

    <u>The intended meaning of the sentence:</u>

    The mayor has given recognition to a grassroots organization (an organization dealing with the basic necessities or with the lowest strata); the organization has helped residents from poor areas unite.

    <u>Concept discussion:</u>

    Idioms: "Aid" must always be followed by "in verb-ing" and not by "to + verb"; for example:

    Correct – I need your aid in finishing the job.

    Incorrect – I need your aid to finish the job.

    Options C, D and E contain this error.

    <u>Note</u>: Like "aid," "skill," "precision," and "interest," too, must be followed by "in verb-ing" and not by "to + verb."

    Diction: Saying "neighborhoods that are impoverished" is awkward because it is equivalent to saying "behavior that is criminal" or "development that is economic"; instead, the best diction is "impoverished neighborhoods," "criminal behavior," or "economic development." Options C and E contain this error.

    <u>Note</u>: This should not be confused with certain ambiguous combinations that are avoidable, such as "moderate alcohol consumption," which is incorrect, and "moderate consumption of alcohol," which is correct. Adding prepositions to phrases generally aids clarity; however, adding a "that" clause lengthens the sentences needlessly. See the table below to get a clearer idea of correct and incorrect structures.

Incorrect (ambiguous)	**Correct (clear)**	**Incorrect (awkward)**	**Correct (appropriately concise)**
Moderate alcohol consumption	Moderate consumption of alcohol	Development that is economical	Economic development
		Behavior that is criminal	Criminal behavior
Nut allergy	Allergy to nuts	Neighborhoods that are impoverished	Impoverished neighborhoods
Internet access	Access to internet		
Rice price rise	Price rise of rice		

    Options A and B contain this error.

    Awkwardness: Option B needlessly uses the noun form "the drawing together of," which is awkward and wordy compared to the verb form of "drawing together."

The correct answer is option A.

152. Concepts tested: Idioms and Concision

    The intended meaning of the sentence:

    The sentence states that a consultant was hired by a pharmaceutical company to supervise a division that was studying the effect that lower salaries would have on employees' morale.

    Concept discussion:

    Idioms and Concision: The correct structure is "effect of something on something else." This is also the clearest and most concise structure possible. Options C and E are unidiomatic. Also, using "as to," "what," etc. are needlessly lengthy, making the structure wordy. Options A, C and E contain this error.

    The correct answer is option B.

153. Concepts tested: Idioms

    The intended meaning of the sentence:

    The sentence talks about the change in the range of performance of the local orchestra. The sentence tells us that local orchestra used to perform everything from Bach and Handel to Bartok. [Note this part emphasizes the range of performance of the local orchestra earlier.] However, now the orchestra appears to have reduced its repertoire to only baroque music. [Note: the range of performance has reduced.].

    Concept discussion:

    Idioms: Idiomatically "from" should always be paired with "to," i.e. : *from X to Y* to express the range of performance of the local orchestra. Using "from Bach and Handel **and** Bartok" is incorrect. Options B, C and E contain this error.

    Also, "appears" should generally be followed by "to + verb." For example: The storm appears to have subsided in magnitude. Any other structure is not appropriate. Options B, C and D contain this error.

    The correct answer is option A.

154. Concepts tested: Idiom, Active/Passive voice

    The intended meaning of the sentence:

    The sentence intends to reflect the view of the average American on sexual harassment and contrast this view with the view of 75 percent of all women. It says that 75% of all women report experiencing sexual harassment in the workplace.

    Concept discussion:

    Idioms: The correct idiom is "think of something **as** something else." Using "to be" or "being" instead of "as" is unidiomatic. Options A, B and C contain this error.

    Active/ Passive: Passive voice is generally best avoided since GMAT prefers active voice. Thus, between options E and D, the best answer is option D.

    The correct answer is option D.

Sentence Correction Guide – Solutions

155. Concepts tested: Parallel structure

    The intended meaning of the sentence:

    The sentence describes what the recently discovered notes of the writer revealed. The notes revealed that the female writer was intellectually exceptional, someone who was guided in both emotional and spiritual activities by strong moral courage.

    Concept discussion:

    Parallel structure "Both" must be paired with "and" and the two parts that this conjunction joins must be parallel. Options B, D and E contain this error. For the sentences that contain a "that" clause in the second part, it is necessary that a corresponding "that" clause appear in the first part. If it does not, then it is incorrect. Options C and D contain this error.

    The correct answer is option A.

156. Concepts tested: Idioms, Concision

    The intended meaning of the sentence:

    The sentence presents a contrast based on views on coffee. On one hand it's not regarded as a drug, on the other its addiction makes it a crucial part of breakfast for many.

    Concept discussion:

    Idioms: To suggest the intensity of any particular thing, "so" or "such" must be paired with "that." Example – The bus was so crowded that I could not board it. There were such crowds I could not board the bus. Options B, C and D contain this idiom error.

    Concision: Using "there is" without any particular referent is awkward and wordy, and 'so much addiction' makes the sentence unnecessarily complex. Option E contains this error.

    The correct answer is option A.

157. Concepts tested: Idioms, Pronoun ambiguity

    The intended meaning of the sentence:

    In a bizarre (weird) case, the judge ruled that because ping-pong ball manufacturers illegally weighted ping-pong balls in order to fix the tournament, these manufacturers were obliged to compensate the four national ping-pong teams.

    Concept discussion:

    Idioms: The correct idiom is *'owed restitution to x for y.'* Option D contains this error.

    Pronoun ambiguity: Using the pronoun "their" or "they" in this sentence is ambiguous because it can refer to "manufacturers" or "teams." Options B, C and D contain this error.

    The correct answer is option A.

158. Concepts tested: Modifiers

    The intended meaning of the sentence:

    The sentence talks about the action taken by ranchers in order to achieve two purposes: shorten the time span and cut the costs needed to raise full-size beef stock. The action is to replace their cattle's regular diet with cornmeal and ground bones. The sentence further tells us that the cattle receiving this diet have been branded generic-grade beef by the ranchers.

Concept discussion:

Modifier: The modifier "branded by them to become generic beef" intends to describe the cattle, not "cattle's regular diet." [What's branded by farmers to become generic beef? Cattle or cattle's diet? Cattle, of course, will become beef, and not the cattle's diet (grass)! Option A contains this modifier error. Option C uses "having been branded," which would refer to "ranchers," making it incorrect.

The correct answer is option B.

159. Concepts tested: Idioms, Meaning

The intended meaning of the sentence:

The US has recessions every 20 years and in the period between the recessions, the economic cycle does not change much, enabling analysts to predict market trends.

Concept discussion:

Idiom and Meaning: The word "between" is important in the sentence in order to convey the correct meaning. The sentence is discussing the economic cycle in the period/interval between recessions/downturns. "Interval" is a phase between two events, and to refer to it, using "between" is necessary. Not using "between" will be unidiomatic and will not convey the correct meaning. Options B, D and E contain this error.

Also, the meaning implies multiple "recessions" (at least two, in which there is an interval period). Simply using "recessing" will not jibe with the rest of the sentence. Using "recessions" is necessary. Option A contains this error.

The correct answer is option C.

Sentence Correction Guide - Solutions

6.12 Diction

160. Concepts tested: Diction, Comparisons

The intended meaning of the sentence:

If the draft (conscription for military service) is not reinstated (put back) in the next decade, the number of people joining the army will be the lowest of all decades.

Concept discussion:

Diction: "Fewer" is used for countable nouns, whereas, "less" is used for uncountable nouns. Countable nouns are those that can be actually counted – 1 star, 2 stars. 3 stars... so on and so forth: Thus, "stars" are considered countable. Uncountable nouns cannot be counted (and thus, cannot be made plural) – 1 rice, 2 rice... cannot be done. Thus, "rice" is considered uncountable.

"People" are countable [1 person, 2 people...]. Thus, we have to use "fewer" and not "less." Options A and B contain this error.

Note:

Countable nouns	Uncountable nouns
Fewer	Less
Many	Much
Number	Amount

Comparisons: "As" always pairs with "as" whereas, "more" or "less" pairs with "than."

Correct – She is *as* intelligent *as* John.

Correct – She is *more* intelligent *than* John.

Incorrect – She is *as* intelligent *than* John.

Incorrect – She is *more* intelligent *as* John.

For the options that contain "fewer" (an equivalent of "less"), we can only use "than" (fewer ... than) and not "as." Options B, C and D contain an error with "as."

The correct answer is option E.

161. Concepts tested: Diction, Comparisons

The intended meaning of the sentence:

There is a lot of fear among people about the obesity epidemic in America, where the average person consumes three times as much as a Japanese person does.

Concept discussion:

Diction: "Thrice" is better than "three times," just as "once" is better than "one time" or "twice" is better than "two times." "Triple" is also awkward. Options C, D and E contain this error.

Comparisons: Using "of" and apostrophe "s" is redundant.

Consider:

Correct: The cart's wheel is broken. [apostrophe "s" denoting possession]

Correct: The wheel of the cart is broken. ["of" denoting possession]

Incorrect: The wheel of cart's is broken.

In the given sentence, using "that of" to refer to "amount of food" is enough. Using "Japan's consumption" with "that of" is incorrect. Option B contains this error.

The correct answer is option A.

162. Concepts tested: Diction, Redundancy

    The intended meaning of the sentence:

    The president implemented some ill-advised (not good) economic policies, which affected both employed people and jobless people; as a result, many people were balanced on the edge of poverty in a very shaky manner.

    Concept discussion:

    Diction: "Amounts," "quantities" and "numbers" differ in their use; "Amounts" and "quantities" are used for uncountable things, whereas, "numbers" is used for countable things. Countable nouns are those that can be actually counted – 1 star, 2 stars. 3 stars...so on and so forth: Thus, "stars" are considered countable. Uncountable nouns cannot be counted (and thus, cannot be made plural) – 1 rice, 2 rice...cannot be done. Thus, "rice" is considered uncountable.

    In the given sentence, we need to refer to people (countable: 1 person, 2 people...) and thus, only "numbers" can be used but not "amounts" or "quantities." Options A, B and E contain this error.

    Note:

Countable nouns	Uncountable nouns
Fewer	Less
Many	Much
Number	Amount/Quantity

    Redundancy: Using "both" and "alike" to reinforce the fact that two groups are hurt by this move is unnecessary. Either "both" or "alike" will be sufficient. Options B and D contain this error.

    The correct answer is option C.

163. Concepts tested: Diction, Idioms, SVA

    The intended meaning of the sentence:

    The prime interest rate has been fluctuating quite a lot in the last month and there has been flight of capital from the economy (people have taken their investments out and invested elsewhere); despite this, the economy has maintained production, currency level, and exports.

    Concept discussion:

    Diction: "Stationery-stationary": "Stationery" means writing paraphernalia such as pen, paper, etc. "Stationary" means "not moving, fixed in a spot or a place." In the given sentence, the meaning needed is that certain things remain fixed, and thus, we need "stationary" and not "stationery." Options A and D contain this error.

Idioms: "Flight" can be followed by "of" or "from" but each means different things.

Flight of something – to show what has "flown away" or left; for example: The flight of the birds to the south happens in winter.

Flight from something – When someone flies away/runs away from something; for example: The criminal's flight from prison was short-lived.

"Flight by" is incorrect. Option B contains this error.

In the given sentence, we need the meaning that "capital/money invested" has "flown away" [from the economy] and not that something has "flown away from capital." Option D and E contain this error.

SVA: What has remained stationary? The economy, in its various aspects. The subject "the economy" is singular and will take the singular verb "has" but not the plural verb "have." Option A contains this error.

The correct answer is option C.

164. <u>Concepts tested</u>: Diction, Grammatical construction, Meaning

    <u>The intended meaning of the sentence:</u>

    Even if the company had lot of money and a large staff, the emission of the poisonous gases could not have been prevented because the plant itself was flawed; this was acknowledged reluctantly by the Bhopal Inquiry.

    <u>Concept discussion:</u>

    Diction: "Number" is used for countable nouns whereas, "amount" is used for uncountable nouns (that are quantities and not numbers). Countable nouns are those that can be actually counted – 1 star, 2 stars. 3 stars…so on and so forth: Thus, "stars" are considered countable. Uncountable nouns cannot be counted (and thus, cannot be made plural) – 1 rice, 2 rice…cannot be done. Thus, "rice" is considered uncountable.

    "Money" is considered uncountable [1 money, 2 moneys is not possible] Thus, we can use "amount." However, "staff" is not a quantity, but neither is it a number. Thus, we cannot use "amount" with "staff" nor can we use "number"; instead a size-describing word such as "big" or "large" can be used. Using "amount" will be absolutely incorrect. Options A and B contain this error.

    Grammatical construction: Since the portion after the non-underlined part contains a verb, forming a clause is necessary. Thus, we need a subject for the verb "could have prevented." "No matter how X or Y" does not make a proper subject for the verb "could have prevented." If the structure were: "No matter how X or Y were, the explosion could not have been prevented," it would be acceptable. Instead "Neither X nor Y" can make a proper subject for the verb "could have prevented." Option C contains this error.

    Meaning: Using "increasing" to describe "staff" would suggest an ongoing activity rather than suggesting "a big staff." However, the sentence does not imply any continuous activity. Thus, option E changes the meaning, making it incorrect.

    Options A and B contain this error.

    The correct answer is option D.

165. Concepts tested: Diction, Comparisons

The intended meaning of the sentence:

The refugees living in the camp revealed, in a survey, that they considered themselves the same as people living in the US.

Concept discussion:

Diction: While "no <comparative> than" is similar in meaning to "not <comparative> than," the former is standard and the latter is not the standard usage. Thus, we cannot use "not worse than" but have to use "no worse than," which is standard and appropriate. Options B, C and E contain this error.

Comparisons: In comparisons, the helping verb depends on the original verb. If the original verb is "to have," the helping verb will also be a form of "to have".

I *have* attempted more exams than my brother *has*. (not does/is)

Similarly, if the original verb is "to be," the helping verb will also be a form of "to be" [forms of "to be" – was, were, am, is, are, will be]

I *am* studying faster than she *is*. (not does/has)

If the original verb is any other action verb, the helping verb will be a form of "to do."

I *study* faster than she *does*.

I *attempted* more exams than my brother *did*.

In the given sentence, the original verb is "considered" and thus, the helping verb should be a form of "to do" but not of "to be" because there is no form of "to be" in the original verb. Thus, "refugees *considered* themselves no worse off than *do* US citizens" is correct but not "refugees *consider* themselves no worse off than *are* US citizens." Option D contains this error.

The correct answer is option A.

166. Concepts tested: Diction, Conjunctions, Comparisons, Redundancy

The intended meaning of the sentence:

A lot of money is being spent on intercepting drugs (getting hold of drugs before the drugs are distributed); despite these efforts, the number of raids has doubled between 1996 and 1998.

Concept discussion:

Diction: "Number" is used for countable nouns whereas, "amount" is used for uncountable nouns. Countable nouns are those that can be actually counted – 1 star, 2 stars. 3 stars... so on and so forth: Thus, "stars" are considered countable. Uncountable nouns cannot be counted (and thus, cannot be made plural) – 1 rice, 2 rice... cannot be done. Thus, "rice" is considered uncountable.

"Seizures," meaning "raids," are countable [1 raid, 2 raids...]. Thus, we have to use "number" and not "amount." Option A contains this error.

Using "size" will not refer to "number" but to the amount seized each time. However, the implied meaning is for the number of raids rather than the amount seized each time. Option B is thus, incorrect.

Sentence Correction Guide – Solutions

Note:

Countable nouns	Uncountable nouns
Fewer	Less
Many	Much
Number	Amount

Conjunctions: "Between" must always be paired with "and," but not with "to." Options A, B and E contain this error.

Comparisons: Using both "more" and "twice" for increased is incorrect. The correct use would be "something increased twice" or "something more than doubled" to convey the appropriate meaning. Option C contains this error.

Redundancy: Using "in the years" along with "between" to denote the years is redundant. Saying "between 1993 and 1996" is sufficient and adding "in the years" is unnecessary. Option E contains this error.

The correct answer is option D.

167. Concepts tested: Diction, Awkwardness

The intended meaning of the sentence:

Three candidates are under consideration to be the replacement for Jones. They all have similar qualifications and are ideal, so selecting one from among them is difficult.

Concept discussion:

Diction: The preposition "between" is restricted to situations involving two entities whereas, "among" is used for situations involving more than two entities. Options A, C and E contain this error.

Also, "its" is a possessive pronoun for third person neuter gender – the dog was wagging its tail; but "it's" is used as an abbreviation for "it is/was/has." Options A and B contain this error.

The correct answer is option D.

168. Concepts tested: Diction

The intended meaning of the sentence:

Urban areas and rural areas have similar levels of incidence of drug abuse, though in some cases the level might be higher in rural areas than it is in urban areas.

Concept discussion:

Diction: Equal-high: Equal can mean number, but it does not have to. Example of "equal" as "number" - "we have an equal number of pets." To talk about number, the word "number" must be mentioned, without which there can be ambiguity, for example: "People are created equal" - not number but quality. Using "as high as" automatically compares incidence of one to that of another. You cannot use these to mean that things are equal/equivalent in quality.

Options A, B and D contain this error.

The correct answer is option E.

169. Concepts tested: Diction, Rhetorical Construction

    The intended meaning of the sentence:

    There has been improvement in the shipping of raw materials; this improvement has become a financial factor in Japan's becoming a world economic power.

    Concept discussion:

    Diction: "Economic" means "related to money or finance" whereas, "economical" means "cheap, affordable, viable"; For example: The economic (money-related) considerations of buying a car are many; Volkswagen is an economical (affordable) car.

    In the given sentence, we need the "money-related" definition, i.e. an improvement has become the (money-related) factor in Japan's transformation. Thus, we need to use "economic" but not "economical" (because the innovation is not necessarily an "affordable" factor in Japan's transformation). Options A, B and C contain this error.

    Rhetorical Construction: The subject of the sentence must always be crisp and clear, as well as be the reason for the sentence. In this case, what has become the factor in Japan's transformation – is it just shipping, or is it the improvement in shipping? It is the improved shipping that has become an economic factor. The subject "improvement in shipping of raw materials" is clear and crisp compared to "shipping of raw materials being improved," which puts the focus on "shipping" rather than on "improvement in shipping." Options A, C and D contain this error.

    The correct answer is option E.

170. Concepts tested: Diction, Parallelism, Rhetorical Construction

    The intended meaning of the sentence:

    Funding for space missions was reduced during the late 60s and 70s; it fell by seventy percent, from its maximum in 1968 to its minimum in 1977.

    Concept discussion:

    Diction: "At" is used for a specific point in time; for example: I will come over at 9:00. "During" is used for a length or duration of time; for example: I will study French during my vacation.

    In the given sentence, we're trying to refer the span of over a decade, during which funding was cut by about seventy percent. Thus, we need to use "during" and not "at." Options C and D contain this error.

    Parallelism: "From X to Y" is a common parallelism marker in which the X and Y parts must be parallel; "from its peak in 1986" is parallel with "to its nadir in 1977" and does not need the word "down." Also, using the word "down" with "fell" is redundant and awkward. Options A and C contain this error.

    Rhetorical Construction: The best placement for the phrase "nearly 70 percent" is right before the "from ...to..." part because if it is put after "from" or after "to," it can be ambiguously interpreted as referring only to "from" or "to"; however, the "by 70 percent" refers to the whole phrase "from 1969 to 1977" and not just to one of them. Options D and E contain this error.

    The correct answer is option B.

Sentence Correction Guide – Solutions

171. <u>Concepts tested</u>: Diction, Concision

<u>The intended meaning of the sentence:</u>

The leader of a seminar on physics wanted to begin the discussions herself because not all knew that the material under discussion related to new theories that were unknown to many physicists.

<u>Concept discussion:</u>

Diction: Not everyone versus everyone did not: If we say "everyone did not know," the meaning would become that *nobody* knew (ALL did not know); however, from the second half of the sentence it is clear that some knew but some did not. To convey "some do but some don't," we need to say "not everyone knew." Options B, C and D contain this error.

For-with: "for" can mean "because"; for example: The nations can complicate matters in international meetings for (because) diplomacy is not easy.

"With" simply suggests "accompanying" in a general manner; for example: The seminar started off with a celebration.

In the given sentence, we need "because" since the sentence indicates that the reason the leader of a seminar on physics wanted to begin the discussions herself was that not everyone there knew the material under discussion. Thus, "because" or its equivalent is required; using "with" will not convey the meaning intended. Options C and D contain this error.

Concision: "knowledgeable" is needless when the verb form "know" can be used; it is direct and less wordy. Options A and D contain this error.

The correct answer is option E.

172. <u>Concepts tested</u>: Diction, Idioms

<u>The intended meaning of the sentence:</u>

A woman promised not to talk about her divorce with the media, but then she decided to do so because she believed that many women might appreciate her message of women rights.

<u>Concept discussion:</u>

Diction: When referring to actions aforementioned using "do so" is appropriate. For example: I asked you to clean your room; did you do so? [Do what? The aforementioned action – "clean your room."]

Similarly, in the given sentence, we need to refer to the aforementioned action (talk to the media); thus, using "do so" would be correct. Options B and C contain this error.

Idioms: "Likely most" is unidiomatic. Options A and B contain this error.

Finally, "likely" must be followed by "to verb" and not just "[verb]" i.e. "She is likely *to study*" but not "She will likely *study*." Options C and E contain this error.

The correct answer is option D.

173. <u>Concepts tested</u>: Parallelism

<u>The intended meaning of the sentence:</u>

The sentence describes the behavioral changes in Miruko: when she is at school and when she is in her home. While at school, she is antisocial and sullen, but she is bubbly and even-tempered at home.

Concept discussion:

Parallelism: The use of the conjunction "but" necessitates parallelism. The first half of the sentence deals with "at school" behavior, followed by "Miruko is XYZ"; thus, the second half, after "but" should be "at home," followed by "Miruko/she is PQR" to make it parallel. All options except A contain this error.

The correct answer is option A.

174. Concepts tested: Diction, Grammatical construction (like vs. as)

   The intended meaning of the sentence:

   Long ago it was found that hummingbirds can hover in a manner similar to insects flitting from flower to flower.

   Concept discussion:

   Diction: "Each" pairs with "other" while "one" pairs with "another." In this case, since "one" is used, we'll have to use "another," i.e. "from one flower to another." Any other combination is incorrect. Options C, D and E contain this error.

   Grammatical construction (like vs. as): 'Like' is used to compare nouns or pronouns. For example: Like Jane, her brother is a teacher. 'As' is used to introduce a clause, a group of words with a verb, including for comparison. For example: Jane teaches English, as does her brother. Using "as" without introducing a clause (containing a verb) is incorrect. Option A contains this error.

   The correct answer is option B.

6.13 Tenses

175. Concepts tested: Tenses, Grammatical construction, Concision

The intended meaning of the sentence:

Some people who believe in civil liberties are of the opinion that the best way to ensure freedom of religion for all citizens is to reduce the importance of the Judeo-Christian god [of Judaism or Christianity] in politics.

Concept discussion:

Tenses: The sentence discusses a general belief of the present, evidenced by "is to reduce…" Thus, we need to use simple present "insist" and not the present perfect "have insisted" [they insist the best way is this OR they have insisted the best way is this?]. Option B contains this error.

Also, option C is needlessly lengthy in using the adjective form "insistent" instead of the direct verb "insist," making it incorrect.

Grammatical construction: Options B contains an error with the past participle in the phrase "can be ensure" (should be "ensured").

Concision: The sentence presents various forms of "ensure," i.e. "for the ensuring of," "can be ensure" (incorrect) and "to ensure." When providing "ways," using "to verb" is the clearest, crispest structure.

For example: The way to solve the problem is patience.

"The way for solving/for the solving of/of solving the problem is patience" will not convey the intended meaning in the crispest possible way.

Similarly, in the given sentence, "the way to ensure something is to reduce something…"

Options D and E contain an error related to this.

The correct answer is option A.

176. Concepts tested: Tenses, Modifiers

The intended meaning of the sentence:

Scientists have found out that the inner ear helps in maintaining body orientation because people with problems in the inner ear have found it more difficult to maintain balance.

Concept discussion:

Tenses: The sentence is in the near present time, evidenced by the use of the present perfect "have determined"; thus, ideally, the other part should also be in the present perfect tense ("have been" rather than the past tense "were"). The past perfect tense is absolutely incorrect because it can only be used to indicate the earlier action of two actions in the past. Option D contains this error. Options A and C contain the passive voice (be + participle), and are also incorrect.

Modifiers: Increasing-increased: Both have different meanings; "increasing" will indicate a continuing activity, while "increased" will mean just "raised." The sentence does not indicate that the "difficulties" are increasing (on an ongoing basis); it seems more like the difficulties have increased with the problems in the inner ear. If the sentence contained some clue word like "progressive disorder" or "more and more" or any other structure indicating an ongoing increase, we could have used "increasing." Using "increasing" in the current structure is incorrect. Options C and E contain this error.

The correct answer is option B.

177. Concepts tested: Tenses, Diction

    The intended meaning of the sentence:

    Campbell became a well-known artist and poet as well as a leading activist for the rights of the mentally-challenged at a time when the differently-abled had very few opportunities.

    Concept discussion:

    Tenses: The sentence discusses a fixed point in the past – at a point in the past, when opportunities *were* few, Campbell *became* something. To discuss a point in the past, we cannot use the present perfect tense "have had" but will have to use simple past tense "had." Options A, D and E contain this error.

    Diction: The sentence discusses a point in the past, but not duration, denoted by the action "became." That is, Campbell became something at a point in the past (not during some time). Duration would have worked for another type of action; for example: Campbell campaigned about rights during the long months of winter. Thus, using words meant for "duration" such as "period," "in" or "during" will be inappropriate. Options A, B and D contain this error.

    The correct answer is option C.

178. Concepts tested: Tenses, Conjunctions, Pronoun ambiguity

    The intended meaning of the sentence:

    Social scientists have found out that caregivers subconsciously (unknown to their conscious mind) enjoy the opportunity to take care of someone; in fact, when their patients get better, the caregivers are disappointed (since they can no longer nurse the person).

    Concept discussion:

    Tenses: When using words like "when" (or "whenever," "every time"), the two clauses joined should be in similar tenses. For example:

    Correct – When I *watch* the movie Titanic, I *become* depressed.

    Correct – When I *watched* the movie Titanic, I *became* depressed.

    Incorrect – When I *watch* the movie Titanic, I *became* depressed.

    Incorrect – When I *watched* the movie Titanic, I *become* depressed.

    In the given sentence, the correct usage will be either "when patients *recover*, the workers *are* disappointed" or "when patients *recovered*, the workers *were* disappointed."

    Options B, C and D contain this error.

    Conjunctions: Using the conjunction "and" with a semicolon is incorrect. To join two sentences, one needs either a semicolon or a conjunction. For example:

    Correct: I need to rest; I am tired.

Sentence Correction Guide – Solutions

Correct: Because I am tired, I need to rest.

Incorrect: I need to rest, I am tired.

Incorrect: Because I am tired; I need to rest.

Option B contains this error.

Pronoun ambiguity: Using the plural pronoun "they" to refer to the noun "caregivers" is ambiguous given the presence of other plural nouns such as "sociologists." Option D contains this error.

The correct answer is option A.

179. Concepts tested: Tenses, Conjunctions, Modifiers

    The intended meaning of the sentence:

    Al Gore was the VP of the US, and similarly, his father had been a senator earlier.

    Concept discussion:

    Tenses: The entire sentence is in the past tense. Al Gore was the VP. Thus, his father must have been a senator even before Al Gore was the VP. Thus, the clause about the father needs to be in the past perfect tense (used to denote the earlier of two actions in the past). Only two options use the past perfect "had been," and the rest don't. Using the present tense or present perfect tense would indicate that the father still is a senator, something that is contraindicated by the "was" in the first half of the sentence. Options A, C and E contain this error.

    Conjunctions: The sentence contains two clauses and thus, needs a conjunction to join the two halves. Not using a conjunction is incorrect. Option E contains this error.

    Also, using "where," which is used to indicate places, is inappropriate. Option B contains this error.

    Modifier: The "earlier" is meant to modify the entire clause about the father being a senator. To place it before "father" indicates that Al Gore has an "earlier father" (and possibly a "later father"), creating an absurdity! Thus, the best placement for "earlier" is either before the clause begins or at the end of the clause, i.e. "earlier his father was a senator," or, "is father was a senator earlier." Options B, D and E contain this error.

    The correct answer is option C.

180. Concepts tested: Tenses, Rhetorical Construction, Meaning

    The intended meaning of the sentence:

    The members of the Smith family lost their money in gambling, and thus, they had to move from their current apartment (in the city) to a suburb near the city.

    Concept discussion:

    Tenses: The sentence discusses two events in the past "lost money" and "forced to move," of which "losing" happened earlier than "being forced to move." Thus, "forced to move" should be in the simple past; past perfect tense is reserved for earlier actions in the past, but only for when the sequence is not necessarily clear. So, we cannot use past perfect tense for "forced to move." Option B contains this error. Using "having" will also convey that it happened earlier, making the meaning incorrect. Option D contains this error.

Rhetorical Construction: The structure "from X to Y" is best used in this order, and not "to X from Y," which is awkward and ambiguous. Option A contains this error.

Meaning: Introducing a new word "withdrew" without any just cause is incorrect. "Withdrew" means to "retreat, possibly after a fight." No such hint has been given in the sentence to justify introducing this word. Option E contains this error.

The correct answer is option C.

181. Concepts tested: Tenses, SVA, Meaning

    The intended meaning of the sentence:

    The sentence talks about an award being given to a musician, Joan White, who is one of the eight musicians who performed in a function held at the end of the year.

    Concept discussion:

    Tenses: Options show different tenses of the verb "perform." The verb "perform" needs to be in the past perfect tense because it is the earlier event of two events in the past, i.e. the University gave an award to a musician who (before the award) had performed in a concert.

    Using "performs" (present tense) or "have performed" (present perfect tense) is incorrect for an action that happened before the university gave an award. Options B, C and E contain this error.

    SVA: Using the singular verb "performs" for the plural noun "musicians" is incorrect. The verb "performs" will not refer to "one of the musicians" but only to "musicians" because of the use of "who." Verbs right after "who," "which," "that" refer to the nouns right before "who," "which," "that." Options C and E contain this error.

    Meaning: Option D is incorrect because it does not match the sentence, as it lacks any verb showing past tense, thus, not correctly conveying the intended meaning of the sentence.

    The correct answer is option A.

182. Concepts tested: Tenses, Diction

    The intended meaning of the sentence:

    The sentence intends to say George Brown has lost more than 180 pounds from the time he had an operation truncating his stomach three years ago until now.

    Concept discussion:

    Tenses: The "losing of the weight" began three years ago when George had an operation and is continuing up to now, or is still in effect. For such events, using the present perfect tense "has lost" is appropriate. Using the simple past tense "lost" suggests that it is a one-time past activity, or that it is no longer valid. However, we know from the meaning that the losing weight is still valid. Options A and B contain this error.

    Diction: "Since" is the best word to indicate "from then on...till now." "Since" automatically draws a connection from past to present. "After" or "subsequently" do not necessarily connect the past to the present. Thus, using "since" in this sentence is necessary. Options D and E contain this error.

The correct answer is option C.

183. Concepts tested: Active/Passive, Comparison, Meaning

    The intended meaning of the sentence:

    The sentence presents a comparison between a student and his fellow students. The sentence states that this student is at least as brilliant as (if not more than) many of his fellow students, but he is very lazy and so he will not complete his thesis.

    Concept discussion:

    Active/Passive: In the second part of the sentence, there are two parts: "he is lazy" and "he will not finish his thesis." They are logically connected and joined by the conjunction "and" and thus, should be parallel too. In some options, the first part is in active voice (he is very lazy) but the second part is in passive voice (and his thesis will be unfinished). Options A and B contain this error. Note: Active voice is preferred to the passive voice in the GMAT.

    Comparison: When presenting dual comparison in the same sentence, i.e. "as <adjective> as" and "more <adjective> than," each comparison should be complete to make the structure grammatical. Leaving out "as" or "more" or "than" will make the structure ungrammatical. Option D contains this error.

    Meaning: The contrast word 'although' is used to express the contrast between the student's brilliance and laziness.' Not using any contrast word will change the intended meaning of the sentence. Option E contains this error.

    The correct answer is option C.

184. Concepts tested: Tenses, Concision

    The intended meaning of the sentence:

    The attorney for the defense made an extremely persuasive argument, weakening the prosecution's argument; the defense attorney was so successful that the jury was almost convinced that the victim did not even exist!

    Concept discussion:

    Tenses: The entire sentence is in the past: the defense attorney weakened... Thus, the jury's "doubting" should be in the past too. Further, the victim's "existing" is the earliest action in the past in this sentence; thus, for such an action the past perfect tense "had existed" must be used. Not using the past tense for the jury's "doubting" or not using the perfect tense for the victim's "existing" will be incorrect. Options B and E contain this error.

    Concision: In terms of crispness, options C and D are unnecessarily wordy.

    The correct answer is option A.

6.14 Conjunctions & Mood

185. Concepts tested: Conjunctions, Awkwardness

    The intended meaning of the sentence:

    Montreal spends a large part of its budget constructing tourist attractions even though it's not certain that constructing such attractions increases revenue from tourism.

    Concept discussion:

    Conjunctions: To indicate contrast, a contrast conjunction should be used [but, yet, though, although, even though]. "Even if" is not as appropriate a contrast conjunction as "even though" or "though." Only if answers cannot be found in options containing "even though" or "though," should we even consider the options containing "even if." Such options are A, B and C.

    Awkwardness: Option E is very awkwardly constructed with the use of "there is," "as to" and "increasing."

    Option D conveys the intended meaning without the use of pronouns (it) or placeholder subjects (there is); the option also shows the intended contrast that the city does something even though it is not sure that doing so increases revenue. Thus, there is no need to refer to the options containing the awkward contrast "even if" - options A, B and C.

    The correct answer is option D.

186. Concepts tested: Conjunctions, Grammatical Construction

    The intended meaning of the sentence:

    In a particular phase, Picasso would paint using bold (deep and vivid) strokes when he was inspired, and then he would be meditative (thoughtful) for days, painting with lightening strokes and shades before adding color.

    Concept discussion:

    Conjunctions: To join two clauses, a conjunction is necessary. In the given sentence, two clauses "would paint a bold stroke" is being joined with "(would) continue with ...," thus, necessitating the conjunction "and." Options A, B and E contain an error with this.

    Also, option C is incorrect because the placement of "but" should have been after the first clause, not before the two clauses, i.e. "Picasso would paint ... but continue..."

    Grammatical Construction: In the given sentence, the verb "paint" needs to function as one of the main verbs in the form "would paint" in order to make a logical statement. Without "would paint," the second verb "continue" would not be sustainable – "Picasso, painting stuff... continue..." "Picasso continue..." will not form a grammatically correct sentence, but if "would paint" is present, then taking "would" as common for both "paint" and "continue" forms a logical sentence: Picasso would paint ... and (would) continue with ..." So, we cannot turn "paint" into a modifier by using "painting" or "who ..." Options B, C and E contain this error.

    The correct answer is option D.

Sentence Correction Guide – Solutions

187. <u>Concepts tested</u>: Conjunctions, Agreement

<u>The intended meaning of the sentence</u>:

Some actors in a particular play have become known for the way in which they interact with the audience.

<u>Concept discussion</u>:

Conjunctions: "Between" must always pair with "and"; pairing "between" with "with," "to," or "or" is incorrect. Options A, C and D contain this error.

Agreement: The word 'actors' is plural. Therefore, the actors have become known as the plural "prime examples" and not the singular "a prime example." Options A and B contain this error.

The correct answer is option E.

188. <u>Concepts tested</u>: Conjunctions, Parallelism, Diction

<u>The intended meaning of the sentence</u>:

In a college, a rule has been passed; according to this rule, students can cook, serve and even buy food.

<u>Concept discussion</u>:

Conjunctions and Parallelism: Whenever we have more than one item in a list, we need a conjunction. For example: I like X and Y. [X, Y are two things in the list of things "I like."

Consider: I like pasta and cheese, as well as chocolates.

This means that I like two things X and Y, and X itself is two things: pasta and cheese.

Thus, in such an example, I need two conjunctions.

Said this way, the meaning is that I like pasta and cheese (together) as well as chocolates. Thus, I don't like just cheese or just pasta, but I like them together, and a separate thing that I like is chocolates.

If I said "I like, cheese, pasta and chocolates," that would not mean the above given meaning. It would mean that I like these three distinct things, not necessarily in combination.

Similarly, in the given example, the rule permits a student two main things: cook food or buy food; the cooking itself contains two activities - cook and serve food. It can't be three distinct activities - "the rule permits the student to cook, serve and buy" - because to suggest that a student who cooks and serves a meal will himself also buy a meal seems ridiculous. Why would a student who cooks and serves himself also buy a meal? Students can cook and serve food [one thing permitted by the rule] as well as buy food [second thing permitted by the rule].

Thus, to separate these two distinct activities of "cooking" and "buying" we need a conjunction, and a conjunction is also needed to separate the two activities that make up "cooking." All options except A contain this error.

Even if we think that there are three things permitted by the rule (cook, serve and buy), no option contains correct parallelism. Either all items in the list should contain "to" or only the first item should contain "to," i.e. I like to swim, to dance and to sing, or, I like to swim, dance and sing.

Similarly, in this example, the option should say either "to cook, to serve and to buy" or "to cook, serve and buy." Option B, C and D contain this error.

Diction: "As well as" can be used to join only 2 things; for more than two things, we can use only "and." In option A, "as well as" is joining two things: (1) to cook and serve, (2) to buy.

However, in options D and E, "as well as" is used to join three things: (1) to cook, (2) to serve, (3) to buy. Such use of "as well as" is incorrect. Options D and E contain this error.

The correct answer is option A.

189. Concepts tested: Conjunctions, Awkwardness

    The intended meaning of the sentence:

    People who consumed very little dairy as kids, notwithstanding the amount they consume as adults, seem to have a disadvantage of being prone to bone fractures; this phenomenon demonstrates the need to consume higher levels of calcium in childhood years.

    Concept discussion:

    Conjunctions: There is a difference between independent and dependent actions.

    For example: She entered the café and ordered a coffee – Entering the café and ordering the coffee are done independently of each other.

    Consider: The volcano exploded and blotted out the sun – the volcano exploded, but did the volcano blot out the sun? The volcano's exploding blotted out the sun. Thus, the volcano is not independently "blotting." Thus, we cannot make it parallel to "exploded." The "blotting" happened because of "exploding"; such dependent actions are presented in "verb-ing" formats or with a noun-modifier clause as follows:

    The volcano exploded, blotting out the sun. (verb-ing)

    The volcano exploded, a phenomenon that blotted out the sun. (noun-modifier clause)

    Similarly, in the given sentence:

    What's a disadvantage that suggests a need for higher calcium consumption in childhood? Being prone to fractures as a result of consuming less dairy is the disadvantage. It's not an independent activity. Do we want to imply that "low dairy-consuming people are prone to fractures and (separately) have a disadvantage"? That's not the intended meaning. The intended meaning is that "some people consumed very little dairy as kids and thus, became prone to fractures as adults, (resulting in) a disadvantage for them." Thus, using "and" will be incorrect as it will imply that the two parts are independent. Options B, C and E contain this error.

    Awkwardness: Using "having a disadvantage that ..." is unnecessary and awkward, making the option wordy. Option D contains this error.

    The correct answer is option A.

190. Concepts tested: Conjunctions, Mood

    The intended meaning of the sentence:

Sentence Correction Guide – Solutions

Both parents worked full-time, so they had a nanny who took care of the children and cleaned the house whenever it needed cleaning.

Concept discussion:

Conjunctions: When paired conjunctions are used, both the joined parts should be parallel.

For example:

Correct – John is either studying English or studying history.

Correct – John is studying either English or history.

Incorrect – John is either studying English or history.

Also, they must be paired correctly; for example "either" can only be paired with "or," and "between" can only be paired with "and."

Similarly, in the given example, "not only" must be paired with "but also"; no other pairing is accurate. Options A, C and E contain this error.

Note: This parallelism rule also applies to the following conjunctions:

(A) either X or Y
(B) neither X nor Y
(C) not X but Y
(D) from X to Y
(E) between X and Y

The X and Y parts should be parallel.

Mood: "Were" and "would" are used when discussing hypothetical situations. For example:

If I *were* you, I *would* not go to the party.

She behaves as though she *were* the queen!

In the given sentence, nothing hypothetical is being discussed. Thus, using "were" for "house" is incorrect. If the sentence were "the nanny cleaned the house as if it were her own," we could have used "were." Option B, C, and E contains this error.

The correct answer is option D.

6.15 Assorted questions

191. **SVA**: What is regarded as salary? The effect of X, Y and Z is regarded as salary, which is singular and will take the singular verb "is" and not the plural verb "are." Options A and B contain this error.

    Comparisons: "twice as much ... as/than"? "As" will pair with "as" and "more" will pair with "than." Options A and C contain this error.

    Awkwardness: Option D contains passive construction ("is paid" — by whom?), making it incorrect.

    The correct answer is option E.

192. **Grammatical construction**: Certain verbs have specific structures that need to be maintained. Verbs such as "require," "recommend," "suggest" have one of the following two structures:

    (1) Verb + that + subject + bare infinitive:
    Example: The doctor suggested that she take her medicine (not takes) [Bare infinitive = infinitive form of the verb without "to"]. Also, in this structure, insertion of "should" or "would" or any other auxiliary is not permitted.

    (2) Verb + object + to + person:
    Example: The doctor suggested some antibiotics to her.

    The non-underlined part contains "suggested" and "that" and so structure 1 must be used.

    The bare infinitive of "to be" is "be." Options B, C and E contain this error.

    Parallelism: "Encourage" should be parallel to "suggest" as both these are the actions of the "representative." Using "encourages" is incorrect. Options A, B and C contain this error.

    The correct answer is option D.

193. **Diction**: Using "the" would mean "specific/definitive/only" and using "a" would mean "general." Do we wish to say that "SAS is the (only and definitive) means to organize" or that "SAS is a (one of the) means to organize"? Since the first half of the sentence says "a database-forming programming language," indicating a general structure, using "the" would be incorrect. Options C, D and E contain this error.

    "Amount" is meant for uncountable nouns whereas, "number" is for countable nouns. The sentence discusses "facts," which are countable. Thus, using "amount of facts" is incorrect. Options A, C and E contain this error.

    The correct answer is option B.

194. **Conjunctions**: "Neither" and "either" are not conjunctions and thus, cannot be used to join two clauses. However, "or" and "nor" are conjunctions and can be used to join clauses.

    For example:

Incorrect – I will wash the car *either* collect the laundry.

Correct – I will wash the car *or* collect the laundry.

Incorrect – I will not wash the car *neither* collect the laundry.

Correct – I will not wash the car *nor* collect the laundry.

Similarly, in the above sentence, to join the two clauses "they did not think of him as the Messiah" and "they did not view him as the son of God," we need a conjunction. Using "neither" will not work. Options C and E contain this error.

Using "but" is incorrect because there is no contrast between the two clauses. If the clauses were "they don't think of him as the M" but "think of him as the son of God," we could have used "but." Option B contains this error.

While D is technically correct, because of the use of conjunction "and" it is not as crisp and direct as option A. option D is awkward.

The correct answer is option A.

195. **Meaning**: Do we wish to say that "partial-birth abortion is a procedure *in* the third trimester" (meaning it normally happens) or that "partial-birth abortion is a procedure *used in* the third trimester"(meaning it is done)? It seems unlikely that it is a normal part of the third trimester. Thus, using "in" would be incorrect. Options D and E contain this error.

    Ambiguity: Using "involving" to refer to "procedure" is ambiguous because the two words are placed very far apart. "Involving" might be confused as a modifier of "pregnancy," as in "pregnancy involving ..." It is better to use "involves" as the main verb of "partial-birth abortion." Options A and B contain this error.

    The correct answer is option C.

196. **Parallelism**: Right before the underlined part, the conjunction "and" is present, necessitating parallelism. What is "and" joining? It is joining the three things that mothers want. Mothers want 1) peaceful conflict resolution, 2) (mothers want) readily available counseling and, 3) (mothers want) decreasing prominence/a decreased prominence? To make it parallel and complete with "mothers want," we'll have to use "a decrease" because "decreasing" does not match with "mothers want." Options A and B contain this error.

    Meaning: What do the mothers want to decrease? Mothers want the prominence of TV shows to decrease or the prominence of violence in TV shows to decrease? Considering the first half of the sentence (discussing ending "violent tendencies in children"), we can infer that the mothers want violence in TV shows, rather than TV shows themselves, to decrease. Options C and E suggest that the mothers want the prominence of TV shows to decrease, making them incorrect.

    The correct answer is option D.

197. **Modifiers**: "Again" is for "attempt" and not for "draft"; thus, "again" must be placed next to "attempt." Consider also the modifying phrase "a program known..." This phrase should appear directly after the noun it is modifying ("draft"). Options B, C and D contain this error.

Idioms: "Known as" is used to discuss names and titles rather than qualities; for example: Elvis is known as the King of Rock and Roll.

To discuss qualities, "known to be" is used; for example, "She is known to be cranky during the afternoon."

In the given sentence, we need to discuss qualities of the draft rather than its title/name. Thus, we need "known to be." Option B, C and E contain this error.

The correct answer is option A.

198. **Redundancy**: Using "over the past decade" with "over the last 10 years" is redundant. Options A, D and E contain this error.

    Tenses: Since the action started in the past and is continuing into the present, using present perfect tense "has increased" is correct and not the past tense "increased" (since the population is still increased). Options A and B contain this error.

    The correct answer is option C.

199. **Pronouns**: "self" pronouns are used when the doer and the receiver of the verb are the same.

    For example: She made tea for herself.

    If the doer of the verb "made" is the same person as the receiver of the verb (who did she make tea for?), we have to use the "self" pronoun here.

    Examples:

    The hunter accidentally hit himself.

    I cannot hear myself in this crowded place!

    She saved money for herself for a future date.

    In the given sentence, human/humans is both the doer and receiver of the action, so a reflexive pronoun is required. Options A and D contain this error.

    Rhetorical construction: Since the sentence discusses a general happening in the current scenario, using a plural would be in tone with the rest of the sentence (organs, pigs, stem-cells); using the singular "a human" does not match the first half. Options A, B and C contain this error.

    The correct answer is option E.

200. **Tenses**: To denote the earlier action of two actions/verbs in the past, the past perfect is used. Two actions in the past are given in the sentence – meteorologists expected something and Hurricane Bradley affected something. Which happened earlier? Meteorologists expected something *before* Hurricane B affected something. Thus, the correct tense is the past perfect "had expected" and not the simple past "expected." Options C, D and E contain this error.

    Meaning: Using "may occur" with "expect" is poor form, as the verb "expect" carries more surety that "may" allows. Options A and D contain this error.

    The correct answer is option B.

201. **Pronoun ambiguity**: Using the singular pronoun "it" to refer to "day" is ambiguous, given the presence of the other singular nouns "humidity" and "fact." Options A, B and C contain this error.

   Meaning: Option E states that is was "the fact shown in the records" that was emphasized by the humidity, but this is not true. The humidity emphasized that the day was extremely hot.

   The correct answer is option D.

202. **Parallelism**: The conjunction "and" necessitates parallelism. What is the "and" joining? Do we want to say "the organization that tries to find pets and (the organization) that returns pets" or that "the organization that tries to find pets and (the organization that tries to) return pets"? It seems more likely that the organization tries to find pets and tries to return them to the owners. To use "that ... and that" would imply that those two activities are separate and possibly unconnected; for example,

   "XYZ is an organization that helps farmers get financing and that helps women get support."

   Thus, using "that ... and that" would be incorrect. Option A contains this error. Option E is also not parallel.

   Awkwardness: "Organization tries to find pets for return to their owners" is awkward and does not convey the meaning smoothly, as does option B. So, option C is incorrect.

   Idioms: "To try at" finding something is unidiomatic and incorrect. Option D contains this error.

   The correct answer is option B.

203. **Tenses**: The use of the word "since" necessitates the present perfect tense "has denied" and not the simple past "did deny." Options B and D contain this error.

   Note: "Since" can be used in two ways:

   1) As "because" – Because/since I missed my train, I am late.

   2) To indicate time – Since 1950, color TVs have been common.

   With the second "since" (time indicator, not "because"), the present perfect tense is compulsory.

   Idioms: "Rights" can be followed only by "to" – ex. the right to freedom, the right to practice any religion, etc. In the given sentence, the "right" under discussion is "right ... to speak freely." Options A and E contain this error.

   The correct answer is option C.

204. **Tenses**: Because of the use of 'in recent years,' a tense that goes back into the past and covers the period up to the present is needed – the present perfect tense "have become." Options A and B contain this error.

   Grammatical Construction: Option C contains a dependent clause, which leaves the rest of the sentence without a main verb, and is therefore, incorrect. **Redundancy**: Using "since" with "in recent years" is redundant. Option E contains this error.

   The correct answer is option D.

205. **Conjunctions**: "Whether" pairs with "or." "If" is used for denoting conditions that have some result attached; for example:

If you help me with the work, I will help you with the presentation. (result)

Using "if" for situations that have no result mentioned or for situations involving "yes-no" answers is incorrect.

Incorrect – Tell me if you're coming to the party (yes-no situation, no result present)

Correct – Tell me whether you're coming to the party.

Since the options contain "or" and the situation involves "yes-no" answers only, "whether" can be used. [Whether the union should fight – yes or no]

Options A, C, D and E contain an error related to this.

The correct answer is option B.

206. **Comparison**: Are we comparing Montreal with any other city or "Montreal's tourist industry" with the tourist industry of any other city? The comparison is between "the tourist industry of Montreal" and "that (the tourist industry) of any other city." Not using "that of" will be incorrect. Options A, C and D contain this error.

Rhetorical construction: To denote "tourist industry of Montreal/Montreal's tourist industry," using "whose" is better than "which has."

Consider:

Awkward – Countries *which have* cities close to ports flourish sooner.

Well-constructed – Countries *whose* cities are close to ports flourish sooner.

Options A, B and C contain this error.

Also, "that of" is singular, referring to a singular "tourist industry" of a singular "city." However, if we use the plural "cities," we cannot say "that of" because many "cities" will have plural "tourist industries." Option B contains this error.

The correct answer is option E.

207. **Diction**: "Less" can be used for uncountable nouns (money, salary, rice, etc) and "fewer" can be used for countable nouns (sources). "Sources" is a countable noun and thus, we cannot use "less" for "sources." Options B and D contain this error.

Lesser is used in comparing two things: Ex. I will choose the lesser of the two evils. Option C contains an error with this.

Also, since the "15,000 dollars" refers to the "salary" and even though it seems countable, money-quantities are considered uncountable.

Incorrect – 15,000 dollars is *fewer* money than he needs to finish his education.

Correct – 15,000 dollars is *less* money than he needs to finish his education.

Thus, in the given sentence, we need to use "less" for the salary. Option E contains this error.

The correct answer is option A.

208. **Parallelism**: Using "and" necessitates parallelism. "First of all" will pair with "second" but not with "secondly" or "secondarily" ("firstly" can pair with "secondly" or "secondarily"). Options A, B and C contain this error.

Also, since the first part contains "first of all, becoming ..." the second should also contain "failing" to make it parallel. All options except E contain this error.

The correct answer is option E.

209. **Pronouns**: Using the noun "convicted murderers" in the sentence is absolutely essential because the non-underlined part contains the pronoun "them," meant to refer to "murderers." Eliminating the noun is incorrect. Options D and E contain this error.

Awkwardness: What is standard practice? Giving notice is standard practice. To say "notice being given" is standard practice or "notice of something to give" is awkward compared to "giving notice about something before executing is standard practice." Options A and C contain this error.

The correct answer is option B.

210. **Modifiers**: Who's distressed by the nutritional content of the junk food sold in the school cafeteria? The PTA is distressed. Thus, this subject (the PTA) must follow the modifier "distressed ... cafeteria" to conform to the rules of modifiers. Options A, B and C contain this error.

Active/Passive: Option D is needlessly passive, making it awkward.

The correct answer is option E.

211. **Grammatical construction**: Certain verbs have specific structures that need to be maintained. Verbs such as "require," "recommend," and "order" have one of the following two structures:

  (1) Verb + that + subject + bare infinitive:
      Example: The doctor recommended that she do yoga for relaxation. [Bare infinitive = infinitive form of the verb without "to"]. Also, in this structure, insertion of "should" or "would" or any other auxiliary is not permitted.

  (2) Verb + object + infinitive + object:
      Example: The doctor ordered her to change her eating habits.

  Similarly, in the given sentence, we can say either "RWJ University requires that professors schedule ... ," or that "RWJ University requires professors to schedule ... " Any other structure is incorrect. Options B, D, and E contain this error.

  Rhetorical construction: Since all the options contain the plural pronoun "their" for the noun "professor," using the plural form "professors" is necessary rather than "a professor." Options A, B and E contain this error.

  The correct answer is option C.

212. **Conjunctions**: "Just as" is paired with "so" and "as" is paired with "so," making the conjunction "just as ..., so ..." or "as ..., so..."; both are used to emphasize the similarity

between two situations or happenings. For example: *Just as* Parliament is the supreme legislative body in the UK, *so* is Congress in the USA.

Not pairing "as" with "so" in such contexts is incorrect. Option D contains this error.

"Like" is used to compare two nouns, not two sentences. For example:

Correct: Like the UK, the USA has an elected body at the helm of legislation.

Incorrect: Like Parliament is the supreme legislative body in the UK, Congress is in the USA.

Option C contains this error.

Awkwardness: Using "similar to" or "in a similar way" instead of "Just as ... so" is awkward. Options B and E contain this error.

The correct answer is option A.

213. **Modifiers**: Who are Jewish immigrants from Poland? Eli and Rivka Schwartz are Jewish immigrants from Poland. Thus, the sentence must continue with "Eli and Rivka Schwartz" after the modifier "Jewish immigrants from Poland" to conform to the rules of modifiers. Options A, C and D contain this error.

    Awkwardness: What was opened by Eli and Rivka Schwartz? Schwartz's Deli was opened by Eli and Rivka Schwartz. Thus, "Schwartz's Deli" should be placed after "opened" for maximum clarity. Option E contains this error.

    The correct answer is option B.

214. **Conjunctions**: When paired conjunctions are used, both the joined parts should be parallel.

    In the given example, correct is "not only had he skimmed ... but he had also..." Options A, B and D do not pair the conjunction correctly. Option E does not contain the requisite parallelism.

    The correct answer is option C.

215. **Rhetorical construction**: What was the attempt? It was an attempt to elect a woman as president of the United States. For clarity, this must stay together and not be interrupted by discussions of time. Option B contains this error.

    Tense: The attempt began at a specific point in the past. Only the simple past tense will work for this sentence. Option E contains this error with its use of the present perfect tense.

    Meaning: What first happened 15 years ago? An attempt to elect a woman. Was that the one and only time? No - it is clearly stated that the Democratic Party is willing to back a woman, so it can be inferred that other attempts have occurred. Option C contains an error with this.

    Awkwardness: Option D's language –attempt "at" electing – is not the clearest way to express the point of the sentence.

    The correct answer is option A.

216. **Conjunctions:** "Whether" pairs with "or." "If" is used for denoting conditions that have some result attached; for example: If you help me with the work, I will help you with the presentation (result). Using "if" for situations that have no result mentioned or for situations involving "yes-no" answers is incorrect.

Incorrect – Tell me if you're coming to the party. (yes-no situation, no result present)

Correct – Tell me whether you're coming to the party.

Since the options contain "or" and the situation involves a "yes-no" answer (and does not contain any result (then ...) clause), then only "whether" can be used. [Whether to execute him – yes or no, or whether to imprison him – yes or no]

Options B, D and E contain this error.

Redundancy: Using "or not" with "whether" is redundant and unidiomatic. Option C contains this error.

The correct answer is option A.

217. **Redundancy:** Using "he is" when the sentence already contains "Albert is" is redundant. Instead of saying "Albert is ... and he is...," one can simply say "Albert is something... and something else..." Options A, B and D contain this error.

Meaning: Who is viewed as the best candidate for the role of the Nutcracker? Albert is. Thus, using "it" instead of "he" is incorrect. Options B and E contain this error.

The correct answer is option C.

218. **Parallelism:** The conjunction "and" necessitates parallelism. "And" is joining 4 things – the forces that may facilitate a dictator's rise to power. These include:

   (A) sudden crashes ...

   (B) discrimination and ...

   (C) inciting/an incitement ... and

   (D) protesting/a protest

Since the non-underlined part contains the nouns "sudden crashes" and "discrimination" and not the verb-ing form, we will have to also use the noun "incitement" and "protest" and not the verb-ing form. Options A, B and C contain this error.

Meaning: Option D implies that one of the things that may facilitate a dictator's rise to power includes current inadequate government making the protest, whereas, the likely meaning is that one of the things that may facilitate a dictator's rise to power includes a protest that the current government is inadequate. So, option D is incorrect.

The correct answer is option E.

219. **Modifiers:** What is like the play that came before it? The new play is like the play that came before it, in that both have been inspired by Othello. Thus, the sentence must begin with the correct subject (the new play) to conform to the rules of modifiers. Options A, B and C contain this error.

Idioms: To imply that something served as an inspiration for some other thing, we can say "X inspired Y," "X is the inspiration for Y" or "X served as an inspiration for Y"; using "Y has an inspiration of X" is incorrect. Option E contains this error.

The correct answer is option D.

220. **Comparisons**: The sentence structure contains comparisons, necessitating parallelism. The sentence is, basically, 'to compare X with Y' is (equivalent) 'to compare P with Q.' X, Y, P and Q need to be parallel. We can compare "the brilliance of Beethoven with the tunes of Britney" with "the value of diamonds with the value of baubles" or "Beethoven's brilliance with Britney's tunes" with "diamonds' value with baubles' value." Any other form will be incorrect. Option E contains this error.

Also, "to compare" should be used with "to compare," or "comparing" with "comparing." Mixing it up is incorrect. Options B and C contain this error.

Also, we can compare "the value of diamonds" with "the value of plastic baubles" (or substitute "the value" with "that" in the second half) or "diamonds with baubles." Any other comparison will be incorrect. Option C and D contain this error.

The correct answer is option A.

221. **Comparisons**: Since the sentence involves comparison, parallelism is necessary. The sentence compares the ease of two things for Grandmother – walking and using a walker. Since the non-underlined portion contains "to walk," we can only say "to use" [i.e. to use a walker will be easier than to try to walk...] Options A, D and E contain this error.

Meaning: Option C does not convey the comparison well enough; the comparison is that *to use* a walker will be easier than *to try to walk*, not that *walker* is easier to use than *to walk*. The sentence does not intend to say that walker itself is easier to use than trying to walk; using something is easier than trying something else. So, option C is incorrect.

The correct answer is option B.

222. **SVA**: What is the molding and smoothing? The steps of the ceramic process in which the students will be involved are the molding and smoothing... Thus, the subject is "the steps," which is plural and will take the plural verb "are" and not the singular verb "is." Options A, B and E contain this error.

Parallelism: With the three steps, we need parallel structure. They all appear in noun form (molding, smoothing, decorating/decoration) While you may be tempted to choose "decorating" as the best noun form in that list, notice that Option C repeats the preposition "in," which is unnecessary, and violates the rule of parallel structure. The non-underlined portion of the sentence already used the preposition (...steps IN which...). Option C is incorrect because of the extra preposition. Options A and E also make errors with parallel structure.

The correct answer is option D.

223. **Modifiers**: Using "which" is incorrect because it refers to "divorce." What's more than had been sued in the past five years? The number 10,000 (and not divorce) is more than had been sued in the past five years. Thus, "which" is incorrect. Options A and E contain this error.

   Pronoun ambiguity: Who is "they" in option C? The sentence does not contain any referent for "they," making it incorrect.

   Diction: To refer to cases, the word "lawsuits" and not "suits" is correct. Options D and E contain this error.

   The correct answer is option B.

224. **Conjunctions**: "Not only" must always be paired with "but also," but not simply "but." Option A contains this error.

   Also, "both" must always be paired with "and," but not with "as well as." Option C contains this error.

   Meaning: Why did Marilyn decide not to go to the hospital despite the doctor's recommendations? Marilyn decided not to go to the hospital because she believed something, not because herbal remedies can actually replace surgery and cure her maladies. This is the intended meaning, which we see from the non-underlined part that says "despite the doctor's urgings that she consider surgery." Options B and E contain an error with this intended meaning.

   Mood: The sentence discusses a hypothetical situation, a belief; thus, using "would" is necessary. "Will" is incorrect. Options B and E contain this error.

   The correct answer is option D.

225. **Comparisons**: What is much more effective? The vaccine will be much more effective than the vaccine was ten years ago. Saying that the vaccine will be much more effective than ten years ago is incorrect because it compares the vaccine to a point in time ("ten years ago"). Options A, B and D contain this error.

   Redundancy: Using "in" is unnecessary. Option E contains this error.

   The correct answer is option C.

226. **Pronoun ambiguity**: To whom does the "they" in "because they usually cause less trouble" refer? This is not clear. Equally ambiguous is the "they" in "than they are for boys." Choices A, B and C are contain this error.

   Comparisons: Choice D has an incorrect comparison: it compares decisions to boys, not girls to boys – "the disciplinary decisions ... are less strict than boys." So, option D is incorrect.

   The correct answer is option E.

227. **Comparisons**: Who gets more independence? <u>Teenagers</u> get more independence *in cities* than <u>they (teenagers)</u> do *in the suburbs*. Not using "they" will compare "teenagers" with "suburbs." Options A, B and C contain this error.

Since the original verb is "get," the comparison verb will be "do"; if the sentence were, "Teenagers *are* more independent in cities than they *are* in the suburbs," we would use "are" in the second half. Option D contains this error.

The correct answer is option E.

228. **Active/Passive**: What has become gentrified? (gentrify - make something sophisticated) Neighborhoods have become gentrified. Thus, we need to use the passive construction, not active (correct – Neighborhoods have been gentrified; incorrect – neighborhoods have gentrified [gentrified what?]). Using "gentrification" will also convey that neighborhoods are gentrifying something rather than being gentrified themselves, i.e. neighborhoods have increased gentrification (of something). Options B, D and E contain this error.

    Awkwardness: Option C needlessly uses noun forms and makes the sentence wordy and awkward.

    The correct answer is option A.

229. **Tenses**: Using the past perfect "had granted" is incorrect because the past perfect tense is used for the earlier of two actions in the past. However, "granting" happened after the code "was enacted," thus, we cannot use the past perfect. We have to use the simple past "did." Options A, C, and E contain this error.

    Idioms: The correct idiom is "right of someone to do something." Options A, B and E contain this error.

    The correct answer is option D.

230. **Modifiers**: 'When' refers to time and 'where' refers to locations. However, we need neither because we're discussing a contrast. So we need a contrast conjunction – "while." Options A, C, and D contain this error.

    Conjunctions: "while" is followed immediately by "verb-ing," not by "verb."

    Correct – I walked to the store while *talking* on the phone.

    Incorrect – I walked to the store while *talk* on the phone.

    Note: If a clause is being joined using "while," then use the verb form according to the context. For example:

    Correct – I walked to the store while I talked on the phone.

    Incorrect – I walked to the store while I talking on the phone.

    Similarly, in option B, if the sentence were "…while *he* spares" it would have been correct.

    Option B contains this error.

    The correct answer is option E.

231. **Tenses**: When talking about a fixed point in the past, only the simple past tense can be used – in 1988, last month, yesterday, at a party.

    Incorrect – I had been born *in 1988*.

Correct – I was born *in 1988.*

Incorrect – *At a recent party,* I have eaten sushi.

Correct – *At a recent party,* I ate sushi.

Similarly, in the given sentence, with the fixed point "at the press conference," we need to use the simple past "announced," and not the present perfect "has announced." Options A, C and E contain this error.

Awkwardness: Saying "the government has a plan" is wordier and more awkward than "the government plans to." Option D contains this error.

The correct answer is option B.

232. **Modifiers**: What's thought to emanate from a tiny gland on the underside of their bodies? Pheromone trails are thought to emanate from a tiny gland on the underside of their bodies. Using the subject "ants" after the modifier "thought...bodies" is incorrect. Options A and D contain this error.

    Pronouns: "Using "this," which is singular, to refer to "pheromone trails," which is plural, is incorrect. Option B contains this error.

    Meaning: The original sentence suggests that the pheromone trails left by the ants can be used. However, option E implies that it is the ants, rather than the trails can be used, making it incorrect.

    The correct answer is option C.

233. **Parallelism**: The paired conjunction "both X and Y" necessitates parallelism. The X and Y parts must be parallel. "(The) rich people" and "(the) poor people" are parallel, so any variation of this is not parallel. No option except D is parallel.

    The correct answer is option D.

234. **Modifiers**: Who's buying electronics? Someone is, either "one" or "you" but not "guarantee." Thus, the "buyer" should be present after the modifier "when buying electronics" to conform to the rules of modifiers. Options C, D and E contain this error.

    Pronouns: If the pronoun "one" is used, the sentence should consistently use "one" throughout, and the same is true for "you." Mixing "one" and "you" is incorrect. The non-underlined part already contains the pronoun "you," thus, using "one" is incorrect. Options A, C and D contain this error.

    The correct answer is option B.

235. **Meaning**: The sentence implies that Brad applied to Ivy League colleges because his counselor suggested doing so. Option B changes the meaning to imply that Brad was suggested by his counselor – When he was suggested by his counselor, Brad – thus, Brad was the suggestion. This happens because the first half has been turned into a modifier. There is the same problem with options C and D: they imply that Brad is the suggestion. So, options B, C and D are incorrect.

    Tip: When unsure of the modifier structure, you should just place the noun that is after the modifier BEFORE the modifier and read it to see whether it makes sense. For example:

Incorrect – Brad, when he was suggested by his guidance counselor, did something.

Incorrect – Brad, a suggestion coming from his guidance counselor, did something.

Incorrect – Brad, a suggestion that came from his guidance counselor, did something.

Correct – Brad, at the suggestion of his guidance counselor, did something.

Awkwardness: "Having" in option E is awkward compared to option A.

The correct answer is option A.

236. **SVA**: What illustrates how complex and peculiar the war ...was ? Quirks do, which is plural, and will take the plural verb "illustrate" and not the singular verb "illustrates." Options A and B contain this error.

    Parallelism: Using "and" will necessitate parallelism between "reveal" (in the non-underlined part) and "illustrate" – revealed and illustrated. Option D contains this error.

    Modifiers: "who" is meant for people and not for things. For things, "which" or "that" can be used. Option E contains this error.

    The correct answer is option C.

237. **Redundant**: The use of 'he was' is not necessary if the subject "Kyle" is mentioned. Options C and D contain this error.

    Meaning: Option A implies that someone was an orphan and Kyle (who may or may not be the orphan) founded the largest orphanage in China. However, that would be absurd and meaningless. We need to suggest that Kyle, who's an orphan, founded the largest orphanage in China. So, option A is incorrect.

    Also, suggesting that because Kyle is an orphan, he opened an orphanage is incorrect because no such meaning has been implied. Option E is incorrect.

    The correct answer is option B.

238. **Idioms**: "Regard" is correctly used as "regard X as Y" whereas, "consider" is used as "consider X Y." Not using "as" for "regard" or saying "regard X Y" is incorrect. Similarly, using "to be" or "as" between X and Y in "consider X Y" is incorrect. Options B, C and E contain this error.

    Tenses: Using "is" for a past time is incorrect; the correct tense would be "was." Option D contains this error.

    The correct answer is option A.

239. **Pronoun ambiguity**: Using the pronoun "their" or "them" is ambiguous given the presence of the two plural nouns "activities" and "citizens," and incorrect because it's trying to refer to "CIA," an organization, which is singular. [What's similar to the KGB? The CIA]. Options A, B and C contain this error.

    Tenses: Whenever time expressions such as "as," "whenever," or "every time" are used, the tenses of the clauses should be similar because these words indicate simultaneous actions.

    Correct – <u>As</u> I *learn* swimming, the water *becomes* less terrifying.

Incorrect – <u>As</u> I *learn* swimming, the water *has become* less terrifying.

Incorrect – <u>Whenever</u> I *eat* pizza, I *became* stuffed.

Correct – <u>Whenever</u> I *eat* pizza, I *become* stuffed/<u>Whenever</u> I *ate* pizza, I *became* stuffed.

Similarly, in the given sentence, "as" is used with the simple present tense ("as citizens *continue*...something *becomes* evident"). Using "has become" is incorrect. Options A, B and E contain this error.

The correct answer is option D.

240. **Rhetorical construction**: The sentence intends to convey that Henry's latest paper could not have been written by him (this part is obvious) because the paper is flawless but Henry had never put in much effort and his essays had been average at best. So, what is obvious? *The conclusion* that someone else wrote Henry's essay *is obvious*. Options A, B and D are unnecessarily wordy.

    Tenses: Using "would have researched" is unnecessary for a simple action in the past; for such an action, the simple past tense "researched" will suffice. Option E contains this error.

    The correct answer is option C.

241. **Tenses**: Using "had been written" is the incorrect tense because the past perfect is used only when there are multiple verbs in the past, of which the earliest takes the past perfect tense. In this case, there are no verbs in the past and thus, the past perfect can't be used. Option A contains this error.

    Modifiers: What is the conjunction "and" in the second half of the sentence joining? It's joining the two modifiers describing the musical "Meet Pauline." These modifiers need to have parallelism. Option B has eliminated certain words from the relative clause ["...musical (which was) written by a large group...."], which is not a mistake in itself, but the second part of the phrase ["...and which was the inspiration..."] includes these same words, and thus, makes the option non-parallel. Options C and E contain similar problems with parallelism.

    The correct answer is option D.

242. **Modifiers**: What's based on the customs of countries? Are historians based on the customs of countries? The inference is based on the customs of countries. Thus, using the subject "historians" after the modifier "based on..." will be incorrect.

    When unsure of the modifier structure, you should just place the noun that is after the modifier before the modifier and read it to see whether it makes sense. For example:

    Incorrect – Historians, based on the customs of countries such as Mexico, have inferred...

    Correct – Historians, on the basis of the customs of countries such as Mexico, have inferred...

    Diction: "Like" is used for comparisons whereas, "such as" is used to enumerate examples.

    For example:

Correct – Fruits, like vegetables, contain fiber. ["vegetables" are not examples of "fruits"]

Correct – Fruits, such as oranges, contain Vitamin C. ["oranges" are examples of "fruits"]

"Mexico" is an example of "countries," thus, "such as" is correct and "like" is incorrect. Options C, D and E contain this error.

The correct answer is option B.

243. **Tenses**: The sentence suggests that "something was thought/imagined not to be tiring," but, in reality, "it turns out to be tiring." Thus, for the "thought/imagined" part, which happened before the actual game, the correct tense would be the simple past tense "seemed" and not "seem." Options B, C and D contain this error.

Also, using "would" or "it" is unnecessary because the sentence conveys the correct meaning without either of those words. Options D and E contain this error.

The correct answer is option A.

244. **Idiom**: The correct use of "substitute" is "substitute X for Y" and not "to." Options A, C and E contain this error.

Parallelism: Using "unlike," a form of comparison, necessitates parallelism. What/Who is unlike conservatives? Mr. Jackson is unlike conservatives. We cannot compare conservatives with Mr. Jackson's stress. Options D and E contain this error.

The correct answer is option B.

245. **Conjunctions**: "Whether" is used to discuss situations involving "yes" or "no" answers – for example:

I asked him whether he was willing to take this job. (yes or no)

"If" is used for denoting conditions that have some result attached – for example:

(condition) If you help me with the work, I will help you with the presentation. (result)

Using "if" for situations that have no result mentioned or for situations involving "yes-no" answers is incorrect.

Incorrect – Tell me if you're coming to the party. (yes-no situation, no result present)

Correct – Tell me whether you're coming to the party.

Since the sentence involves a "yes-no" answer, and does not contain any result clause, only "whether" can be used. [Whether the company was as responsible for the slander as the newspaper was – yes or no]

Options A, B and C contain this error.

Concision: Between options D and E, E is better because E is more concise.

The correct answer is option E.

246. **Modifiers**: What's added to the increase in monthly wages? Are the dining hall employees added to the increase in monthly wages? "Improved insurance coverage" is added to the increase in monthly wages. Thus, using the modifier "added to…" with the subject "dining hall employees" will be incorrect. Options A, B and C contain this error.

Incorrect – Employees, added to the increase in monthly wages, are asking …

Correct – Employees, in addition to the increase in monthly wages, are asking …

SVA: What was discussed last spring? An increase in wages was discussed last spring. Increase is singular and will take the singular verb "was" and not the plural verb "were." Options C and D contain this error.

The correct answer is option E.

247. **Comparisons:** In comparisons, one of the following structures can be used:

    (A) X is more … than Y

    (B) X is as … as Y

    (C) *Rarely, a variant of the second structure* – X is so … as Y

    Using any other combination is incorrect. In the given sentence, the third structure is being used: "Ripe peaches are marked not so much *by* their color ___ by their firmness…" Since "so" is used in the first half of the sentence, we have to use its pair "as" to make "not so much by … as by …" All options except D contain this error.

    The correct answer is option D.

248. **Pronoun ambiguity:** Using "it" in options A and B is ambiguous because it is trying to refer to "a number of students" but such a noun isn't present in the sentence. It can't refer to "ten percent" because then the sentence would suggest that "(it) ten percent is five percent." So, options A and B are incorrect.

    Awkwardness: Saying "the percentage of students is ten" is awkward compared to "ten percent of students." Options D and E contain this error.

    The correct answer is option C.

249. **SVA:** What has demonstrated that women's sports are still lacking dedicated fans? The contrast has demonstrated that women's sports are still lacking dedicated fans. "The contrast," which is singular, will take the singular verb "has" and not the plural verb "have." Options A, B and C contain this error.

    Idiom: The correct idiom is "contrast in X and Y" but not "contrast in X over Y." Options B, C and D contain this error.

    Comparisons: The sentence intends to contrast "sales in certain sports" with "sales in other sports." Comparing "sales in male-dominated sports" with "female-dominated sports" is incorrect. Options B, C and D contain this error.

    The correct answer is option E.

250. **Grammatical construction:** To cite reason, a "to verb" should be used, but not any other form.

    Correct – I went to the theatre to watch a movie.

    Incorrect – I went to the theatre for watching a movie.

In the given sentence, we need to use "to improve" to provide the reason. Options A and D contain this error.

concision: Option B is unnecessarily wordy.

Agreement: In option E, the verb "is improved" does not agree with the noun that goes with it (aspects).

The correct answer is option C.

251. **Pronoun mismatch**: Using the plural pronoun "they" to refer to the singular "plus-size woman" is incorrect. Options B, D and E contain this error.

    Meaning: What will result in fashion failure? Wearing clothes meant for smaller-sized people will result in fashion failure. Thus, the correct subject is "wearing clothes..." Not using the correct subject will create an awkward structure. Options B, C and D contain this error.

    The correct answer is option A.

252. **Parallelism**: The conjunction "and" necessitates parallelism. "To have" should be parallel with "to be handicapped" or "having" should be parallel with "being handicapped." Any other combination is incorrect. Options D and E contain this error.

    Modifiers: Who has difficulty refraining from eating? One that is handicapped by an excess of weight has difficulty refraining from eating. Options A and B do not use a proper relative clause for this portion of the sentence, and make the sentence appear to mean that it's "an excess of weight" that has "difficulty refraining from eating." Use of a conjunction and proper signal words for the relative clause will make this sentence correct.

    The correct answer is option C.

253. **Comparisons**: In comparisons, "more" always pairs with "than." Since the non-underlined part contains "more rights...," we have to choose "than"; if it had contained "as many rights..." we could have chosen "as." Options B, C and D contain this error.

    Also, "of" denotes possession, as does "apostrophe 's.'" Thus, to denote possession either one should be used.

    Correct – The cart's wheel is broken.

    Correct – The wheel of the cart is broken.

    Incorrect – The wheel of the cart's is broken.

    Option E contains this error.

    The correct answer is option A.

254. **Idioms**: "Just like" is always incorrect. Idiomatically, "just as" or "like" is acceptable, but not "just like." Option A contains this error.

    Analogies [X : Y : : P : Q] are worded as X is to Y what P is to Q. Similarly, in the given sentence, an analogy is being made that machines are to modernity what servants were to former times. Thus, we have to use "what" to join the two comparable analogies. Options A, B and E contain this error.

Tenses: Since the second half of the sentence is dealing with a time in the past, the simple past tense "were" is correct and the simple present tense "are" is incorrect. Option D contains this error.

The correct answer is option C.

255. **SVA**: What affects the learning experience of the entire class? Misbehavior affects the learning experience of the entire class. Thus, the subject "misbehavior," which is singular, will take the singular verb "affects" and not the plural verb "affect." Options A and C contain this error.

Redundancy: 'Because' is more efficient than 'for the reason that,' 'for the reason,' and "in that," and "because" is a word preferred by GMAT. Options A, B and C contain this error.

Idioms: The correct idiomatic expression is 'on the part of someone' and not 'on the parts of someone.' Option E contains this error.

The correct answer is option D.

256. **Tenses**: Since the sentence discusses actions in the past ("after the revolution," "older ideologies"), we have to use the simple past tense "embodied" and not the present tense "embodies." Options C, D and E contain this error.

Pronoun ambiguity: Using the singular pronoun "it" to refer to "The Communist Party" is ambiguous given the presence of other singular nouns "revolution," "Country X," "ideology," etc. Options C and D contain this error.

Awkwardness: "Older ideologies" is concise and well-constructed compared to "ideologies that were older," which is awkward and lengthy. Options B and D contain this error.

The correct answer is option A.

257. **Diction**: "Population" is not a countable noun (you can't say 1 population, 2 populations). Thus, we cannot use "fewer" for "population." We can say "less." Option E contains this error.

"Lesser" is always incorrect for simple comparison; "lesser" is restricted only to philosophical discussions – for example, "this is the lesser of the two evils." Option C contains this error.

"Lower" is a specialized word, best used for "number." For example: The number of people is lower than it was last time. Using it for population is not ideal. Option B contains this error.

"Soldiers" are countable and thus, "fewer" is correct and "less" is incorrect. Options B and D contain this error.

The correct answer is option A.

258. **Tenses**: The sentence discusses actions in the past. Thus, the past tense "could" is correct and the present tense "can" is incorrect. Options A, C and D contain this error.

Idioms: "Rely" is paired with "on" and not with "for" – the depositors could not rely on the savings. Option E contains this error.

The correct answer is option B.

259. **Meaning**: What's favored by popular radio stations? Playing songs on the radio often is favored by popular radio stations.

    If "a practice favored by popular radio stations" is used as a modifier, the correct subject after it should be "playing songs ..." and not "a song" because the "song" itself is not the "practice favored by popular radio stations." Options C and D contain this error.

    Conjunctions: Using "and" to join the clauses "a song is played on the radio often" and "favored by popular radio stations" implies that these two are separate, independent characteristics. However, the sentence suggests that playing songs on the radio often *is the practice* favored by popular radio stations. Thus, these two clauses should not be independent of each other. Options B and E contain this error.

    The correct answer is option A.

260. **Pronoun ambiguity**: Using the plural pronoun "they" to refer to "treaties" is ambiguous given the presence of the other plural noun "Americans." Options A, B and D contain this error.

    Parallelism: If "that" is present before the conjunction, it must be repeated after the conjunction too, i.e. "Most think *that* ... <u>but</u> *that* ..." Options A and C contain this error.

    The correct answer is option E.

261. **Tenses**: When were hunters thought to extract oil? It is thought now that hunters extracted oil, evidenced by the use of other present tense verbs in the sentence ("believe," "serves"). Thus, the present tense "are" is correct, whereas, the past tense "were" is incorrect. Options B, C and E contain this error.

    When did hunters actually first extract oil, now or back then? The hunters first extracted oil earlier, not now. Thus, using the present tense for "extract" is incorrect, and we need the present perfect "have extracted" to indicate that it was first done some time ago. Options B, C and D contain this error.

    The correct answer is option A.

262. **Conjunctions**: The correct idiomatic conjunctions are "neither...nor" and "either...or." Any mismatch or different pairing is incorrect. Options A, B and C contain this error.

    Meaning: "Nor" is a better choice than "and ... not." Also, there are three things being discussed in the sentence: 1) leading to better times, 2) a more relaxed sense of national security and 3) actually destroying the terrorists. None of these three things is happening despite the war on terrorism. In the correct answer (E), "not leading" is connected to both "better times..." and "relaxed sense...," and in the third part ("destroying..."), another negative is used. Thus, the first two things should be separated by their own conjunction, with the third part taking a different one, i.e. "not leading to X... or to Y..., nor is it doing Z," instead of saying "not leading to X..., Y and it is not doing Z." Repeating "to" in the second item will also add to clarity by showing that "not leading" is being used for both. Options A and D contain an error with this.

The correct answer is option E.

263. **Pronoun mismatch**: What will expand the amount that can be used? Finding additional sources will expand the amount that can be used. However, the pronoun "it" can only be used to refer to singular nouns and not to clauses or phrases. Options A, C and E contain this error.

    Diction: "Amount" can "increase" rather than "expand." Option B contains this error, apart from being awkward because of its double use of "that."

    The correct answer is option D.

264. **Tenses**: When did people rekindle their faith? After a meteor shower was observed, some people rekindled their faith. Thus, "rekindling" should be in the past tense "rekindled" or the present perfect tense "have rekindled" to indicate it was done in the past but not in the present tense. Options A and E contain incorrect present tenses.

    Awkwardness: Using the placeholders "there are" is unnecessary and awkward. Options C and D contain this error.

    The correct answer is option B.

265. **Modifiers**: What has the potential to cause errors in judgment? Is it overtime itself or working an excessive amount of overtime? It's not overtime itself but rather the practice of working an excessive amount of overtime that has the potential to cause errors in judgment. Thus, using "that has the ..." without using the word "a practice" to refer to the situation of "working an excessive amount of overtime" is incorrect because then the sentence will suggest that the "overtime has the potential to cause errors in judgment." Options A, B and C contain this error.

    Redundancy: "Can" is shorter and clearer than "has the potential to," making the latter redundant. Options A, B and D contain this error.

    The correct answer is option E.

266. **Comparisons**: In comparisons, "so" pairs with "as"; for example: they are not <u>so</u> much friends <u>as</u> colleagues. Similarly, in the given sentence, the non-underlined part contains the phrase "not so much because ..." Thus, we'll have to use "as" and not "but." Options A, D and E contain this error.

    Parallelism: In the comparison structure "(not) so (much) X as Y," the X and Y parts should be parallel. Option B contains this error.

    The correct answer is option A.

267. **SVA**: Using the singular verb "was" to refer to the plural "cities" is incorrect. Options A and B contain this error.

    Conjunctions: To join multiple items in one list, a single conjunction is sufficient; using multiple conjunctions is incorrect.

Correct: ...cities, characterized by 1) ornate gold decorations, 2) (characterized by) large populations, **and** 3) (characterized by) wonderful natural beauties.

Incorrect: ...cities, characterized by 1) ornate gold decorations, 2) **and** (characterized by) large populations, **and** 3) (characterized by) wonderful natural beauties.

Options B and D contain this error.

Parallelism: The multiple items in one list must be parallel in terms of the structure – either all items should have prepositions or the preposition should be a single common one used before the first item.

Correct: ...cities, characterized by 1) ornate gold decorations, 2) (characterized by) large populations, **and** 3) (characterized by) wonderful natural beauties.

Correct: ...cities, characterized 1) by ornate gold decorations, 2) (characterized) by large populations, **and** 3) (characterized) by wonderful natural beauties.

Incorrect: ...cities, characterized by 1) ornate gold decorations, 2) (characterized) **by** large populations, **and** 3) (characterized by) wonderful natural beauties.

Option C contains this error.

The correct answer is option E.

268. **Modifiers**: What had been damaged? The tome (book) had been damaged. If we don't use "it" to refer to "tome" in the clause about being damaged, the clause will become a modifier suggesting that the librarians have been damaged! Options A, B and E contain this error.

    Tenses: The past perfect tense must be used only for the earlier action of two actions in the past. What happened first – the damage or the reading? The damage happened before the reading. Thus, the damage should be discussed in the past perfect tense ("had been damaged") whereas, the reading should be in the simple past ("were able to read"). Options B and D contain this error.

    The correct answer is option C.

269. **Idiom**: "Result" when used as a verb should be followed by "from," but "result" when used as a noun should be followed by "of." For example:

    "Result" used as a verb: This resulted *from* your carelessness.

    "Result" used as a noun: This is a result *of* your carelessness.

    In the given sentence, "result" is used as a noun ("a result"), and thus, "from" is incorrect.

    Option B contains this error.

    Meaning: "Costing reconstructions" is nonsensical.

    Option C contains this error.

    The original sentence implies that "negotiation" happened with European governments and not that "reconstruction was undertaken with European governments," which is what Option D incorrectly suggests. As well, "negotiated costs" does not convey the same meaning as the original sentence; reconstruction was negotiated, not costs.

    Option E has a problem in its phrasing about costs. Costs are not going to be undertaken, reconstruction is.

Sentence Correction Guide – Solutions 297

The correct answer is option A.

270. **Conjunctions**: To denote contrast, contrast conjunctions should be used. The two parts of the given sentence contain a contrast : "she scorned romance books" and "she had a bookcase full of such books." Thus, a contrast conjunction is necessary. "For all" and "in spite of" denote contrast. However, options B, C and D don't contain any contrast indicator, so these options are incorrect.

    Meaning: Option E uses the word "activities" instead of discussing "books," making it incorrect.

    The correct answer is option A.

271. **Meaning**: What was thought by some detectives to have occurred around midnight? The monk occurred at midnight or the immolation occurred at midnight? It's the immolation that occurred around midnight. Thus, to convey the correct meaning, the subject of the sentence should be "immolation" or "immolating" but not "monk." Options A, B and E contain this error.

    Option C is nonsensical.

    The correct answer is option D.

272. **Idioms**: "Desire" should be followed by "to verb." For example: I have no *desire to walk* any further. Options C, D and E contain this error.

    Redundancy: "To be in sympathy with" is needlessly wordier than "to sympathize with." Option A contains this error.

    The correct answer is option B.

273. **Comparisons**: Scores of minorities are below what of white students? Scores of minorities must be below *scores* of white students. To refer to the plural noun "scores," we can use "those of" but not "that of." Options A and B contain this error.

    Awkwardness: "Economic differences that are shrinking" is awkward compared to "shrinking economic differences." Options A and E contain this error.

    Pronoun ambiguity: Using the pronoun "their" is ambiguous given the multiple plural nouns "minorities," "scores," and "students." Option E contains this error.

    The correct answer is option D.

274. **Comparisons**: In comparison, "so" pairs with "as"; for example: they are not <u>so</u> much friends <u>as</u> colleagues. Similarly, in the given sentence, the non-underlined part contains – "not <u>so</u> much by their virtue ... " Thus, we'll have to use "as" and not "and." Options B and D contain this error.

    Parallelism: In comparison structure "(not) so (much) X as Y," the X and Y parts should be parallel. Since the non-underlined part contains "not so much <u>by their brute effort</u> ...," we will have to use "as <u>by their strategic planning</u>." Options A and E contain this error.

    The correct answer is option C.

275. **Conjunctions**: "Between" always pairs with "and" and not "with." Options A and B contain this error.

Modifiers: What produced extreme radiation and high temperatures? Interchange, not neutrons, produced extreme radiation and high temperatures. Using "which produced ..." will refer to "neutrons." Options C and D contain this error.

The correct answer is option E.

276. **SVA**: What has played a large part in deciding what to perform? The opinion has played a large part in deciding what to perform. The subject "the opinion" is singular and will take the singular verb "has" and not the plural verb "have. Option D contains this error.

Parallelism: "As" needs parallelism - "*it is* common *in* ... as *it is in* ..." Options A, B and D contain this error.

Grammatical construction: To follow the phrase "it is common...," the word "that" is required. Options A and E contain this error.

The correct answer is option C.

277. **Parallelism**: "From" must always be paired with "to." Option D is incorrect because it pairs "from" with "with."

"From X to Y" needs parallelism in the X and Y parts. Options A and E contain this error.

Meaning: The original sentence implies that agencies collaborating in a coup d'etat should be criticized and agencies collaborating to overthrow foreign governments should also be criticized. Options A, B and E do not make it clear who does the collaborating to overthrow the foreign governments.

The correct answer is option C.

278. **Awkwardness**: The expressions "developed after when" and "Developed after there being" are awkward compared to "developed after someone supported ..." Options A and E contain this error.

Also, "speculators supported construction" is better and more direct than "speculators' support of construction by foreign speculators," which is awkward and redundant. Option C contains this error.

Tenses: The verb "develop" needs to be parallel to "lagged" because of "and." Thus, "develops" is incorrect. Option D contains this error.

The correct answer is option B.

279. **Conjunctions**: "Not only" must be paired with "but also." Options A, B and C contain this error.

Parallelism: The conjunction "not only X but also Y" necessitates parallelism in the X and Y parts. Since the non-underlined part says "not only *gather*..." the correct option would be "but also *damage*..." and not "causing." Option E contains this error.

The correct answer is option D.

Sentence Correction Guide – Solutions

280. **Meaning**: If we use "caused by," ambiguity is created because it could mean "crime caused by" or mean "decrease caused by." "Because" poses no such problems because it will be the cause of the overall sentence before. For example:

    Ambiguous: There is drastic reduction in rainfall caused by opposing convectional currents. [rainfall caused by opposing convectional currents OR reduction caused by opposing convectional currents?]

    Clear: There is drastic reduction in rainfall because of opposing convectional currents. [reduction caused by opposing convectional currents]

    Options A and D contain this error.

    Idioms: "Surveillance" is correctly used as "surveillance by someone of something." No other prepositions are correct (though the order of the two prepositional phrases may be reversed, i.e., "surveillance of something by someone"). Options C, D and E contain this error.

    The correct answer is option B.

281. **Diction**: To discuss more than two of something, "among" is used, whereas, "between" is reserved for only two things. In the given sentence, more than two cultures are being discussed. Thus, "among" is correct. Options D and E contain this error.

    Comparisons: "Misunderstandings" are being compared. Thus, we need to use "those" and not "that" to refer to "misunderstandings," which is plural. Options B, D and E contain this error.

    Also, "greater" must be paired with "than"; "as great as" is correct but "greater than" is correct. Option A contains this error.

    The correct answer is option C

282. **Parallelism**: "Either X or Y" needs parallelism in the X and Y parts. Option C and E contain this error. Going beyond a purely grammatical standpoint, the meaning of the use of "either...or" is wrong in these options as well because no choice is actually involved.

    Grammatical construction: "Require" will be followed by "to verb." Thus, the best possible construction would be "required to destroy" rather than "required to have destroyed" or "required to have had destroyed." Options A and B contain this error.

    The correct answer is option D.

283. **Grammatical construction**: "So" and "such" can work with an adjective in the following ways:

    So + adjective
    Ex. Your house is so beautiful!

    Such + adjective + noun
    Ex. You have such a beautiful house!

    Options A and B deviate from the rule above, and are incorrect. Option D begins with the correct grammar, but then becomes awkward at the end ("of the kind today's have"). Really, the meaning of the original sentence is to convey a kind of comparison, which Option C does in all the right ways. Option E begins with a less common, but still correct, usage of "so" (so + adjective + noun), but it doesn't follow through with correct grammar in the comparison part of the sentence ("of the kind...")

The correct answer is option C.

284. **Diction**: "Frequent" means something happening at regular intervals: for example – Lightning is frequent in this area.

    "Common" means "prevalent": for example: Orchids are common in NE India.

    In the given example, the sentence does not imply that couples earn at regular intervals, but implies that when more couples earn incomes, something will happen. Thus, the correct word is "common" and not "frequent." Options A and B contain this error.

    Meaning: "Should" changes the meaning, making it different from the original sentence. Option C contains this error.

    Option E is needlessly wordy and awkward.

    The correct answer is option D.

285. **Comparisons**: "Wines" should be compared with "wines" whereas, "wineries" should be compared with "wineries." Any mismatch is an incorrect comparison. Options A and D contain this error.

    Option C compares Germany's (wines) with New York, making it incorrect.

    "Those from" in option E is ambiguous because the sentence later discusses "wineries in New York" as well as "wines." So, option E is incorrect.

    The correct answer is option B.

286. **Modifiers**: The word "consequence" is necessary to refer to "discovering the need for glasses" as a result of "sitting close to the TV screen..." Without "a consequence," using "affected" will imply that the "glasses" or "middle age" have been affected, not the "eyes." Options D and E contain this error.

    Idioms: "Consequence" is followed by "of" and not by "from." Also, "to" cannot be used with "near." Option B contains this error.

    Redundancy: Using "consequence" and "result" is redundant. Option C contains this error.

    The correct answer is option A.

287. **Conjunctions**: Three similar things are being joined and so contrast conjunctions will be incorrect. Option C contains this error.

    "As well as" cannot be used to join more than two things. Options A and E contain this error.

    Awkwardness: "Student misbehavior that is persistent" is awkward compared to "persistent student misbehavior." Options A, B and E contain this error.

    The correct answer is option D.

Sentence Correction Guide – Solutions

288. **Modifiers**: What's touching on subjects like greed and corruption in corporate America and delivering a scathing condemnation of contemporary capitalism? The novel is touching on subjects ... contemporary capitalism. Thus, the sentence must begin with the subject "the novel" after the modifier "touching on...capitalism." Options C, D and E contain this error.

    Awkwardness: "Is going to depict" is not the correct tense for a generalized statement. For a general statement, the simple future tense "will depict" is also appropriate. Option B contains this error.

    The correct answer is option A.

289. **Tenses**: What happened first in the underlined actions? The "buying on rumor" happened first. Thus, it should be in the past perfect tense ("had bought") to denote the correct order. Options A and E contain this error.

    Punctuation: A semicolon is used to join two clauses. Using a fragment after a semicolon is incorrect. Option B contains this error.

    Redundancy: Using "those" and "these" to refer to investors is redundant and repetitive. Option D contains this error.

    The correct answer is option C.

290. **Comparisons**: What tells psychologists more about what? Something tells psychologists more about children than X. Do we wish to convey that something tells psychologists more about children than (it tells them about) IQ, or do we wish to convey that something tells psychologists more about children than IQ (tells psychologist about children)? Clearly, we're not saying that psychologists know more about children than they know about IQ! We're saying that children's adaptation tells psychologists more than IQ **does**. Thus, using the auxiliary verb "do" for IQs is necessary to convey the meaning. Options A, B and D contain this error.

    Pronoun ambiguity: Using plural pronouns "they" or "their" to refer to "children" is ambiguous given the presence of another plural noun "psychologists." Options A and E contain this error.

    The correct answer is option C.

291. **Parallelism**: Since the non-underlined part uses "people exercising daily," subsequently too we need to use "people exercising" to maintain parallelism in comparison. Options C and E contain this error.

    Comparisons: GMAT prefers "no adj-er than" to "not adj-er than," i.e. "no healthier than" is preferred to "not healthier than." Thus, we need to use the former and not the latter. Options B and C contain this error.

    The correct answer is option A.

292. **Idioms**: "try" should be followed by "to" and not by "and" or "for." For example:

    Correct: I will *try to* study tonight.

    Incorrect: I will *try and* study tonight.

Incorrect: I will *try for* studying tonight.

Options B and D contain this error.

"Retrieve" must be followed by "from" and not "out of." Options C, D and E contain this error.

The correct answer is option A.

293. **Comparisons**: "Conductors" are the people who direct orchestras. The sentence intends to compare "(film) directors" to "conductors." Options D and E imply that "conductors" are something that is directed by other people. So, options D and E are incorrect.

    Modifiers: Using "which" for people is incorrect. Option B contains this error.

    Parallelism: Since the non-underlined part uses "directors who create...," we should use similar structure in the underlined portion to make the comparison parallel. So, we should use "conductors who direct" instead of "conductors directing." Option A contains this error.

    The correct answer is option C.

294. **Parallelism**: "X is Y" needs parallelism. Since the non-underlined part says "something is to see ...," we have to use "to verb." Options B, C and D contain this error.

    Also, since the non-underlined part says "to see" and not "to have seen," using "to have witnessed" would be incorrect. Option E contains this error.

    The correct answer is option A.

295. **Modifiers**: "Depending on his talent" refers to the "male musician." Options A and B imply that "degree in music" depends on his talent. So, options A and B are incorrect.

    Who graduates from college? The male musician graduates from college. Options C and E imply that the talent of the male musician graduates from college, making these options incorrect.

    The correct answer is option D.

296. **Conjunctions**: "Not" pairs with "but." Option E contains this error.

    "Not X but Y" needs parallel structure. If a verb is present after "not," a verb must be put after "but" too. Ditto for prepositions and other structures. In the given sentence, any of the following structures would be parallel:

    (A) *not resulted from* failures in teaching *but resulted from* insufficiently supportive home environments

    (B) resulted *not from* failures in teaching *but from* insufficiently supportive home environments

    (C) resulted from *not* failures in teaching *but* insufficiently supportive home environments

A, C and D contain this error.

The correct answer is option B.

297. **Conjunctions**: To denote causes, the best conjunction is "because" and not "since" or "rather." Options B, C and D contain this error.

    Tenses: Since the sentence is in the past tense, evidenced by the verb "thought," we need to use the past tense "seemed." Option A contains this error.

    Idioms: "Seem" should be followed by "to." Options A and C contain this error.

    The correct answer is option E.

298. **Idioms**: "Distinguish" can be correctly used as:

    (A) distinguish between X and Y
    (B) distinguish X from Y
    (C) distinguish X from Y from Z

    No other structure is acceptable. Options C, D and E contain this error.

    Prepositions: The preposition "between" is used to distinguish between two things, yet the original sentence discusses four things (between A and B, plus between C and D, but not between A/B and C/D). Option A is therefore, incorrect.

    Either "much more + adjective" or "far more + adjective" may be used in this sentence, but only Option B is grammatical in all parts of the sentence.

    The correct answer is option B.

299. **SVA**: "Both listeners and fans" will take the plural verb "know" and not the singular verb "knows." Option B contains this error.

    Tenses: The sentence is in present tense ("says") and using the simple past "knew" is incorrect. Option C contains this error. Similarly, using "was" or "had been" is incorrect because the fans "will know." Options C, D and E contain this error.

    The correct answer is option A.

300. **Modifiers**: Whose few slashes of the sword? The fencer's slashes of the sword defeated her opponents. Thus, the sentence must begin with the subject "the fencer" after the modifier "with ... sword" to conform to the rules of modifiers. Options A and E contain this error.

    Meaning: Are the two actions ("defeating" and "capitalizing") independent of each other, or is it that "defeating" happens by "capitalizing"? The "capitalizing" is the way the fencer "defeats" her opponents. Thus, using "and" between the two actions is incorrect because it will imply two independent actions. Option D contains this error.

    Also, the sentence wishes to convey that "defeat happens by capitalizing" and not that "capitalizing happens by defeating." Thus, the correct structure would be "fencer defeats ... capitalizing ..." Option C contains this error.

    The correct answer is option B.

Chapter 7

Talk to Us

Have a Question?

Email your questions to info@manhattanreview.com. We will be happy to answer you. Your questions can be related to a concept, an application of a concept, an explanation of a question, a suggestion for an alternate approach, or anything else you wish to ask regarding the GMAT.

Please mention the page number when quoting from the book.

Best of luck!

Professor Dr. Joern Meissner
& The Manhattan Review Team

Manhattan Admissions

**You are a unique candidate with unique experience.
We help you to sell your story to the admissions committee.**

Manhattan Admissions is an educational consulting firm that guides academic candidates through the complex process of applying to the world's top educational programs. We work with applicants from around the world to ensure that they represent their personal advantages and strength well and get our clients admitted to the world's best business schools, graduate programs and colleges.

We will guide you through the whole admissions process:

- ✓ Personal Assessment and School Selection
- ✓ Definition of your Application Strategy
- ✓ Help in Structuring your Application Essays
- ✓ Unlimited Rounds of Improvement
- ✓ Letter of Recommendation Advice
- ✓ Interview Preparation and Mock Sessions
- ✓ Scholarship Consulting

To schedule a free 30-minute consulting and candidacy evaluation session or read more about our services, please visit or call:

 www.manhattanadmissions.com   +1.212.334.2500

Made in the USA
Middletown, DE
09 September 2024